Best Dearborn Stories

Voices From Henry Ford's Hometown

Volume III

Edited by
David L. Good and L. Glenn O'Kray

Published by the Museum Guild of Dearborn
Dearborn, Michigan

*To those who walked before us – creating stories,
remembering stories, telling stories.*

*Best Dearborn Stories: Voices From Henry Ford's Hometown
Volume III*
Copyright 2013 by the Museum Guild of Dearborn

ISBN 978-1-62890-368-3

1. History. 2. Stories.

Book layout & design by Carl Johnson at Saint Creative
www.saint-creative.com

Printed in the United States of America.

www.thedhm.com

Table of Contents

Best Dearborn Stories: Voices From Henry Ford's Hometown
Volume III

Author Index

Foreword

*Best Dearborn Stories: Voices From Henry Ford's Hometown,
Volume III* is most probably the final publication in a series meant to
accomplish two ends. The first is to raise money for the Dearborn
Historical Museum. The second is to record residents' histories.

The city of Dearborn, like most municipalities, has been
hard hit by the financial meltdown that has devastated the state of
Michigan as well as the entire nation. The Dearborn City Council
has attempted to strike a balance between providing essential
services such as police and fire protection and supporting the
cultural and recreational pursuits of its residents. The council felt
it necessary in 2012 to make drastic cuts to the Museum, reducing
the city subsidy to covering only legacy costs.

The council has reinstated some operating funds for the
Museum in the 2013-14 fiscal year. However, these funds are well
below the level of prior years, especially those years during which
as many as 18 full- and part-time employees serviced the Museum.
Income from this book helps sustain the Museum.

The Museum Guild of Dearborn has promoted the
preservation of Dearborn history by supporting this publication.
This book has preserved in some ways a sense of the collective
memory of the past and present residents of Dearborn. Some
anecdotes reflect events that happened on one particular day.
Others reflect the span of a person's entire life. Still others reflect
the mindset of the author, explaining what he or she believes. Some
stories are descriptors of organizations in the community, in many
ways reflecting the values of the community.

Some authors write about encounters with Henry Ford himself. These individuals are becoming fewer and fewer. This publication may be the last to tell personal stories of interactions with that captain of industry.

This volume may also reflect a dying breed – those who like to tell tales and write anecdotes, especially about themselves, their lives, their beliefs.

A special note of thanks goes to Jane O'Kray and Janet Good, supporters who are long-suffering spouses of the editors.

A note of thanks also goes to Joe Fetter and Carl Johnson for their fine work on this publication.

- L. Glenn O'Kray

Chapter 1

Loving Dearborn

Camp Dearborn:
The Roar of the Panther,
The Smell of the Skunk

By Tom Connell

The first time a family member discovered Camp Dearborn in 1967, she secured a tent at the beginning and again at the end of summer with her four children. She has continued her annual tent rental.

During the last 45 years, we've had great memories and celebrations at Camp Dearborn, initially securing tents on the lower D row until several years ago when D row was converted to a field and we found a new location. In 2012 we had 12 tents/cabins for the family. Some of us come every year, others not as often. Our family travel from Illinois, Michigan, Minnesota, Wisconsin, Ohio, Iowa, California, Florida & New York to be together during our Camp Dearborn week.

We have stories to tell about:

- Mass on the hill on Saturday evenings.
- Hauling pails of water from the water pumps near each tent.
- The boys (ignoring parental directive) having scary experiences when going to the dam.
- Being on the lookout for the "panther" spotted near Camp Dearborn.
- Our kids needing to soak in tomato juice to get rid the smell of the skunk they chased in the field.
- Flashlight tag in the field at night.
- Waking to doughnut deliveries and "Chicken Fat" every morning and on some days, long ago, waking and finding the field by D row littered with occupied sleeping bags.

- Celebrating Peggy's 40th birthday with a truck driving through the field flashing lights and singing "Lordy, Lordy, Peggy's 40" and our annual photo on the hill or near the tent, where for some years there were 100+ family and visitors.

And then there was the canteen with dancing for all ages, ice cream and evening entertainment; the weekly talent shows and other camp activities -- euchre tournaments, children's crafts and of course the campfires which created opportunities to make new, now lifelong, friends.

Camp Dearborn has come to be our place for sharing, caring and celebrating. The first Sunday of our camping week is reserved for celebrating births, graduations, birthdays, anniversaries and other life events. For some years it served as our place to support each other through divorces and deaths of family members. Last year we created a "Circle of Love," supporting each other in grieving the death of a family member.

The evening campfire is a place to gather and share, ask questions, seek wisdom from the elders and enjoy each other's company. Camp Dearborn offers us the opportunity to be with each other for an extended time in a relaxed atmosphere and for our children and grandchildren, providing a chance to play and get to know their cousins, aunts and uncles in an environment like no other!

Viva La Camp Dearborn!!!!

Tom Connell is 79 years old. He, his wife and five children have been going to Camp Dearborn since 1970. Their kids, brothers, sisters and their kids and their grandkids currently have nine tents and two cabins.

Warming up to the Big City

By Werner and Joan Frank

We came to Dearborn in 1957 fresh out of college and newly married. Our first residence was an upper flat on Mead near Ford Woods with no air conditioning. It was an ideal place for us to live and get to our jobs, airport and the food industry.

Coming from a small town and farm, we were pretty much in awe of this big city. We enjoyed this new area with shops nearby and Joe's Meat Market and the wonderful Dearborn Pizzeria on Chase Road.

We had a new baby girl and needed more room, so we bought our first house on Steadman in 1959. This was just a great neighborhood, with Mr. Brown's Drugstore on the corner just a half block away and several small markets nearby.

We moved to west Dearborn (Lodge Lane) in 1970. This also was a great neighborhood. We felt very welcome. The neighborhood had many block parties and other gatherings through the years. We were close to our favorite stores—Crowley's Jacobson's and the wonderful Sanders ice-cream store.

Several of the men on the street played golf, and I, Werner, was invited to play with them the very first week. We had many good times golfing and telling stories. Later on I played the Dearborn Hills course, where I met two fine gentlemen, Fred Schreiber and

Punch Yinger and many others. They counted every stroke.

During our 56 years in Dearborn we have maintained a relationship with many of our longtime neighbors. Sadly some have passed on.

Our daughter keeps in touch with many of her junior high and Dearborn High friends through Facebook and e-mail. They get together several times a year.

Werner Frank retired from a 30-year career as a store manager at Farmer Jacks. Joan Frank retired from American Airlines, where she was a secretary for 40 years. They split their time between Morley Manor and Sun City West, Arizona.

Savoring the World

By Geraldine Grunow

When I got a call in the summer of 1990 from the then-chair of the English Division, Ed Chielens, to tell me that the Hiring Committee was offering me a position as English Instructor at Henry Ford Community College, I was thrilled to think that I'd be teaching composition and literature full time at an institution where I had already been happy as a part-time instructor.

And I have, indeed, enjoyed this wonderful opportunity to research and practice good-writing pedagogy, as well as to reread favorite writers in order to teach old and new works of literature. In addition, however, as a wonderful and unexpected bonus, I've had many years to explore the amazingly rich cultural and culinary landscape of the college and of its hometown. Here's a tiny sampling.

To begin with, right here on campus, I've feasted on delicious and exotic cuisine regularly at the 5101 Restaurant, where food is prepared and served by our culinary arts students. These students are trained by instructors who can retrieve thousands of ethnic recipes from up the starched white sleeves of their chef's uniforms. Meal costs are minimal; service is earnest and efficient. Among the best events for showing off the college to friends and family are the international buffets during spring semester, a German Oktoberfest and a hearty pre-Thanksgiving dinner.

On a more intimate level, a unique combination of food and culture-sharing with kindred spirits was offered at a simple breakfast meeting a couple of years ago, hosted by our Arab Cultural Studies Department and the Center for Teaching Excellence and Innovation. During this meeting, two women authors – Suad Amiry, architect-author from Ramallah, and Karen Connelly, Canadian writer and traveler –spoke of their lives and works. These visitors quickly established community among a diverse group of women faculty, and we went on to share stories and concerns from our own life journeys. A magical morning....

And a magical evening at the beginning of November, this time with students, members of the HFCC Amnesty International Club.... I've been an activist with Amnesty International (an independent, grass-roots, human-rights movement) for many years, but I'd been unsuccessful in establishing a student group at HFCC until a few years ago, when a smart, popular student, straight from high school, asked me to. The club took off running, and we've been crowded with members ever since.

With the cooperation of the always-helpful Student Activities Department, we began a tradition of celebrating the Mexican Days of the Dead in our own way. We've used this occasion to remember all the martyrs and victims in the struggle for universal human rights, as well as those on death row everywhere awaiting the ultimate inhumane, cruel and unusual punishment. At the first candlelit vigil, held on a chilly evening around the wildflower garden in the middle of campus, one of the members, who had spent a year in Mexico as a Rotary Youth Exchange student, explained the history of this beautiful celebration. Afterward we enjoyed a treat of new Michigan apple cider and light, sweet, skull-decorated pastries (*Pan de Muertos*) from a nearby Mexican bakery.

Thinking about Dearborn itself, I feel a little melancholy about the loss of many once-vibrant establishments: Annam, the elegant Vietnamese restaurant; Einstein's Bagels on Michigan Avenue; the original La Shish, where we would often take guest speakers with the Cultural Activities Program for lunch; the Little

Professor Bookstore, where I used to purchase books for teaching, especially for my children's literature course.

Fine places remain in Dearborn, of course, all providing nourishment for the body and for the soul. Many of us in the (newly named) Communications Division like to meet at Chinatown in Fairlane Mall for a buffet lunch the first day of the semester; its vast seating area accommodates as many of us as want to come and to catch up with all our vacation news and review our plans for the next semester's teaching. Members of our instructors' union, AFT Local 1650, also enjoy St. Patrick's Day with the Dearborn Rotarians at Park Place. The beautiful music of Inis-Ceol and a tasty corned-beef-and-cabbage dinner bring yet another world culture to Dearborn and HFCC.

Finally, there's my favorite restaurant in the world, located just beside the Arab American National Museum: M and M's, serving a variety of Middle Eastern and American dishes – all home-cooked, with fresh ingredients, to individual request. I've spent many hours there with colleagues, discussing how best to address professional issues and carefully assessing final exam essays so that we can feel confident that the grades are appropriate. The utterly delicious food and the wonderfully friendly, welcoming atmosphere make it easy to see the world from the windows of Dearborn as a beautiful mosaic of humanity.

Much gratitude to Dearborn for giving me so many reasons to savor the world!

Geraldine Grunow was born and educated in Scotland; her husband, Ken, grew up in Dearborn Heights. They met when they were both volunteer teachers in Ghana over 40 years ago; they have three children and three grandchildren. They have been active volunteers with Amnesty International in Detroit since the children were young.

HFCC Lures a Visitor Back After 40 Years

By Dr. Stanley E. Jensen

My first exposure to Dearborn occurred over 40 years ago when I visited Greenfield Village along with some of my college friends. Who would have guessed that four decades after my first visit I would not only be living in Dearborn, but I would be the president of Henry Ford Community College?

I was born and raised on a farm in northeastern Iowa. Today the fifth generation of my family is being raised on that same farm. I know what it is like to come from a community with deep roots and long-term relationships. In my new home in Dearborn, I find that many residents are very proud that they have lived here their entire lives or their families for generations. I certainly can identify with that, and I can also identify with many who have moved here recently.

After graduating from high school, I moved to Grand Rapids and spent most of the 1970s earning my baccalaureate degree from Cornerstone University and my master's as well. Then I moved back to Iowa and, while earning my Ph.D. from the University of Iowa, established a church in eastern Iowa. After serving as a dean in a small college, I established my own consulting company which accomplished many leadership and team-building results for businesses and colleges for over 20 years. I then served as president of Colorado Mountain College for nearly five years. On the first day of May 2013, I became I the fifth president of Henry Ford Community College.

My wife and I still remember with fondness the day we moved to Dearborn. It was early spring and the trees were white with new blossoms. The weather seemed perfect and we started to meet new friends. I deeply value the culture of Dearborn because of its breadth of diversity and the pervasive Midwest work ethic. Education is highly valued in Dearborn, and Henry Ford Community College has served the Dearborn area for over 75 years by providing education that effectively transfers skills and knowledge to the workplace. I believe that Henry Ford Community College is the best value in higher education in Dearborn.

The entire country and much of the world have benefitted from the innovative ideas and products that originated in Dearborn. After the tough economic times of the recent past, southeast Michigan is rebuilding. The same innovative spirit that changed the world is being seen again in neighborhoods that are rebuilding and companies that are rising to meet the challenges of the 21st century. Working together and working wisely will be important to our future.

Great things ahead!

Dr. Stanley E. Jensen and his wife, Teresa, live in Dearborn. They have six children and nine grandchildren, all residing in Iowa.

How Many City Workers To Change a Light Bulb? Only One - And Fast!

By John Malone

People always wondered what Mayor Hubbard was like. From my viewpoint he was amazing.

While attending Dearborn High School, I was given an assignment to attend a meeting of the City Council. I arrived early and was waiting for the meeting to begin when I ran into my uncle Duane Dunick, who was deputy city attorney. He asked what I was doing at the meeting, and after I explained, he excused himself and said he would see me after the meeting.

The meeting was all routine business, and I kept busy writing notes so I would be able to remember the details later. The meeting seemed to last forever, but I'm sure it wasn't more than an hour or so. The meeting was adjourned and I packed up my papers and started to leave. I was stopped by my uncle, who said he wanted to introduce me to some of his friends. We walked down the hall and went into a large office.

I was surprised to see all the men who were present at the meeting. My uncle introduced me to the mayor, who couldn't have been nicer. The mayor introduced me to all the department heads and council members, who had stayed after the meeting. He and the others spent at least a half an hour explaining what was behind each of the items they had discussed in the meeting.

They were so kind to a high school student that it was easy to understand why they were elected and re-elected. It also showed the reason the city of Dearborn ran so smoothly.

An example of the way things were handled in the city was brought home to me one evening when my girlfriend (now my wife of 49 years) and I were talking about our jobs. She was working at Levagood Park pool, and I was working for the Dearborn Historical Museum. Somehow the conversation worked itself around to how efficiently things were handled by the city.

She wasn't so sure about the efficiency, so I decided to test things. We were sitting on her front porch on Gregory Street, and I had noticed that the streetlight on the corner was burned out. I called down to City Hall, and within an hour, a truck with a cherry picker showed up and a worker replaced the bulb. This has always stuck in my mind because I think it is the only argument I have ever won from my wife.

John Malone is retired and living in the Upper Peninsula town of Laurium. It, like Dearborn, is a friendly town of many nationalities. It has more than 200 inches of snow each year.

La Belle Epoque

By Evelyn Gorden Marshall

My brothers and I grew up with one parent. My dad was killed in an auto accident in 1947. Life was tough, but it didn't seem bad. We didn't suffer. We had enough to eat. We had a home. We had wonderful relatives and good times. The neighborhoods were clean and neat thanks to "Orvie." We went to Greenfield Village Day Camp all summer. We went to the Ice Capades, zoo, circus, parades, rodeo, Camp Dearborn, the Rotunda, the art museum, the library, the Calvin and many other places, all without a car. And in winter, the sledding, skating and all-around snow fun kept us busy. We also frequented Seashore Pool and Muirhead's.

The schools were well cared for, too. The teachers wore business casual. There were standards to be kept. We took classes like music and gym. As students, we performed in programs, complete with sets and costumes, which included singing and acting. During gym, we learned tennis, field hockey, basketball, kickball, golf, track and synchronized swimming, to name a few. We had art class and made things. We didn't need to pay for supplies.

There was a nurse if you got sick (and I did once take advantage of that when I threw up all over my locker). Never did find out who cleaned that up! We had fluoride treatments and polio shots and were monitored for scoliosis.

Almost everyone walked to and from school. There were parties, too, right at school in the lunchroom. I still have the picture of me with two guys at a table. The other girl didn't show up. That never happened again.

Just about the time I thought my mom would live to be 100, she died a few months before her 97th birthday in 2009. She was able to stay in her home until a few years before her death. The neighborhood remained safe, neat and clean. The schools are still good, but where did all those programs go – the athletic, art and health-related programs?

My brothers and I lived during a great time. I hope those of you who are my age realize that a better time, a safer time and a time of plenty was part of our past. Did you see the movie, *Midnight in Paris?* The movie reminds me of now, thinking back on what we see as a better time and longing to be there. Unhappy and somewhat unsatisfied with the present, I search for *la belle époque*. I really feel like I have lived it!

Evelyn Gorden Marshall is a retired nurse. She lives in Westland and is pursuing a career in writing. Her latest book is Recipes from the Junk Drawer, *and next will be* Recipes from the Fruit Cellar.

From Camp Cook To Miss Paint-Up

By Cynthia Parrelly

My father and his parents and his four siblings were born and raised in Dearborn, and consequently, so were my three siblings and I. In fact the four of us have remained in Dearborn and have raised seven more Dearborn residents.

While growing up during the 1960s, I thought I lived in paradise: beautiful schools, homes, parks, shopping, etc. Our neighborhoods were safe and fun, and no one locked the door. Most families had a working dad and a stay-at-home mom. It was heaven on earth.

Every summer, my family, as well as other neighborhood families and extended family members, would rent tents at Camp Dearborn's Tent Village. There were enough families to take up an entire row of tents. These two weeks were so exciting for my family that it was hard to wait for the time to come.

Looking back, though, I don't think it was much fun for my mom, as she had to practically bring her entire kitchen with us to cook. She seemed to enjoy it at the time, though.

Days were spent at the many playgrounds, the paddle boats, the pool, the beach and the famous Canteen, where we ate great hamburgers, hot dogs and ice cream. I can still remember waiting in line and smelling the food. At night, we (as teen-agers) would get all fancy to attend the dance at the Canteen. We would walk there in groups and hang out and dance. A lot or Righteous Brothers and Crosby, Stills, Nash and Young music. We could stay until the dance ended and then walk back. We would then stay up on the tent patio playing cards. It was a blast!

All of the families would visit each other, eat each other's food, sleep over and enjoy the practical jokes we played on each other. During our stay, the Camp Dearborn photographer would come by and take group photos. I still have all of them. Black and white and everyone is smiling!

Another great memory for me is the Clean-Up, Fix-Up, Paint-Up parades that the city and the schools co-produced each year. I can remember working with my classmates to design our message and couldn't wait to walk in the parade. One year, to my surprise, my mother was named Miss Paint-Up and was given a crown and a sash and walked in the Memorial Day parade that year with Miss Clean-Up and Miss Fix-Up. I was so proud! Only way-back Dearborn residents will remember the crowning of the three ladies. My heart will always be in Dearborn. It is a part of me.

Cynthia Parrelly is the administrative specialist for Enrollment Services at Henry Ford Community College. Previously she spent 10 years as the executive assistant to the president of the college. She is an advocate for the disabled and has served on the Dearborn Disability Concerns Commission.

Learning to Crawl, Walk and Run With Museum Volunteers

By Michael "Jack" Tate

In early 2012 the Dearborn City Council drastically reduced the annual subsidy traditionally given to the Dearborn Historical Museum. The council agreed to pay only for legacy costs, those related to retirees. In response the city had little choice but to release the chief curator, Kirt D. Gross, and two of four part-time employees. The other two employees resigned.

The mayoral-appointed Dearborn Historical Commission then decided that the Museum should operate primarily through the use of volunteers. As I have had a strong interest in the Museum most of my life, the mayor appointed me as acting chief curator, effective in July 2012. This marked the first time, to my knowledge, that the Museum has had a volunteer chief curator.

Looking back now, I can honestly state that the journey has been the ride of a lifetime. We have had many challenges. We have had many things to figure out. And, with the extraordinary assistance of our current part-time employees, Craig Hutchison and Marguerite Baumgardner, we have had many successes. We could not have achieved all that we have without the amazing dedication of a great group of volunteers. The team that has been assembled and that is still growing is one of the most intense, hard-working groups I have ever known. And they all do it out of a love for the place and its history.

I want to list just a few of our accomplishments so far and in the process to recognize this dedicated group that has become the backbone of this Museum.

A number of organizations have played key roles in keeping the Museum going. First among them is the Museum Guild of Dearborn, a 501(c)(3) nonprofit that serves as the fund-raising arm of the Museum and has supported the Museum through volunteers since 1957. Under the leadership of its president, Rick Danes, the Guild has sponsored a long list of fund-raising activities, including its first annual golf outing last August. Chief planners for the event were Danes, L. Glenn O'Kray and Walt Baumgardner.

In addition, the Guild in 2013 sponsored the museum's annual volunteer brunch, the opening of a Sports Legacy exhibit, an annual Pioneer School Program and an annual garage sale. The group is also sponsoring publication of this third volume of *Best Dearborn Stories.* The Guild is continuing as well to host the Victorian Christmas Tea in December. Thank you to the Guild for this wonderful event and all the others.

The Sons of Union Veterans of the Civil War has supported the Museum through innumerable events for many years under its president, Rick Danes.

Another group, the Herb Society, headed by Cookie Tapp, is restoring the side doors of the McFadden-Ross House.

Among the numerous tasks undertaken chiefly with volunteers, we have begun the process of logging every single item in the collection (accessioned and nonaccessioned) and documenting each one with a photograph. This information is then cataloged into the Museum's software, PastPerfect. The collections cataloging crew includes Sarah Eubank, Alex Osborne, Michelle Yowler, Jim Bumgarner, Danielle Bixler, Rob Bazzi, Alex Nakhleh, Rick Danes, Claire Boie, Brenda Purkiss, Ruth Bruce, Marge Montrief, Tom

Saroglia and Kelly McGuire.

We have refurbished the Pioneer Room floor thanks to Harold Rahrig and Jim Bumgarner.

The Pioneer School Program is starting to thrive again. Every second-grader in the Dearborn Public Schools visits the Museum for an orientation to the early history of the city. In 2014 we will be including private schools in the program. This would not be possible without the volunteers who love this program and make it work. They include Gretchen Ackermann Moss, Shirley Banick, Joseph Borrajo, Ruth Bruce, Mary Bugeia, Julia Casey, Susan Dabaja, Shirley Damps, Rick Danes, Teresa Danyliw, Jilda Franks, Barbara Goldi, Carmen Gudan, Karen Jewell, Michael Kieltyka, Patricia Meyer, Rose Marie Mouhot, Mary Nuznov, Jerry Olson, Mary Olson, Shirley Painter, Brenda Purkiss, Nancy Rahrig, Moe Sion, Linda Stegner, Dee Waldron and Sharon Reid.

The Teddy Bear Picnic, sponsored by the Dearborn Historical Society, has been brought back and looks to be an event that will grow after a very successful first year back. The volunteers who worked the event really put their heart and soul into it: Leeanne Abu-Zahrah, Andrea Abu-Zahrah, Marguerite Baumgardner, Ed Binkley, Claire Boie, Leona Bretsik, Ruth Bruce, Julia Casey, Rick Danes, Irma Danes, Teresa Danyliw, Tara Gnau, Barbara Hall, Fred Levantrosser, Ed Maurus, Anne McGraw-Mueller, Sheila Mistecki, Marsha Mistecki, Marge Montrief, Rose Marie Mouhot, Jerry Olson, Mary Olson, Shirley Painter, Anita Polzin, John Polzin, Brenda Purkiss, Nancy Rahrig, Jennie Soltau, Lisa Wincent, Dee Waldron, Mary Bugeia and Susan Saroglia.

Our first Party at the Museum was a tremendous success, with attendees at the September event numbering over 1,200. We had been hoping for 500. This was an intense event because of the turnout, and a sincere thank-you goes out to the Dearborn Historical Society for sponsoring the event and to those volunteers who hung in there despite the circumstances: Colleen Murphy, Jim Lane, Mary Nuznov, Julie Hirina, Sharon Murphy, Craig Champagne, Denny Clark, Betsy Bommarito, Cathy Saroglia, Sue Saroglia, Tom Saroglia, Jenny Saroglia, Nicole Mouchet, Heather Stetz, Dave Gorden, Sharon Bledsoe, David Bilko, Anna Kopcha, Lindsey Kisslinger, Leo Early, Teresa Danyliw, Isamay Osborne, Mary Olson, Karen Wisniewski, Marguerite Baumgardner, Craig Hutchison, Tara Gnau, Steve Guibord, Joe Palukus, Amy Stegner, Jamie Croskey, Sarah Eubank, Rick Danes, Aaron Schrader, Howard Fite, Ken Roberts, Ed Binkley, Kelly McGuire and Jerry Olson.

Rounding out the Museum's list of planned activities for 2013 are two Halloween events, Historic Halloween at the Museum and the Motor City Ghost Hunters' Adult Ghost Walk. Thank you to the volunteers behind both events: Brenda Purkiss, Clair Boie, Ruth Bruce, Marguerite Baumgardner, Marge Montrief, Rick Danes, Rob Bazzi, Ed Maurus, Mary Nuznov, Shirley Mayland, Barb Goldi, Mary Bugeia, Lisa Wincent, Mel Waldecker, Irma Danes and Karen Wisnewski.

A hearty thanks to John Polzin, who has acted as the Museum's custodian for the past few months. This is one of those thankless jobs that gets noticed only when it is not being done.

We now have docents who are helping to keep the McFadden-Ross House and the Commandant's Quarters open and who give tours when needed. Thank you to Ed Binkley, Lynn Brewer, Ruth Bruce, Karen Bumgarner, Dave Gorden, Pat Long, Shirley Mayland, Jane McCormick, Jennie Soltau and Mel Waldecker.

L. Glenn O'Kray, the Historical Commission vice chair, has spearheaded the comeback of the cable show *Through the Arsenal Gates*. The mayor was so pleased with Bill Hackett's interview on the Battle of the Overpass that he sent a copy of the program to

Ford Board Chairman Bill Ford. O'Kray also is coordinator and co-editor of the *Best Dearborn Stories* series, which has raised more than $21,000 in profits for the Museum over the last two years.

The Museum's quarterly journal, *The Dearborn Historian*, after a hiatus of four years, is once again being published and is thriving under the leadership of Historical Commission Chair David L. Good. The Historical Society of Michigan awarded the publication a prestigious State History Award in Communications in 2013.

In terms of exhibits, the Museum had a wonderful Christmas display set up in its meeting room cases and at City Hall. The Sports Legacy exhibit was masterfully built and designed from a variety of items. The Party at the Museum had a beer-related exhibit in the meeting room and an assortment of beer paintings in the hallway. Rotating exhibits are part of the lifeblood of a Museum, and we send a hearty thank-you to Jamie Croskey, Mary Nuznov and Amy Stegner.

The operation of the Museum would cease if we did not have a crew that did some heavy lifting, restoration and technical work. This crew includes Tom Saroglia, John Eldrington, Harold Rahrig, Rick Danes, Jim Bumgarner, John Polzin, Walt Scaramucci, Chet Doughman, Terry Hutchison, and Brian Kutscher.

There is always miscellaneous computer work to be done. This rests in the capable hands of Jill Franks, Michelle Saad, Sandra Sitkowski, Kelly McGuire, Sarah Eubank, Colleen Murphy and CeCe Cantineri.

The archives are a treasure to be preserved and accessed by researchers. We are very grateful to have this resource in the very capable hands of Karen Wisniewski and Karen Krepp.

There is still much to do. But this is a great start. And the progress we have made so far is because of the people mentioned above. I have found that these folks are not only dedicated and talented, but that they have helped create a bridge between the community and the Museum. One of our next major tasks is to build the Museum structures that have been drawn up for many years now. But for now, we must work with what we have, and these wonderful people are helping do just that.

I loved my job as an engineer with Detroit Diesel, but I live for each day as the curator of the Museum, working side by side with people that have a heart to maintain and teach the history of Dearborn.

Michael "Jack" Tate is a lifelong resident of Dearborn and was a member of the Junior Historians at the Museum as a youth.

From Adray to Zither

By Jane Jones Vos

Dearborn has always had a small-town feel, even now. When I was young, under 10 years old, I'd go to the corner grocery store, Bluebird Market, or Lily's at the corner of Tenny and Monroe. They knew me by name. They knew my family, friends and neighbors. At Bluebird, you would pick out your groceries, and at the end of the month you'd settle up.

That was also the era when Mike Adray of Adray Appliance sponsored what seemed like hundreds of baseball teams. Children all over Dearborn wore the cool Adray jerseys. Everywhere you went, grocery store, summer Stephens pool, Crowley's, you'd see people with Adray tshirts.

The Music Man would make his rounds at the local neighborhood parks, bringing his zither. The first time I saw it, I thought it was the coolest thing around. It really did help spark a love of music. I had eight siblings, so music lessonson came at a premium. But being exposed to the zither was definitely top-notch music education. "When would I get to see it again?" I wondered. "Would I ever be able to play it?"

Gimp was a big thing. Most children and moms made key chains with four strands of gimp. One of my brothers made a really thick key chain out of gimp; it must have had 16 strands. His key chain made it into the city wide summer art show. I was so excited for him!

The Junior Olympics at Ford Field was one of the big summer events. Hundreds (if not thousands?) of children participated from Dearborn. Their were officials with stopwatches and measuring tape keeping track of events such as the softball throw or 100-yard dash. The winners would then participate at another event; they were the cream of the crop in all the track and field events from around the state. I had never heard of Lapeer or Metamora until I was a winner at Junior Olympics and went on to face the statewide competition. I learned a lot of geography, too. The Junior Olympics always started with a parade of all the participants from the dozens of Dearborn parks. The flag was carried and the national anthem sung with joy.

Terry was the name of my big sister's beau. Jones was a big family name–like Sarb, Oulette, O'Connor, DeLage and other hard-working folks in the community.

These were some of the highlights from my childhood in Dearborn, Michigan.

To this day, Dearborn still has a small-town atmosphere. One of my daughters worked at Biggby the past couple of years, and customers recognized her as being part of the Jones clan. The roots go really deep here in Dearborn.

Jane Jones Vos has lived in Dearborn most of her life. She is a wife to Doug (33 years), mother to five children plus two sons in laws and a daughter in law, oma to several grandchildren, bookkeeper, but most importantly a Christ follower.

Chapter 2

Henry Ford

A Forgettable Introduction To Mrs. Prunk's Uncle

By John Altenburger

Two houses down the street from us in Dearborn lived Horace and Grace Prunk; their son, Tommy; and a dog, Smokey. They lived in a corner brick house on Mohawk and Denwood. Grace was a niece of Henry Ford; her name before she married was Bryant. As I recall, Horace was a veterinarian.It was understood by the neighbors that "Uncle Henry" was the source of this house for the Prunks.

From time to time "Uncle Henry" would come over to visit. It just so happened that I was over at the Prunks' playing with Tommy when "Uncle Henry" dropped in. It must have been in 1946. I was 8 years old and had no idea of the level of this dignitary. It was a very casual introduction, and Tommy and I just kept doing whatever it was we were doing.

Word must have gotten back to my parents of this meeting because Mom explained who this man was. I still was too young to comprehend the significance and, frankly, hardly remember it.

John Altenburger moved to 741 S. Denwood at age 3 when it was a dirt road. About 30 percent of the lots had houses on them. His two closest neighbors were executives at the Cadillac Motor Car Company, where John worked. At retirement, he had lived in Dearborn from 1940 until 1996.

One Farmer to Another

By James Brand

January 1, 1940, found my parents, Farwell and Mary Louise Brand, hosting their usual New Year's Day party at our home on Gulley Road. Mother had warned my brother and me that we would be dressed appropriately and washed or else! She had pointed out that along with many relatives and friends, Henry and Clara Ford, old friends of my maternal grandparents, were also invited. We, of course, knew of the Fords, for in those days it was not unusual to see Mr. Ford driving of being driven around town. Then, there were some of us who were driven to the engineering labs every Friday after school. Dressed in our best knickers, we would spend an hour learning square dancing and waltzing under the tutelage of Benjamin Lovett. Occasionally Mr. Ford would show up and sit for a short time, watching us doing the old dances.

The party was in full sway and the Fords did attend. Mr. Ford, however, was not too fond of parties and as a 14-year-old, I wasn't much interested beyond the food. So we both ended up in my father's study with plates of food, and we began to talk. We had eighty acres, lots of horses, chickens, turkeys, and a goat. We had an old Fordson tractor for power on the farm. I told Mr. Ford a few things about the farm and the tractor. He got interested and started telling me how he grew up on a farm. We talked about animals and then farm equipment. He became very animated about the new Ford-Ferguson tractor that had just come out and said that I should talk to my father about it. I told him I already had all the literature.

I think we sat and chatted about half an hour. It was just like talking to my late grandfather. I do believe he enjoyed it, too, for we covered a lot of subjects, mainly rural. He did not talk down to me, but as man to man. It was an experience I will never forget.

James Brand is a retired professor from Ferris State University. He grew up in Dearborn and graduated from Dearborn High in 1943. He has been retired for 26 years. He has traveled the USA, Canada, Mexico, New Zealand, Australia, and Scandinavia in a recreational vehicle.

Ford Road and Greenfield

By Jerry Brown

First memory: I was born in 1929. I grew up at 5830 Steadman. I well remember Henry Ford's farm on Ford Road and Greenfield. He used to grow soy and wheat. Three friends and I frequently went to play in Mr. Ford's barn. There would be a pile of straw, and my friends – Tom Morris, Pat McIlvey, Virgil Vel – and I would swing on a rope and jump into the straw.

The auto magnate would frequently come to the barn. He would arrive at about the same time of day in a chauffeured Model A or Model T. He looked pretty much like pictures showed him – slender and wearing a flat straw hat. He would walk into the barn and ask how we were doing. We would say, "Fine, Mr. Ford." He would tell us that we could play in the barn as long as we didn't get hurt. If we got hurt, we couldn't play there anymore.

I think his reason for coming there was to visit the gravesite of his dog in back of the house.

Another memory: I had a big police dog named Duke. I loved that dog. He was my buddy. He went just about everywhere with me. These were the days before there were leash laws. Dogs could run around the neighborhood, and nobody thought anything of it. One day Duke was running with a pack of dogs in the Victory Gardens at Ford and Greenfield. The cops came and shot all the dogs. I was devastated.

Jerry Brown spent 38 years as a conductor for the Chesapeake and Ohio Railroad. He then made real estate his career. He and his wife, Jennie, have been married for 59 years.

The Business World According to Henry Ford

By Henry Fischer

Our library book discussion group, Classics Revisited, discussed Henry Ford's autobiography, *My Life and Work,* on April 17, 2013, the year of his 150th birthday. As usual, we were to meet at 7 p.m. in the Ford Collection Room at Henry Ford Centennial Library, a fitting location to discuss the man who has been called the greatest success story in the history of industry.

It rained heavily that day. One of my co-workers said, "I wonder how many will come for Classics?" At about 6:59 p.m., only one person had shown up. Then, a few minutes later, people of all ages started pouring in. There were about as many men as women. The table in the Ford Room seats 12, but this time people had to bring in extra chairs or sit on the couches along the wall. (The Ford Room has a 1970s feel and is rich with the smell of old books.)

Everyone seemed eager to discuss Henry Ford; many wanted to discuss this strange book they had never heard of before. I had seen a few documentaries on Henry Ford, but I didn't remember any mention of his autobiography. When you watch or read biographies of Henry Ford, you get someone else's take on the man and the myth. When you read his autobiography, you get to hear from Henry Ford himself. And when you hear it from his perspective, he comes off a little differently. Yet in a sense this only adds to the mystery, since (as one member pointed out) earlier editions claim it was written in collaboration with Samuel Crowther. For the rest of this piece I'd like to share a sampling of our discussion, focusing on some of Ford's ideas, observations and discoveries, many of which are as relevant today as when the book was first published in 1922.

He speaks passionately about service, how "service comes before profit" and how profit is a natural result of excellent service. He emphasizes the importance of giving his employees a good living wage. To him, the basic question is not "What should we pay the employee?" but rather "What can the business stand?" When he started paying $5 a day, many business people thought Ford Motor Company would go bankrupt. In fact the opposite happened. The workers could afford the machines they made and sales soared. As Ford says of working men and women: "The scale of their living — the rate of their wages — determines the prosperity of the country." Imagine if one of the big retailers or fast-food franchises started paying a comparable wage in today's dollars. What might that do for our country? Interestingly, Ford goes a step further: "There is something sacred about wages — they represent homes and families and domestic destinies. People ought to tread very carefully when approaching wages. On the cost sheet, wages are mere figures; out in the world, wages are bread boxes and coal bins, babies' cradles and children's education — family comforts and contentment." What if we started to think of wages in this way?

Henry Ford's love of all things mechanical shines through in his writing. He describes how he always had nuts and bolts in his pockets whenever he drove to town. He says a real mechanic "ought to know how nearly everything is made." Imagine a mechanic today knowing how nearly everything is made. Now that's hardcore! Henry Ford says the machine is the mechanic's book. He talks about his farm "at Dearborn" and his museum full of his "mechanical treasures."

Reading his book gives you a bird's-eye view of how he came to build his "universal" car, the Model T. From the scraps of a French racing car, he finds a steel that is lighter and stronger than any other steel he is familiar with. No one knows what the steel is, so he has his colleagues send it to the lab to be examined. They find out it is vanadium steel. Henry Ford decides to use it in the mass production of Model T's. As it turns out, Ford Motor Company was the first business to produce vanadium steel commercially. Henry Ford stresses over and over again that excessive weight is the motor vehicle's greatest enemy. He strives continually to make the lightest and strongest car possible at that time, which to him is the Model T. He wants to make a car that will last a lifetime (there is no planned obsolescence in his business). But he repeatedly tells the reader: If you learn one thing from this book, it should be the realization that however well you're doing something, it can always be done better. What if Ford Motor Company designed a new Model T using today's standards while staying true to Henry Ford's principle that the car be so simple that anyone could understand it?

Henry Ford buys a school, a hospital and a railroad and tries to make them all self-sufficient. He says even jails should be self-sufficient. All should produce. Imagine if jails were self-sufficient instead of costing taxpayers thousands of dollars per inmate. When this was brought up, a member of the group said, "Let's bring back Henry Ford!"

Another thing Ford talks about is the jobs in his factories. He has them classified in such a way that he can tell the level of difficulty of each job and which ones can be done by blind, deaf, armless, legless or convalescent people. A blind man he hires ends up doing the job of two employees. Ford says that when they hire people, everyone starts out at the bottom. They don't look at the applicants' job histories: "We do not hire a man's history, we hire the man." And "He is equally acceptable whether he has been in Sing Sing or at Harvard." They also get rid of job titles as much as possible because, according to Ford, a title is an excuse for a man to do nothing and think he's superior. And Ford says he never hires "experts" because that is a sure way to have mediocre results. This reminds me of the old joke: An "ex" is a has-been, and a "spurt" is a drip under pressure.

Ford focuses diligently on ways to make jobs more efficient to improve productivity. For instance, he calculates the exact number of movements it takes to do a job and keeps thinking about how to reduce that number. He says if someone wants to be a manager, he has to take his work home with him; that a manager's real work begins at the end of a work day. He says that a manager should be working alongside the laborers in the foundation of the business to find out what is wrong, what can be improved.

His book is filled with quotable passages. I believe I read this one (among others) to the group: "More men are beaten than fail. It is not wisdom they need or money, or brilliance, or 'pull,' but just plain gristle and bone. ... It is failure that is easy. Success is always hard. A man can fail in ease; he can succeed only by paying out all that he has and is."

On the night of our discussion, 17 people showed up, a record number at that time. People still really want to know who Henry Ford was. Well, if you want to hear from Henry Ford himself, check out his autobiography (from the library – we have many copies). You may be pleasantly surprised. With this book you can catch a glimpse of his extraordinary mind. Here you can find the man, the mechanical genius, Dearborn's Henry Ford.

Henry Fischer lives in Dearborn with his wife and two young children. He moderates Classics Revisited, a book discussion group that meets at the Henry Ford Centennial Library.

A Keen Student of Human Nature — And the 'Sweet Science'

By David L. Good

The yellowing newspaper clipping didn't really belong in the old album, pasted alongside a bunch of faded family photos. It seemed to date from the same period as the photos – the 1920s – but what was its connection, if any, to our family?

In a style the writer no doubt supposed to be slyly humorous, the clipping recounted a brief anecdote about the almost mystical powers of the man in charge of the lobby at the Ford Motor Company office building in Dearborn. Unlike most of the photos, the article was coy about identifying its subject, simply labeling him a "keen student of human nature." But I know now who he was, with absolute certainty, even without the name or much else in the way of clues.

He was my grandfather, Oliver E. Jones.

I know because, for a number of years in the 1920s, Grandpa Jones was the guy you had to talk your way past if you wanted to see Henry Ford. I know because, during his time there, Grandpa collected the autographs of Mr. Ford's most famous visitors – Thomas Edison, Amelia Earhart, Charles A. Lindbergh, among many others. My Uncle Leon, who owns Grandpa's autograph book, has been kind enough to share some of the signatures. My brother, Ray, has the "March King," conductor-composer John Philip Sousa. On my living room wall, I have the poet Carl Sandburg, a three-time Pulitzer Prize winner who appended the line "Mule skinner and Phi Beta Kappa" to an autograph dated 1928.

Beyond his well-verified job credentials as a screener of the rich and famous, Grandpa Jones did indeed on occasion seem to display some almost mystical insights into human nature –although in the end, his emotions got the better of his insights, sparking a bizarre confrontation that cut short his unforgettable career at Ford's after just a few years.

Apprenticed as a cabinetmaker in the late 1800s in Birmingham, England, Grandpa Jones moved to Dearborn from Toronto about 1920, along with his French wife (my grandmother, Jenny), a young daughter (my mother, Marcelle) and a younger son (Uncle Leon). Before that, in 1912, a Toronto newspaper noted that Oliver E. Jones had made quite a favorable impression on the local citizenry, leaving a crowd cheering in the street as he performed an act of selfless heroism. The paper credited Mr. Jones, employed as an insurance agent at the time, with pulling off "a feat of no little daring" by stopping a runaway horse that had already injured two people. In the best stock Hollywood Western style, he had jumped aboard a cart pulled by the horse and made his way forward, finally grabbing the reins and bringing the creature to a halt.

With the outbreak of World War I a few years later, Grandpa Jones enlisted for his second military stint, joining the Canadian Army and serving as chief armourer at the Toronto Armory. Some two decades earlier, as a young man, he had served in the British Army.

In peacetime, Grandpa Jones turned toward the United States and the auto industry for work. Before long he was at Ford's, first as a gateman and a serviceman, then supervising two crews working the pits at the former Wagner Brick Yard near Oakwood and Beech to excavate what became known as the Twin Ponds. One day Henry Ford stopped by to inspect the work and talk with the men. As Grandpa recalled it, Mr. Ford liked something about the tall, almost gaunt crew boss, well beyond the fact that they shared the same English heritage – perhaps that this man talked a bit better than the other workers, that he dressed a bit better or even that he looked a little like Henry Ford himself, both facially and in body type.

In any case, not long after that, Grandpa Jones found himself working in the lobby of the old Ford office building, interviewing visitors who wanted to see Mr. Ford or other company executives.

According to the newspaper clipping, which looked as though it might have come from the Detroit News, the article's writer provided his name and the name of the man he wanted to see. At that, the lobby receptionist asked, "And what is the name of your paper?" After pointing out that he hadn't identified himself as a newspaper man, he was told: "I can tell them. You look like a newspaper man and you talk like one."

Further, the receptionist claimed he "could almost invariably tell the character of a caller's errand." As evidence, he mentioned a well-dressed woman who had visited the building recently: "The minute she opened the door, I said to myself: 'She's got a patent she wants to sell.'" And he was right.

The writer wryly concluded, "Callers at the Ford office are counseled to have their more intimate garments in a good state of repair."

Actually, his grandchildren have their own story about his knack for telling people things about themselves. He loved to reminisce about the time he encountered a swarthy man with a Turkish surname who bet that Grandpa couldn't figure out where he was from. Listening to the man talk for a few minutes, Grandpa detected traces of a Cockney accent – and said offhandedly that he wouldn't be surprised if the man had grown up "within the sound of Bow bells." To the English, that's a familiar description of east-end Londoners, and the astonished man had to acknowledge that Grandpa had nailed him exactly.

It must have been a wonderful job. But it had to end – just not so soon had Grandpa Jones not been so proud of his English ancestry. This is what happened: Grandpa was in the men's room at the same time Mr. Ford's closest aide, his private secretary, Ernest G. Liebold, was washing up. As perhaps the most powerful man in the company next to Ford, Liebold apparently was accustomed to saying what he wanted, to whom he wanted. He was also known to hold strong views about certain ethnic groups; these views brought Henry Ford wide personal censure when they made their way into Ford's anti-Semitic newspaper, the Dearborn Independent, as edited by Liebold during its eight-year run in the 1920s.

Whether or not he was aware of Grandpa's background during the washroom encounter, Liebold nonetheless felt compelled to make a crack about "English SOB's." That did it. Still fit and wiry at age 50 or thereabouts, Grandpa Jones also knew something about boxing. I remember the leather "speed bag" hanging from the ceiling of his basement. Even into his 80s, he could keep on punching that thing in a rapid "rat-tat-tat-tat" rhythm that would have done a professional exponent of the "sweet science" proud.

And I don't know now whether it was one punch or a succession of them that Grandpa Jones administered as a corrective to an ill-mannered Ford Motor Company executive on that particular day in the men's room of the Ford office building in Dearborn. But history records that the aforementioned executive was knocked cold, and suffice it to say that Mr. Ford had no choice but to summarily dismiss the Englishman he had recruited from the Wagner Brick Yard mud pits only a few years before.

Grandpa Jones held a succession of jobs over the ensuing years, inspecting bars for the Michigan Liquor Control Commission, selling real estate, working as a receptionist at Kelsey-Hayes, but he never did anything approaching his job at Ford's. My sister, Marilyn, still has the black metal sign he had anchored in his front yard on Beech Street for many years. It read, "Antiques Repaired, Restored and Refinished." Relying on boyhood skills learned in England, he established his own home-based business as an authentically old-school restorer. He also charged old-school prices: $5 here, $10 there for hours of painstaking work, all the while using techniques that dated back to when many of the pieces were made, right down to mixing his own glue.

Grandpa and Grandma Jones lived in their house on Beech Street near Monroe until the city decided in the mid-1970s to put up another of its senior citizens' apartments, Hubbard Manor West, right smack where the house was. They were offered a unit in Sisson Manor, already in operation on Mason right behind them, so they didn't mind selling the house. My grandparents lived at Sisson Manor until they died, Grandpa Jones at 95 in 1975, Grandma Jones at 94 in 1978. I remember visiting Grandpa at Oakwood Hospital as he lay, semi-comatose, during his final days. He couldn't hear me, but I could hear him. Very softly, he was murmuring the words he had often yelled up from his basement workshop: "I'm workin' on a job, Mother. I'm workin' on a job."

That could be the end of the story, but it isn't, quite. Some seven or eight years later, while I was the editor of Michigan Magazine at the Detroit News, a pair of Michigan State University faculty members came in to pitch a story. One of them, a redhead in his 30s, introduced himself as Bill Liebold, who I later learned had been a Dearborn High School classmate of my brother's.

Toward the end of our meeting, I asked Bill Liebold the inevitable question: "You wouldn't happen to be kin of the old Ford's big shot, E.G. Liebold, would you?" Understandably, he puffed up just a little as he replied, "Why, yes I am, as a matter of fact. His grandson."

I could scarcely contain my glee when I told him: "Well, my grandpa knew your grandpa at Ford's more than 50 years ago, and my grandpa beat the crap out of your grandpa."

As a footnote to the story, Grandpa Jones wasn't the only person of interest in this story to be sacked by Henry Ford. In 1944 E.G. Liebold told the newspapers that his 34-year connection with the company had ended, explaining only, "I didn't quit and I didn't resign."

Well, maybe you never heard that old cliché, "What goes around comes around," eh, Mr. Liebold?

David L. Good is chair of the Dearborn Historical Commission. He was a reporter and editor at the Detroit News for 34 years and is the author of the 1989 biography of Mayor Orville L. Hubbard, Orvie: The Dictator of Dearborn.

Oliver E. Jones

Why Didn't My Grandfather Lend Henry a Pen?

By Sandra Doman Horton

Families usually have some stories that are passed down from parent to child – never anything that can be proven to be true – but believed to actually have happened by those who hear the tales. Here's one of our family stories – true or not?

My grandfather, William Lab, came to the Dearborn area around 1916. Along with his wife, Ida, and daughter (my mother, Marguerite Doman), he lived with my great-grandparents in their farm home on Ford Road. My grandfather helped them work the farm. Eventually my grandfather got a job working on the Ford Farms, which could be seen from Ford Road near Southfield Road. When my mother was about 8 or 9, my grandfather and his family moved to a house on Silvery Lane in Dearborn. Family lore has it that this house was moved from somewhere on the north side of Ford Road to its present location. It is still there today and looks like an old farm home with a big, screened-in porch across the front. The one thing I remember about this house was the chicken coop out back.

According to another story, when my grandfather became too old to farm any more, Henry Ford offered him a job as the watchman on the back gate to the Fair Lane estate. Most people remember the main gate to the Ford home off of Michigan Avenue – a very impressive entrance. But not many people may be aware that there was a back gatehouse located on Ford Road. I know it was there for sure because my mother would on several occasions drop me off to visit with my grandfather if it was close to the end of his shift. I would sit with him in a little green gatehouse. Occasionally someone would come through or a delivery truck might enter. My grandfather always had to call up to the big house to announce a visitor. When his shift was over, we would walk to his car – parked some distance from the entrance. He would drop me off at my house, on Waverly just off of Ford Road, on his way home. So just where was this gatehouse? It must have been somewhere on Ford Road between Evergreen and what is now Edward Hines Drive. I do remember a thick woods. Of course nothing looks the same now, and this place is just a fleeting memory of images in my mind.

As the family story goes, Henry Ford would occasionally ride his bike down to the back gate and sit and visit with my grandfather for a while and then ride back. Apparently Henry visited with my grandfather shortly after my birth, on May 12, 1942. The proud, new first-time grandfather informed Henry of the event, and Henry congratulated him and then signed his autograph on a piece of paper and said to give it to the new granddaughter. My mother was carefully keeping a baby book for me and included the signature, which is dated May 24, 1942. I'm not sure if the date is Henry's handwriting or my mother's.

Many, many years later my mother and I had a discussion about this signature and wondered if it would be worth any money. I did some research and decided it might be worth $1,000. (A recent serch on eBay listed a signature dated July 16, 1928, for $1,500.) When I informed my mother, she told me that the signature was originally written in pencil, and over the years, as it began to fade, she traced over it in ink! Well, that was the end of my fantasy of cashing in for some bucks. Of course I probably never would have sold it. I love the story and I believe it is true. My grandfather was a much-loved person in my life, and this memento of him and Henry Ford is very special to me.

Sandra Doman Horton was born in Dearborn and graduated from Dearborn High in 1960. She now lives in Beverly Hills and has two children and five grandchildren. Her mother still lives in Dearborn.

Ford's First Recall

By Ken Jess

I am a longtime Dearborn resident. I was born in 1942 at the Dearborn General Hospital, located on Morley and Oakwood. It is now an office building. But the story I would like to share happened a long time before that.

My grandfather came from Scotland, and my grandmother was a Finn. They met in Calumet in the copper country of the Upper Peninsula. My grandfather, along with his brother, worked in the mines before 1900. My father, Joseph, was born in 1901, followed by Robert in 1903 and Clare in 1905.

The family grew up in Calumet with Grandpa still working in the copper mines until he was injured in an explosion in which he lost a leg in 1917. Grandpa could no longer work the mines, and with no other jobs available to raise a family, they decided to move south to the Lower Peninsula and a larger city.

They ended up in Highland Park, where the mayor gave Grandpa a job picking up papers and debris with a stick with a nail at the end. With his job not bringing in enough money, he told my father to go out at the age of 16 and see if he could find something to help out. So Joseph started out early the next morning going to stores and small businesses. He came upon a small diner where he could rest a little and maybe get a drink of water. When he entered, he saw a man sitting at the counter eating. He sat by the man, who spoke to him. After Dad told his story, the man bought him breakfast and asked him if he had a bicycle. The man gave him an address and told Joseph to bring his bike and to be sure to be there before 7 the next morning.

When Joseph got home, he told his family of his experience. His father was very proud of his son, and they checked out the bicycle, and Grandpa told Dad about the importance of being on time.

The next morning he set out with his bike, address in hand. After looking for a while, he came upon an odd-shaped building that looked like an army quonset hut, but there was the address on it, big and bold. He laid down the bicycle and approached the door. After knocking, he heard a voice telling him to come in. Slowly he opened the door enough to see a man sitting behind a desk. The man was the same one who bought his breakfast the day before. Joseph then noticed a sign on the desk that read *Henry Ford*.

"Good morning, Joseph," Mr. Ford greeted him. "You're a little early. That's good. Come in and sit down. Did you bring your bicycle?"

"Yes, Sir."

"Do you have a basket?"

"No, Sir."

"Well then, if you want that job I was talking about, you'll have to take that bike down to the third shed and ask for Max. Then come back here and see me."

Joseph did what he was told, and Max put a basket on Joseph's bike. Upon completion, Joseph returned to see Mr. Ford, who told him to return the next morning to begin work. He was to use his bike to deliver notes, letters and packages throughout the Ford complex. He had just become Henry Ford's personal mail boy! His job continued for almost two years.

On August 10, 1919, Mr. Ford called him to the office. "Tomorrow is a special day, Joseph. It's your 18th birthday. If you're interested, you can work on the assembly line starting at $5 a day." Joseph could hardly wait to get home and tell his mother and father.

His first day on the job was rough. Because he was small, Mr. Ford had told the foreman to give him a job to fit. The foreman had Joseph put small hubcaps on every car on the assembly line. He put two on the one side of the car and then had to jump over the belt that pulled the cars along and put two on the other side, then jump back over the belt. This rotation lasted all day. When he got home, he talked to his father, saying he didn't mind being tired because he knew he would get used to it after working that job for a while. He showed his father his hands, swollen from hitting all those hubcaps into place.

As usual, Grandpa had an idea. He told Joseph to go out into his workshop and get the rubber mallet off his bench and take it to work the next day.

Joseph went to work the next day, mallet in hand. He not only kept up, but his hand did not hurt and he actually got ahead of the line. All of the sudden, he heard, "Joseph! Joseph! Look down the line and tell me what you see," the foreman yelled.

Joseph's mouth dropped open as he looked at all the cars down the line and noticed a small dent in each hubcap. Not funny at the time, but in later years he told many friends that he caused Ford's first recall!

Joseph remained at the Ford Motor Company and moved to Dearborn, raising a family there. He worked at Ford's for 46 years. He went from mail boy to the third-shift superintendent of the Rouge complex.

I worked for 32 years at Ford's, and my brother Bill worked there for 36 years. Henry Ford was Dearborn and Dearborn was and is the Ford Motor Company.

Ken Jess lives in Dearborn Heights with his wife, Karen. He has coached athletics not only for St. Sebastian School but also for Dearborn District #7. He has coached Annapolis High School's girls' basketball and softball for 15 years.

The Only Time I Saw Henry Ford

By Loren Moore

The only time I saw Henry Ford was in 1946 when I was 6 years old. It was at Ford Field in July. Local 600 of the United Auto Workers and the city of Dearborn wanted to honor him on his birthday.

My mother, dad, brother, sister and I were standing up by the flag pole. I had never heard or seen fireworks before, and they scared me. I thought the war had started again. My dad put me up on his shoulders so I could see down below. A big open car drove onto Ford Field with an old couple in the back seat. My dad said, "That is Mr. and Mrs. Ford!" as they waved to everybody. It was dark, and a big spotlight shined on them and played over the crowd. I had never seen so many people in one place before. Ford Field was packed everywhere with people.

Henry Ford died the next year.

Loren Moore is a retired firefighter. He and his wife, Margaret, have been married for 34 years and are the parents of Laura Lee and Mike and have a grandson, Pauly. Moore is the secretary of the Early Ford V8 Club of Dearborn.

'If It Hadn't Been For the Fords...'

By John Roring

My uncle, Howard Simpson, worked in the office next to Henry Ford, who signed his paycheck. His son, Bruce, had attended the Village school and was the head of Ford Engineering. Bruce played the violin, and Henry Ford gave him a valuable violin, which he sold a few years ago for a significant amount of money. My uncle got my mom, Ruth, into Ford's, and she became the head librarian for Ford Engineering. Henry used to bring Edsel Ford's kids into the library, and she would chase them. One of my mom's jobs was to clip *Little Orphan Annie* cartoons and paste them in a book for Henry. My mom danced with the auto giant in the library.

My grandfather was Norwegian and was a sea captain. He paid for his home in Norway by taking his shipping fleet out for whaling expeditions. The socioeconomic system at that time was like the company store. My family would sell the town its provisions while waiting to be paid with fish.

Henry used to hire Norwegians and Swedes to captain his ships. My dad also was a seaman, and Henry hired him to be an officer on his ships. My dad told me of taking Henry together with Thomas Edison on the ship. Henry didn't like that Edison chewed tobacco and would spit on the wooden deck. My dad remembered Henry's changing the course of his vessel, saying, "I can do this. This is my ship." Once a year my mom would go out on one of Mr. Ford's ships, where she met my dad, who worked as a captain.

Even though my mom and dad were in love, they couldn't get married because Henry did not allow married couples to work for him.

My parents used to live in the Brady Street apartments, which were flooded on the night of Henry's death. I remember seeing pictures of cars with only the roofs showing in the flood.

As a kid, I used to deliver newspapers on Wagner Court when there were just a couple of homes, including the Wagner mansion. I used to ride my bike by Greenfield Village and jump over the wall. There used to be a market by the Village that sold corn. I remember Boy Scout campouts at the Village. My dad also worked for the Boblo Boat organization. Through him I got free passes for the island, and I would have great fun for days on end.

I guess I got my love of ships from my dad. I worked on ships on the Great Lakes. Then I worked at the Rouge for 30 years.

At Fair Lane I attended the 150th anniversary celebration of Henry's birth. I used to sneak around the place and eat apples from the trees growing on the estate. At the celebration I spoke with Edsel Ford. I told him I had gone to Edsel Ford High School. I told him if it weren't for the Fords I wouldn't be here. He said, "If it hadn't been for the Fords, I wouldn't be here either!"

John Roring has a daughter and three sons, two of whom work for the Ford Motor Company.

John Roring at the launch of the Edmund Fitzgerald.

The Simpson-Ford Connection

By Bruce H. Simpson

The Simpson family connection with the Ford Motor Company, and particularly with Mr. Henry Ford, started in 1918 when Howard W. Simpson went to work at the Henry Ford & Son tractor plant in Dearborn. Howard had graduated from the University of Michigan in mechanical engineering in 1917. In 1921 he became Chief Engineer on Fordson tractor design and testing. He reported directly to Henry Ford on many special projects, including new tractor concepts, transmissions and farm machinery.

In 1939 Howard decided that he wanted to concentrate on his own designs, and he left the company. He went on to design tractor-driven power mowers and other farm equipment, but he primarily concentrated on planetary gear transmissions. His 42 patented inventions included many new planetary gear arrangements. Each of the "Big 3" and several foreign automakers adopted one particular three-speed planetary gear arrangement, known by engineers around the world as the "Simpson gear train," for their automatic transmissions.

The Simpsons' association with Ford was not limited to business. Mr. Ford was well known for his love of Early American dancing and particularly square dancing. He had frequent formal evening dances to which Howard and his wife, Gertrude, were always invited. In fact Gertrude Simpson was one of Mr. Ford's favorite dance partners. Gertrude was also a friend of Henry's wife, Clara, and Clara agreed to host a meeting of the Dearborn Women's Winter Study Club at "the residence" (Fair Lane Estate) when it was Gertrude's turn to host a meeting. Years later Clara Ford invited the Greenfield Village School girls to swim in the pool at Fair Lane and the Simpsons' daughter, Charlotte, often went swimming there as Mrs. Ford's guest.

Howard and Gertrude's son, Bruce, had his first contact with Henry Ford in September 1929, when he joined the first class of students at the Greenfield Village School. Classes were held in the Scotch Settlement School, the very school Henry Ford attended when he was a boy. Bruce has a picture of Mr. Ford shaking his hand on the first day of school.

After about a year, the school started having a short, nondenominational chapel service before each school day, held in the Martha-Mary Chapel. Mr. Henry Ford usually attended these chapel services, so we saw him almost every school day. The chapel services usually consisted of a hymn or two, a popular song (*Home on the Range* was a favorite), the Lord's Prayer (yes, prayer in a school activity!), a responsive reading from the Bible and a special number. The special number might be a vocal solo (Susan Alderdyce, Catherine Miller and Margaret Voorhees were Mr. Ford's favorites), an instrumental solo or a reading. And so it was at these chapel services that Bruce played the violin on many occasions when Mr. Ford was present.

One such occasion Bruce will never forget. After a service at which he played a violin solo, Mr. Ford came up to him and said he had a suggestion about his violin playing (Mr. Ford was a fiddler). It had to do with the way Bruce changed the direction of the bow. To make his point clear, Mr. Ford took the violin and demonstrated just what he meant. So Bruce is probably the only person in the world who had a "violin lesson" from Henry Ford.

And Mr. Ford was very supportive of Bruce's efforts on the violin. When Bruce had progressed to the point where he could appreciate a really good violin, Mr. Ford loaned him a fine 1750 Gagliano violin from his collection. Bruce played this violin for four years, and it was a great inspiration for him. To this day, at age 85, he still plays regularly in the Dearborn Symphony Orchestra.

Mr. Ford provided support and encouragement for all

the students in many ways. The girls were given the opportunity to learn and work at weaving, silk making, pottery, secretarial skills, photography and homemaking; the boys at wood working, machine shop, foundry, glass blowing, auto mechanics (working on Model T's), besides everybody being involved in music, sports of all types and, oh yes, academics. When someone showed particular interest or a flair for something, they were given every opportunity to pursue it. Bruce's sister, Charlotte, who also attended the Village Schools, was especially interested in weaving and horseback riding. She still has some very fine fabric she wove in the Village and some ribbons for her riding skills.

We never ceased to be amazed at the scope and diversity of Mr. Ford's interests and involvements. His mechanical genius was undoubtedly his greatest talent, but close behind was his interest in and concern for people. All people – great people and common people, including kids like us. He had many famous people among his friends – statesmen, industrialists, entertainers, musicians and movie stars. His special friends were other pioneers like himself, people like Edison, Burbank, Firestone and George Washington Carver. We saw many such people who would come to our chapel services with him.

In spite of his great fame and fortune, Mr. Ford always impressed us as being a very natural, even humble, person. He also enjoyed having a good time, whether square dancing or showing us a newly restored steam engine – he really enjoyed himself. And he enjoyed doing things for other people, which he did in many ways. Mr. Ford was, without a doubt, a truly great man and he left the world a much better place than when he found it.

In 1947, after Bruce had served three years as an officer in the U.S. Army Air Corps during World War II, and completed his college education in mechanical engineering and gotten married, he was hired by Ford as a product development engineer. For the next 40 years he had a very interesting and rewarding career with the company. Some career highlights included making yearly prototype vehicle test trips to the Arizona desert to select the proper engine cooling systems, receiving a patent on a sealed cooling system, establishing a product reliability program, developed the first production package of vehicle safety features and representing Ford at many government meetings and hearings on vehicle fuel economy and emissions control.

Bruce retired from Ford in 1986 as executive engineer, fuel economy, emissions and noise control planning. After retiring from Ford he worked for the American Supplier Institute for nine years as vice president, quality standards and awards. There he developed a universal quality standard and a quality assessment system for automotive suppliers, conducted seminars on several quality-related subjects and served on the Board of Examiners of the Baldrige National Quality Award for two years.

Along the way Bruce and his wife, Alice, had four sons. The oldest of them, Dick, has been following the Simpson family tradition of working for Ford for the past 38.6 years. Dick was a test instrumentation technologist in the Ford Advanced Engineering Center, where his basic task was to make vehicles and vehicle components more pleasing to the ear.

Altogether, the Ford Motor careers of Howard Simpson (21 years), then Bruce (40 years) and Dick (38.6 years) come to a total of some 99.6 years. We were indeed very fortunate to have either actually known Mr. Henry Ford or been employed by the Ford Motor Company.

Bruce H. Simpson (1921-2010) wrote this story in 2003.

Chapter 3

Growing Up

Fording the Rouge on Rubber Ice

By John Altenburger

If you took Cherry Hill toward the eastern end, it would be close to South Brady Street. Turning left (north), Brady Street would parallel the Rouge River and be within a mile of the Ford Estate.

One winter in about 1955, Bob Lockhardt and I took my 1928 Model A Ford up Brady Street until we could conveniently park and walk down to the river. We knew Henry Ford's estate was there close by, but we had never seen it. And, since it was an extremely cold winter, the river was iced over.

As we walked down to the river, we could see little patches where the ice had not formed, so our strategy was to keep clear of those spots. As we got on the ice, we could see it give way to our weight. We would shuffle and not step so as to minimize the stress on the ice, and in so doing we invented the expression "rubber ice." We'd keep moving, and the ice would depress, but we'd be fast enough that it didn't break through. Also, one person did not follow the other one, as "double dipping" might be more than the ice could handle. We walked until we could see the large expanse that must have been a garden, and the home building also came into view.

Our concern turned to returning safely to the car, and we crossed the river again, avoiding the ice path that we had taken previously, and safely made it to the car.

John Altenburger moved to 741 S. Denwood at age 3 when it was a dirt road. About 30 percent of the lots had houses on them. His two closest neighbors were executives at the Cadillac Motor Car Company where John worked. At retirement, he had lived in Dearborn from 1940 until 1996.

The Only Thing Missing Was the Feathers

By Anonymous

It was a hot, late Saturday, summer afternoon in the 1970s in Dearborn. There were about eight of us looking for something to do. We had walked up to the Westborn shopping center, checked the stores that we might be interested in and found nothing.

Walking back home through the alley, we noticed that a crew had started to retar the flat roof of the Penn Electric building on Outer Drive, south of Michigan Avenue. Up on the roof some of us scampered. The 50-pound cans of tar said, "Asbestos." Someone said, "Let's see if it burns."

Off the roof one of the cans fell. It split open and the black stuff oozed out. We found a tennis ball nearby and scooped up some tar. Someone struck a match or lighter, and the tennis ball soon was blazing.

A concerned citizen driving past the alley stopped and yelled, "Hey, what are you kids doing?" I thought it was obvious. It was a science experiment. Whoever was holding the blazing tennis ball dropped it into the broken-open can of tar, and in no time, traffic on Outer Drive in both directions came to a screeching halt because of the roiling black smoke from the asbestos/tar. The eight of us all split at this time.

At the other end of the alley I met up with Harry. We talked for a second and hurried back to try to extinguish the inferno we had started. I found a small tree branch, raised it over my head and brought it down hard. Flaming liquid flew in all directions. A small piece landed on my hand and burned into my skin. It really hurt. I looked over at Harry. He had found the large push-broom used to spread the hot tar. He had it poised over his head and was bringing it down on the pool of flaming liquid.

I hollered, "No," but it was too late. I think he saw it coming and lifted his head because his neck was covered in burning goo.

The police arrived about this point and asked what we were doing. We said we were just walking home from shopping, saw this fire that some miscreants must have started and were just trying to put it out. One officer was talking to me and one to Harry.

While talking to the police, I decided to remove the piece of now-cool tar from my hand. To my shock and horror, the tar took a couple of layers of skin. When I glanced at Harry, he was removing large chunks of the tar and skin from his neck. I went to him and his officer and told them they needed to get Harry to the hospital to remove the stuff. My guess is that the police knew we were involved but had no proof.

That's the last time I played with burning tar!

The names have been changed to protect the guilty.

A Walk Down Memory Avenue

By Julia A. Archer

Back in the 1940s during my years at Sacred Heart School, I frequently walked the two long blocks on Michigan Avenue east to the office of my father, Dr. F.J. Kronner, in the Calvin Theater Office Building just before the main library, now known as the Clara Bryant branch.

Across Michigan on the northeast corner was a gas station with an L-shaped building around it. Bays faced Michigan Avenue, and a white, two-story building with huge plate-glass windows faced Military. Next was a vacant lot. Remember when Muirhead's had the Styrofoam igloo and another year when the corral for reindeer was there? Following was the small brick Sloss Office Building. There followed a strip of stores. C.R. Smith grocery store had tin ceilings that you could later see through the dropped ceilings in the Bally Building.

There was also a record (yes, record) store in that strip and several other shops. Then a big red horse barn, the odors drifting out. Finally, after some space, in a large brick two-story building with a porch across the front was Dr. Ray Eilenfeldt and his wife's home. Their living quarters were on the second floor, and his offices were on the first. He was an osteopath and also took care of medical doctors' patients because MD's were commissioned officers in the World War II military. Here we are at Howard, the cross street.

A solid row of storefronts followed. Theilman's drugstore

with a soda fountain in the back, clothing stores, Gus's Greek Restaurant, the marquee to the Calvin Theater (with fake icicles indicating air conditioning), a shoe-repair store, the Sweet Shop, the entrance to the three-story Calvin Office Building, a travel agency, Dr. Firestone's eye practice and the library.

The walk certainly provided me with great memories!

Julia A. Archer is a lifelong Dearborn resident. She grew up within a mile of Sacred Heart and her present home. She has seven children. Six live in Dearborn. She has seven grandchildren and one great-grandchild.

A Swing Down Memory Lane

By Joan Dziadzio Boudreau

As I reflect on my childhood in Dearborn, my friendship with Peggy Pheney comes to mind. We have been friends from the age of 7, having attended school at Joshua Howard. For the sixth grade, my parents had me transferred to Sacred Heart.

Every morning all through the summer, Peggy and I would get together in her back yard and sit in her garden swing. We would swing back and forth and make all our plans for the day. We would set aside time for playing with our dolls, riding our bikes and playing with other neighborhood friends As it turned out, Peggy and I both became teachers. Maybe those hours of planning on the swing prepared us for the lesson plans that we would be faced with in our chosen careers.

Our times together would last just through each summer from Memorial Day to Labor Day. Peggy was truly my summertime best friend. It was almost like a rule; she was a "public," and I was a "parochial." We just couldn't mix the rest of the year. Looking back, I see much humor in this behavior; at the time I felt it made perfect sense.

As an adult, I have related stories about my friendship with Peggy to my husband and children. I have told them so much about the garden swing that for my 60th birthday they surprised me with one for our cottage. On the dedication day, they wanted

Peggy to be there for this wonderfully meaningful moment. I was overwhelmed with happiness as my summertime memories came flashing back through my mind.

Peggy remains a very special friend, and we often enjoy walking down memory lane together. Oh those lazy, hazy days of summer during our childhood!

Joan Dziadzio Boudreau has been married to Cyril (Cy) Boudreau since 1967. She has two children, Chris (married to Tracey Esper) and Amy (married to Sal Gencarelli). Joan has six grandchildren including a set of triplets. She is a graduate of Sacred Heart High School and is a retired Detroit Public School Teacher.

Surf's Up!
Down the Rouge
From Gulley to Southfield

By James Brand

In the spring of 1947, the Rouge River was at a very high level of flooding. Melting snow and then spring rains found the placid stream rampaging way beyond its normal confines. The rolling flood made a lot of news in the papers and also drew the attention of two curious teen-agers. Henry (Sandy) Brand and Jim Strang were standing on the Gulley Road bridge, watching the water boil under the structure and remarking on the high water.

Timing is everything. As they looked upstream, they saw a footbridge from a county park come bobbing along, handrails and all. As the footbridge hit the Gulley Road bridge, it got stuck. The boys ran down, grabbed the footbridge and beached it. They ran over to a downed tree, broke off a couple of stout branches, leaped on the footbridge and shoved off. They ducked as they went under the road bridge and soon found themselves sailing free toward Dearborn.

Bounding along the flats south of Dearborn Hills, they soon passed Telegraph Road and then Outer Drive. Hanging on like leeches, the two mariners flew by St. Joseph Retreat, Military Avenue, and Ford Field. A quick glimpse of the Brady Street apartments showed them the water was in the front doors. As they approached the Ford estate, the flooded powerhouse became apparent. Unknown to our two seamen, Henry Ford was on his deathbed as they shot past his home. Mr. Ford died that night by candlelight.

As the bridge/boat approached Southfield Road, the two crewmen finally woke up to the fact that they better get off before they wound up in the Detroit River. Using the branches they had picked up, they managed to steer the craft to a rather bumpy landing in some brush along the shore. Scrambling through sticky, muddy ground, they made it to dry land. Getting back home, they realized was going to involve a call home for transportation. There would also be a lot of explanations as to how they got where they were.

James Brand is a retired professor from Ferris State University. He grew up in Dearborn and graduated from Dearborn High in 1943. He has been retired for 26 years. He has traveled the USA, Canada, Mexico, New Zealand, Australia, and Scandinavia in a recreational vehicle.

The '60s: Past Perfect

By Cheryl Frank Brotz

Growing up in Dearborn in the '60s was almost picture perfect. Everyone knew the neighbors back then. And for a kid in the '60s, this was good and bad. I could jump on my bike, go to Brown's Store and grab ice cream for a quarter. Ride my bike to Ford Woods and be in the water all day. Walking from home on Steadman to Oakman School with the older kids was pretty cool. If I did something wrong in the neighborhood, my parents knew by that evening. We could take the bus to Schaefer and spend the afternoon shopping, then stop at Sanders for a cream puff.

Going to Oakman School had wonderful memories for me. The Clean-Up Parade was held every year, and children were asked to make signs for improving the community. Back then, we didn't realize we were starting the green movement.

The graduating sixth-grade class at Oakman always held a BBQ picnic that was great fun. I often think of that time as a child. I was lucky to be a part of a great community and one rich with history that most kids will never experience today.

I graduated from Dearborn High in 1977. Even then I felt the sense of community with people working together to improve Dearborn. I was a lucky kid.

Cheryl Frank Brotz now lives in Macomb with her husband and two daughters who are both attending college.

Clean Up, Paint Up, Fix Up

By Judy Byrwa

Being born and raised in Dearborn and living here most of my life, I have many special stories about my experiences, but one stands out that I don't believe any other city in the country had – the Dearborn "Clean-Up, Paint-Up and Fix-Up" parades.

I was attending St. Clement Catholic School in the 1950s, and every spring our entire school as well as all Dearborn schools would have out annual "Clean-Up, Paint-Up and Fix-Up" parade. We would march through the nearby streets carrying paint cans, paint brushes, rakes, brooms and the like, along with our homemade signs saying, "Clean-Up, Paint-Up and Fix-Up." Dearbornites took such pride in their homes, lawns and clean streets, and this was instilled in us at an early age. I was always so excited to participate in these parades. All the Girl Scouts and Boy Scouts would wear their uniforms, and there was always a Boy Scout who carried the big United States flag at the beginning of the parade.

They were wonderful times that gave us kids a sense of pride in our schools and in our neighborhoods, along with the knowledge that we could make a difference.

Judy Byrwa is retired and is planning to publish her first book on spiritualism.

'Round the Campfire, We Laugh and We Sing'

By Patricia "Tris" Bovich Caserio

"We're up at Camp Dearborn, the land of our dreams, where the water, it sparkles and glistens and gleams, so come along and join us for we are never blue, be a member of our happy camping crew – you too!

"At night round the campfire, we laugh and we sing, give a cheer for Camp Dearborn and let the echo ring. Give a cheer for our counselors for they are never blue, give a cheer for our campers – you too!"

From the summer of 1965 to the summer of 1970, my sister Mary Bea (Marnie) and I left the parking lot behind the Youth Center in a big bus for two weeks at Camp Dearborn Resident Camp. We each had a big suitcase and a rolled-up sleeping bag. Joining us were friends from Sacred Heart Grade School, including my best friend, Lynne Labardee, and our cousins.

The Resident Camp is long gone, but it was fabulous – it was wooded and up a hill. We were divided by age. Minnitonka starting at age 7, Nanatoga, Wee Tompi Woods and TopaWinga for the 14-year-olds. Each village had a song: "Oh, Nanatoga is the greatest, it is the greatest of them all.... You can always tell we're on the run, because we live in the land of the setting sun..." I can still sing every one, but that is another story. Music was a big part of the camp; we started each meal in an outdoor patio area. "High-Ho – the boatman go, up and down the river on the Ohio." "Want

72

to go on a bear hunt?" "Eddie Koochie- kachie-kamma-toesinarra-toesinocah-samma-kamma-waukee Brown." (Anyone who spent time at the camp is now singing along.) We sang outside before we went into the lodge for breakfast, lunch or dinner. We sat at tables of seven. Always one counselor, always a hostess, said grace before we started, and we were on teams to do set-up and clean-up chores.

During each session we would have a secret Indian ceremony for which we prepared. We fashioned candlesticks out of pieces of wood, sanded and waxed them until they gleamed. We used these for the ceremony, which involved HUGE magical bonfires and lots of dancing. I know the counselors enjoyed it as much as the kids because in my 21st year, I went back to work for the city of Dearborn as a counselor and saw what went on behind the scenes. It was one of the best summers of my life, the only time I lived outdoors in a tent for 12 weeks. My youngest brother, John, was a camper that summer in the boys' camp. Needless to say, he got a few extra privileges because his big sister was a counselor next door in the girls' camp. I think he went to every session that year.

One of the most memorable events at camp occurred during the summer of 1969. It started out as a normal day. We probably lashed a frame together with twigs in our craft session. We probably walked down the big hill to the lake for swimming, singing all the way. We may have had canoe practice for our upcoming three-day canoe trip. We probably had riflery or archery or fishing as an activity. We may have had a cookout over a campfire. We most certainly had our regular nighttime campfire. "All my bags are packed, I'm ready to go, I'm standing here outside your door"... "and the seasons they go round and round..." (Did I mention we sang a lot?) Anyway, that night we retired to our canvas-covered tents with the wood floor and an occasional mousy visitor only to be awakened probably around 10 p.m. We walked through the woods with flashlights and packed into the lodge that night. It was July 20, 1969, and we gathered around a very small television set probably 12 inches in diameter that one of the counselors had brought to camp. The crickets were chirping, and the night air was blowing through the screens. After some fuzzy reception, the black-and-white picture became clear, and at 10:56 p.m. we saw Neil Armstrong land on the moon. Everyone was silent as we tried to hear what he said through the static. We clapped and cheered at the sheer magnitude of the event. I will never, ever forget it.

I was sad when I heard that the camp shut down. It was such an amazing experience. Part of the closing ceremony each session included writing ourselves notes and sealing them in envelopes. The city of Dearborn mailed them back to us at Christmas—we were to open the letters and read about what fun we had at camp, (I think it was also to remind our parents to sign us up for the next session.) I still have one unopened letter I have kept all these years as a souvenir.

My sister Marnie and I used to talk about how some kids at other camps would be homesick and cry about going to an overnight camp. We cried when the session was over and it was time to leave, knowing we would have to wait a whole year to do it all over again.

I dedicate these memories to my dear sister Marnie (1954-2012), who passed away from brain cancer.

There is a wonderful link, full of many of the songs we sang at camp: http://www.ultimatecampresource.com/site/camp-activities/camp-songs.html.

Now sing along with me...

Oh, I was born one night, one morn, when the whistle went "Toot, Toot."
You can bake a cake or fry an egg, when the mudpies are in bloom.

Does six and six make nine, Does ice grow on a vine.
Is little Joe an Eskimo, in the good ole summertime.
So, loopty-loop through your noodle soup, just give your
socks a shine.
I'm guilty judge, I ate the fudge, three cheers
for Auld Lang Syne.
I cannot tell a lie, I ate an apple pie.
It's up a tree, beneath the sea, above the bright blue sky.
If Easter eggs don't wash their legs, their children
will have ducks.
I'd rather buy, a lemon pie, for forty-seven bucks.
Way down in Patagonia, I fell into the foamia
But that is all baloney-a, Paderewski blow your horn
"Toot, Toot."

*Patricia 'Tris' Bovich Caserio is a free-lance advertising art director
living in Los Angeles with her husband and two sons.*

Skinny-Dipping at Clara Bryant

By John A. Covert

In 1955 my family moved to Dearborn. Prior to enrollment in Dearborn Public Schools I had been attending parochial schools. On my first day at Clara Bryant, I was told that I would be attending physical education and that, among other things, I would need a jock supporter.

I wasn't sure what a jock supporter did or why I needed one, but I concluded it had something to do with my manhood. I did not discuss the matter with my parents, but instead pedaled my bike over to a dry-goods store at Ford and Telegraph. I was embarrassed when a lady sales clerk approached me and asked how she could help. I mumbled, "I need a jock supporter." She replied, way too loudly, "You need a sock supporter?" I gulped and belted out, "No, I need a jock supporter." "What size?" She asked. I eventually departed with a medium, but this was only the beginning of my gym class adventure.

I soon discovered that swimming was part of class–nude swimming. After a few days it was no big deal, but there were the persistent rumors of secret peep holes where the girls could spy on the boys or vice-versa.

Years later, during the twilight of my own service as a public school teacher, I was relating all of this to some of my much younger colleagues, who were shocked that students could actually be required to swim in the nude. After I described how the boys would – one at a time – spread their cheeks to show the teacher they had washed properly, one fellow remarked, "Well, I'll never complain about taking attendance again."

John A. Covert is a retired Livonia Public Schools teacher. He is an environmental activist.

The Flying Eggs
And the Cardboard Caper

By Maury Dean

To get back to the Old Scooter Gang (*Best Dearborn Stories, Vol. I, p. 93*), we required five years growing up on Elizabeth Street, shimmering in the west Dearborn sub-teen glow of Glenn O'Kray's Aunt Helen Bandyke's streetlight, at the magical corner of Doxtator and Elizabeth. Like the *Don't Stop Believin'* dude (Journey, #8, 1981), and maybe YOU, I was actually born and raised in south Detroit.

Well, middle Detroit, for my first nine years. It's a mile from Motown's three four-square West Grand Boulevard studio buildings, where Doug Warren's Greasytones and I found sketchy employment from Smokey Robinson and Berry Gordy somewhere in the scintillating '60s. Ed McCoy and I cranked out hopeful Soul/ Rockabilly/Teenpop hits with Big Mack and Fortune Records.

My ultimate fortune was basically reality – "Son, don't quit your day job, and yes, you've gotta work at it for 40 years." Which I did, thanks to grudgingly following my power-house engineer John Dean's hard-nosed Work Ethic. So zoom back with me to the red-gold maple fall 1952-1959 zone, singing rock and roll ballads with Glenn, Toby Kuta and the davishing Doxtator streetlight dudes on Elizabeth Street.

As Hallowe'en glimmered in the Dearborn High orange tiger sky, some of us were often up to no good. It was getting late early, so three local guys (Greg, Gary and Don) and I invested in some eggs to go with our adventurous, newly teen-age minds. We walked a block toward Sullivan's Bar. Sure, we soaped windows, doused shaving cream and practiced Applied Tomfoolery. But we were 13 now and needed to amplify our street-cred courage via some really foolish, semi-idiotic prank, like our hero Bugs Bunny might pull off on rootin'-tootin' stooge Elmer Fudd.

I was a Wheaties/Cheerios/Frosted Flakes guy anyhow. I couldn't look an egg in the eye and dream of eating the gooey thing, unless it sneaked into a devil's-food cake or something. "Arsenic in little white shells" was my favorite Tom Schmitz teen-age-curmudgeony egg quote.

We kids had no SmartPhones or octagon thugs or daily major league color TV baseball. When some vampirish vandal said, "The only good egg is a flying egg," we jumped onto the Smart-Alecky Flying Egg Bandwagon.

Eggs! Sullivan's was a nifty neighborhood west Dearborn shot-beer-martini watering-hole my "uncle," John Sullivan, attended after his humdrum accounting day bloomed into Jimmy Buffett's *It's Five O'Clock Somewhere*. A beery thirst sent Sullivan to Sullivan's Bar to witness celebrants to October glee, glory and hangovers. Since we ran half a mile in Coach Jack Johnson's Bryant Junior High just yesterday, we egg-chuckers figured we could outrun ANY old guy maybe 45, or 39, or 26, or 71.

We snuck up like goblins at the back door, as October frost glazed our ungloved young macho hands. We fondled raw eggs and hung fire to unleash a barrage of eggy terror. Greg, later a Taylor cop, opened the back door and gazed inside Sullivan's Bar. Unrelated pal John Sullivan was not there on bar-stool row (that would have nixed our nasty scheme). After-work dudes sat in the smoky choking glow, chugging Goebel and Stroh's beer in their finest work suits. Logo T-shirts were a thing of the future, and Levi's forbidden in many '50s bars. Their Pop Standard jukebox bubbled with sophisticated Sinatra strings and sleepy midnight escapes into Oktoberfest brews and booze. We saw enough. No one there was young or fast enough to dream of catching us fleet-footed teen-age terrors.

"Ready, aim, fire!" Our fearless foursome heaved our two dozen oval barrage down the bar-stool line, and splat–beer buffs now got egg in their beer. No one cared about cholesterol back then, but flying eggs became very bad news that evening for a whole lot of us. Amid a chorus of eggy splats on silk suits and a rebound roar of cursing unheard of on '50s black-and-white TV, Sullivan's Bar erupted in chaos, consternation and a bunch of old guys over 25 in wing-tip running and stampeding after us. Uh oh.

No problem. We knew the perfect getaway escape route. No scooters yet, just fast feet. We hotfooted down the alley between Elizabeth and Martha, dashing from Ford Road a long block down to our safe-haven Doxtator, where these old guys would never find us. We flew down the grubby alley at Olympian pace, whisking by trash cans, growly dogs and grass clumps. We heard no swift footsteps chasing right behind, as we speedily escaped this outraged growling mob of raging, egg-spattered bar patrons. As we dashed onto our home-turf Doxtator to teen-age freedom, our tranquility exploded.

This '53 Ford Customline shrieked around the corner on two wheels, brakes in a soprano screech. An angry, eggy 6-foot-3 bruiser jumped out and grabbed Gary, firing our pal into the car. We couldn't exactly call the police in that cell-phoneless era, could we? We three frozen fugitives shivered in Johnny Walz's parents' shrubs for an hour. We sweated Gary's fate and traded safety and security for frostbite. Finally, we figured the coast was clear and headed to my nearby place for cider and doughnuts. It was the perfect crime, we chortled, but we had to find out what happened to Gary, and we hoped he was OK.

The beefy bruiser who grabbed Gary was sitting in my living room with Gary's father, Greg's father and Don's father. My Golden Gloves middleweight Windsor boxing champ father looked very serious, and I was hoping for maybe just getting grounded for about nine years. Gary was there, too. Nobody blamed him for implicating us all.

"Why'd you do it, Maury?" my father asked. I thought

up a story of the "Do WHAT?" variety, but the big tough elderly 25-year-old dude with the egg-splat suit had us dead to rights. We confessed our "perfect crime," and our folks were crestfallen at the lack of perfection in their teen-ager lads. Or were they?

Gary's dad, who worked like everybody else in Dearborn for Ford's auto empire, had just met my General Motors power house engineer father. The two of them gave the burly bruiser a beer for his trouble, and the three rehashed various scrapes they'd all encountered as nighthawk lads. I think they were glad we kids actually HAD adventures, not just vicariously WATCHED them on TV.

Gary's dad asked, "Maury, didn't you and Gary sit on this big flat cardboard box chunk right here in Sullivan's vacant lot on Ford Road in a snowstorm last year and count whether more Fords passed than Chevys?" Yep, we did, we confessed. Gary was sad to agree that Chevy edged out Ford 237 to 235, with Oldsmobiles crunching 142 sightings and Buicks at 111, and 99 Mercurys, 88 Pontiacs, 79 Plymouths, 59 Dodges and 16 DeSotos, 15 Cadillacs, 12 Lincolns and 10 Chryslers, plus the odd Studebaker, Willys, Jeep, Hudson, Packard, Kaiser, and mini-car Crosley. And one Volkswagen.

Decades down the pike, '70s and '80s and '90s Cardboard Kids discovered Toyotas, Nissans, BMWs and whatever else. Our '50s survey, though, was nearly vintage all-American mobiles strutting down the white-ribbon concrete boulevards of the World's Greatest Suburb, Dearborn; its parent, the Arsenal of Democracy Detroit; in the World's Greatest State, Michigan; in the World's Greatest Auto-Birthing Country, the United States of America. Zowie. But then the conversation morosely drifted back to flying chicken embryos. Eggs, arrrgh,

The four fated fathers, not forefathers, the men whose egg-flinging sons had beaten back boredom by a gutsy prank (albeit a stupid one) decided they'd better go over to Sullivan's Bar to pay back the suit-cleaning fees, since we aimed low on purpose and no one got hurt. No shots were fired, and no animals harmed.

You see, we all listened to our moms' lectures ("Be careful. Don't put somebody's eye out"), and aimed for cloth, not flesh. My three equally guilty friends were sent home to do penance and atonement, while our fathers and their wallets marched right off to Sullivan's Bar to make reparations for the Terrible Teen-age Flying Egg Bombardment.

Seems the fathers had an extremely excellent and eggless time at Sullivan's Bar. Seems it took our dads until the bar closed at 2 a.m., and they had to show up in the bleary-eyed shop at 6 or 7 a.m. at Ford's or GM. Apparently, our moms weren't too overjoyed about THE DADS EITHER, saying the four dads had too much fun themselves at the pub. So our gender was in the collective doghouse.

But wait. So the great egg-splat news was this. My mom, Liz Dean, was a bit of a Prohibition-era rebel herself growing up in Butte, Montana, and my dad left Scotland at 13, with a couple of teen-age pranks under HIS belt too. So nobody got busted or belted for egg-chucking, and nobody was real happy. Miraculously, I plea-bargained my punishment into two weekends grounded and extra chores and the promise of a helmetless 40-mph motor scooter when I became an adult the next year on my 14th birthday.

Those were the days, my friends. We thought they'd never end. Look at my poor Detroit birthplace today, and our Atkinson house there still stands, but the neighborhood is pretty much gone. Look at our Dearborn Elizabeth Street block. Aside from a little new multiculturalism, it is still the semi-innocent wonder that was my America of the '50s and beyond. Praise be.

Maury Dean got his doctorate from the University of Michigan and taught at Suffolk Community College in New York. He has written The Rock Revolution, Rock and Roll, Gold Rush, *and* This'll be the Day: The Life and Legacy of Buddy Holly.

My Introduction to Dogs — And Old People

By Mary DiPaulo

There were several old people residing all in a row to the east of my childhood home on Prospect Street in east Dearborn– and to the next corner, where my best friend lived. Back then, "old" is what we called anyone over the age of 50.

Growing up in the '60s, I remember thinking that if I ever needed lemonade or a cookie as I was hiking the150 steps from my house to my friend's house on the corner, I could rely on either Mrs. Vanderpanz (my immediate next-door neighbor to the east), or Mary Gizzard (her next-door neighbor to the east), or Helena O'Hara (yep, you got it – her next-door neighbor to the east) if necessity dictated.

Not that it ever happened, but it was certainly nice to know I had so many available old ladies living one right after the other between my house and the corner.

Their dogs, however, represented a very different story. Prince was the German shepherd next door. He wasn't a prince at all in my estimation; he was a loaded and lethal weapon used to scare little girls like me right into orbit. Prince was Mrs. Vanderpanz's dog, and only a flimsy chain link fence about 4 feet high separated us. Even though I liked Mrs. Vanderpanz, Prince really and I do mean REALLY scared me. I remember at the time thinking I should always watch his tail. If it moved back and forth, that was a good thing. If it didn't move, STAY AWAY FROM THE FENCE!

I know that Mr. Vanderpanz (when he was alive) must have realized this too because he often encouraged me to come over to the fence and "meet" Prince proper-like when we were outside at the same time. Silly me – thought if I was being invited to meet the dog with Mr. Vanderpanz there, maybe the dog knew that he had to be nice back at me. WRONG!

Although I don't remember the incident, my mother said Prince bit me when I was around 4 years old. He could have bitten my head off for all I can recall, but what scars I do carry are limited to my forehead, fingers and knees. So maybe Prince bit me from bottom to top or top to bottom. I don't know. What I do know is that I never thought dogs would be a welcome part of my world for forever and a day after Prince showed me his choppers up close and personal.

Yet, as God would have it, Prince wasn't the only German shepherd living in "the row" between my house and the corner. Helena O'Hara had one too, but hers was a girl named Duchess. Thankfully, however, Duchess really WAS a nice dog and not at all like Prince. (Even though they could pass for twins separated at birth in the looks department.) Funny how that worked out. The first time I thought Mrs. O'Hara had the same dog as Mrs. Vanderpanz, I almost fainted dead away on the spot. This was probably a year or so after the bite incident with Prince. But Mr. O'Hara brought Duchess right up to me (leashed and on a lead) so she could sniff me and therefore find me acceptable in my skin. And ever since that moment, Duchess and I became great friends. I spent more days during the summers going over to play with Duchess than I think I did with my best friend on the corner. I loved that dog. I am also thankful that Helena didn't have any other kids in her house to compete with me for Duchess's time and attention.

Residing in between Prince and Duchess, Mary Gizzard's dog was some orange-and-white, yappy little thing that didn't even look like a dog in my opinion. I should have probably given it a chance in that it was about 10 times smaller than either Prince or Duchess, and it seemed to be loved to bits by Mary and her husband, Elmer. However, when a kid like me has already met the two biggest dogs she'll never ever forget for the remainder of time and space, a little yappy thing cannot compare in the least. As did none of the other small fries that came and went on our street and throughout our neighborhood during all the years I lived there.

Epilogue: 50 years and two rescue beagles later, I waited until age 41 before fully understanding the benefits of canine ownership, the healing power of pets, and the benefits of raising dogs under 20 pounds each.

Mary DiPaolo, M.A., LLP, is a Northville-based psychotherapist whose radio talk show Sunday Sessions *aired on WJR-760AM. She is also a former small-business columnist with the Observer & Eccentric newspapers, wife of 32 years, and mother of three (one human and two canine). Her blog may be found at www. yourweeklysession.blogspot.com*

A Shout-Out to Old Pals, Teachers, Coaches

By Claude Dillard

Many of my recollections were passed on by my late parents, Herb and Jean Dillard, and my older brothers, Herb Jr. and Louis.

Ford Motor transferred my dad from Memphis, Tennessee, to Dearborn in 1948. We lived initially in the historically furnished Patrick Henry House behind the Dearborn Inn.

We moved to 22312 Hollander, a block from York School, later renamed Joshua Howard. Although I was already 6 years old, I was placed in kindergarten because I had no prior schooling in Tennessee (but I did wear shoes!). Supposedly I caused numerous disruptions and was moved into first grade rather quickly. My close friend was Jim Flake. My first crush was Margaret Bond. (You knew, right, Jay?) I was on the Safety Patrol and enjoyed the free musical instrument program. I enjoyed walking to the park, playground and ice rink.

In the 1951 Dearborn High yearbook, there is a photo of Herb Jr. and friends in front of our house titled "The Gang's All Here." I'm the one in sailor hat.

Ford transferred our family to North Kansas City, Missouri, from 1951-1954 for my dad to work at the Claycomo Plant, where bomber wings were being built for the Korean Conflict.

We returned in 1954 and lived at 1512 Nightingale near Divine Child and Levagood Park. I attended Clara Bryant Junior High. Many of the students remembered me from grade school and recalled my funny Southern accent. My first "love" was the late Jill Markley, who became a great writer, publisher and editor. I thoroughly enjoyed the time I got my braces and the class "forced" me to kiss one of the girls with braces to see if we would lock together.

I was greatly influenced by my coaches, Jack Johnson (basketball, gym) and Sherm Collins (basketball, tennis). Because of them I chose to pursue college at Eastern Michigan to become a teacher and coach, although my career path turned into computer programming and system design. I still keep in touch with both of them.

I remember school plays like *HMS Pinafore* with Bob Cushman; great musicians like Paul Ganson (bassoon) and Chuck Feger (tenor sax), who had highly successful musical careers. Google Chuck's group, The Showcasemen. I really had fun on Saturday mornings at open gym, playing basketball against high school and college players. Fred Drilling was already a great tennis player at that time and has played in over 70 international events, winning numerous titles, including the 2007 ITF Super Singles World Championship in New Zealand and the 2012 USTA National Men's 70 Clay Court Singles and Doubles Championships. He is currently ranked fourth in the world. He is still "volleying" with Coach Collins in Florida.

My ninth-grade year was at the "old" Dearborn High on Mason. The building was ancient and intimidating. It was fun, though, having teachers who taught Herb Jr. like Dorothy Wolfe, English, who said she hoped I was a better student than he was, and Coach Carl Flegle. One of my favorite teachers was Coach Herb

Schroeder. In gym class, he was showing me wrestling moves and accidentally (?) broke my wrist. He was so embarrassed to have to call and explain it to my dad. We remained friends until his death in 2009.

It is no surprise: Coaches Flegle, Schroeder and Johnson are in the Michigan High Schools Coaches Association Hall of Fame. And Coach Collins, who also coached many successful teams at Henry Ford Community College during a 30-year career, received the Dearborn Sports Hall of Fame Legends Award in March 2013. It has been my honor to have been coached by each of them.

The new Dearborn High School opened in 1957. We were the first sophomore class. My homeroom was held in Ranald Becker's machine shop. He was a stickler for being on time. He relished sending us, especially the girls, to the office for being late, even if the tardy bell was still ringing. I always sat next to Fran DeLuca in homeroom and in every class we had together where seating was alphabetical. Our first and only date was to the senior prom, which was a great choice.

I also remember Ed Lanzi's class where he deducted points from our class scores if we referred to his wrestlers as "guys" and not "men." But he also added points when we attended their meets.

One of the many benefits of Ford Motor's generosity was sponsorship of driver training cars and driving track across the street from school. Having a whole semester of driver training instilled mental and physical driving skills that are missing in today's weekend driving schools.

One of my dearest friends from high school was Bill Angell. Over the years we talked about the politics of the day, but mostly about our years in Dearborn and how lucky we were to have been raised there during the '50s and '60s. He recalled my encounter with Mr. Becker in shop class that almost came to blows. Bill said he actually respected him more after that and was thankful for it.

Another memorable classmate who achieved worldwide success because of Dearborn and the arts programs is Ben Franklin, aka Ralph Archbold. Ralph is the "official" Benjamin Franklin in Philadelphia. Coincidentally, he shares a January 17 birthday with Benjamin Franklin! In the past 35 years, he has portrayed Ben Franklin more than 7,000 times at political events as well as community events. He also married Betsy Ross (Linda) July 3, 2008, in Independence Hall, Philadelphia.

One of the funniest, although dangerous, pranks I recall was due to the 1959 TV series *The Untouchables*. It inspired (?) a fake kidnapping in front of the Dearborn Theatre, with real guns and a hearse. I don't recall the culprits, but this time the Dearborn Police Department was not amused.

We lived at 240 N. Mildred at Myrtle from 1959 until my parents moved to San Diego in 1975.

In 2010 I attended our 50th reunion. It was really nice to see many of my classmates, teachers Jack Johnson, Tony Russo and especially Dorothy Wolfe, who stayed to the very end, outlasting the majority of us. Thanks to David Gorden and the many others who organized this event and for maintaining e-mail communications with all of us over the years.

Along with most Dearborn residents, I have very fond memories of the great school system with the music, arts, sports programs and our FANTASTIC teachers. We had excellent parks throughout the city, with free tennis lessons, tobogganing at Ford Field, day camp at Camp Dearborn, Greenfield Village and Edison

Institute. My mom had Mayor Hubbard's direct phone number on the refrigerator and used it often! Also, I was fortunate to have worked for the Recreation Department at several parks and playgrounds, especially, on the east side, where I met many, many wonderful people from diverse ethnic backgrounds. A shout-out to the Berry clan.

I will be forever grateful to Henry Ford and the city of Dearborn.

Claude Dillard has been living in San Diego since 1975, retiring in 2006. He is married and has three children, 49, 24 and 20.

Recollections of a Survivor

By Marguerite Lab Doman

One of the things I remember about growing up in Dearborn in the 1920s is that my grandparents lived on a farm covering many acres. My favorite meal for breakfast was fried cornmeal mush. It was quite a treat. My grandma would prepare the mixture the night before. We would serve it with maple syrup. The only place that I know that serves it now is Bob Evans'.

All cars had a running board on them. I remember that I was occasionally allowed to stand on the running board while my dad drove. We owned a Model A. It was a lot of fun. I remember when it would rain. You didn't just roll up the window. My dad would stop the car and we would pull up the icing glass. As Ford Road wasn't paved, we were always getting stuck. We would have to get out of the car and push!

My mother wore a corset that seemed to me to be a pain in the neck. My aunt was the one to tighten the corset. My mother would say, "Pull it tighter. Pull it tighter!" I thought that she couldn't breathe, but she survived.

In the winter we would go skating on Twin Ponds by Oakwood Boulevard. Everybody went there. You could meet all of your friends there. We loved going to Muirhead's Department Store at Christmas.

When somebody did die as I was growing up, black was

placed on the front door of the house of the deceased. This would tell everyone that somebody had died. The coffin was shown in the front room. The oldest child was expected to sit by the casket overnight.

Memories keep me going.

Marguerite Lab Doman is a retired school teacher and is 97 years old. She has lived in Dearborn all her life. She now lives in Oakwood Common.

Exploring Ford Country

By Charles R. Dysarz

I was born and raised in east Dearborn on Palmer Street, just two short blocks west of Greenfield Road and about one mile south of where Henry Ford was born. There was a gate on the north end of my street where the pavement turned to gravel. A sign on the gate read, "Private Property No Trespassing." This was Henry Ford's original homestead, with a large red barn that housed farm implements. There were crops in the field, and at this place in time, rows of Ford tractors were stored there waiting shipment. Henry's birthplace farmhouse was still there across Greenfield Road on the corner of Ford Road. He also had a large barn behind the house that, upon inspection, was full of enormous pipe organs and other furnishings that he was collecting for his museum.

There were six streets in our little neighborhood, all less than a mile long and running north from Michigan Avenue, surrounded on three sides by Ford's property. Even our school (Henry Ford) at the end of Driscoll Street was surrounded the same way. Looking west from the schoolyard toward Southfield Road, you would see all Ford farmland, and if you looked real hard, you could see the barbed-wire fence on the other side of the road all the way down from Michigan Avenue north to Ford Road. That was the back yard of Henry Ford's Estate. He tilled a few acres of land on his side of the fence to feed the animals that roamed his property, mainly deer that could be seen grazing out in the field.

With so much wide-open space around, where was a kid

to play? On Ford's property, of course. There were always three or four of us kids from the neighborhood looking for adventure. We would spend all week at school planning our weekend jaunts, and when Saturday came around, it was through the soybean fields, across the railroad tracks and into Ford's woods behind the Ford Foundation.

There was a huge poured-concrete sewer pipe stuck in the ground at the edge of the Rouge River that ran through the property; it provided us with shelter from the elements as well as a meeting place. We would build a campfire, swing on vines that hung from the trees and work on a raft that we were building to float down the river. Life was good and no one bothered us. At the end of the day, the sun going down and our bellies empty, we would head for home to a nice warm meal and the comfort of our family.

During summer vacation we pitched a tent in a patch of woods near our homes and adjacent to Ford's cornfield. We could ride our bikes there and still be home within minutes. The tent stayed there all summer long, and we would take turns sleeping overnight and roasting corn over an open fire, and still no one bothered us. We would do the usual activities during the day like swimming, biking, baseball and then congregate at the tent later in the day. It was fun sitting around the campfire telling jokes and stories of the day.

One day we got the idea to venture into the Henry Ford estate and take a look around. That part of our realm was always a mystery to us, so the consensus was that we were going in. Our point of entry was under the barbed-wire fence where it crossed over a creek running through the property along Southfield Road. We crawled along the edge of the creek like real commandos until we were close enough to the woods to make our entry unnoticed. We had to be stealthy and keep an eye out for Ford's security guards who patrolled the property. They would drive their cars slowly through the woods, and although we were scared, we hid behind some trees until they passed.

We came across a neat little cabin that had a sign on the chimney, "Santa's Workshop." There was no lock on the door, so we went in. It had a smooth, wooden floor with a rope bed in the corner, a big wooden table and chairs and a fireplace. It was cool, dark and very quiet inside, as if the occupants had moved out. There was a manger out back with hay or alfalfa in it. We stayed there a while and watched silently through the windows at the deer that came to feed; then a security car drove slowly by and the deer ran off.

We then took to the woods again and discovered bridal paths about 8 feet wide winding through the woods and birdhouses everywhere. The bridal paths were easy to walk and quiet compared to walking on fallen branches off of the paths, but we started to worry about a horse rider coming around the bend, and we wouldn't be able to outrun a horse, though we hadn't seen one all day. We saw a small horse barn through the trees, but didn't dare go over there and look inside because it was out in the open and we didn't want to be seen. We saw the mansion way down through an open area, but didn't venture too close for fear of getting caught.

After a while, the feeling of vulnerability set in, and we were definitely on the wrong side of the fence, so, having had enough sightseeing for the day, we found our way back to the creek and made it out of there without incident.

In early fall Ford farmhands harvested soybeans right in the field next to our school. We kids would jump up on the trucks and stuff our pockets with the beans to use for ammunition in our pea shooters. We would walk down the street shooting at each other, dogs, cats, flower pots, empty milk bottles on the porches, whatever. It was all in fun and it didn't hurt.

In the winter the farm fields were desolate, and our weekend jaunts across the railroad tracks were fewer. We would go skating at Ford's twin ponds on Oakwood Boulevard in west Dearborn or sled down the hill at Ford Field. Our school was open for recreation in the evening so we could swim or play in the gym as we waited for spring and a new lease on life away from the bonds of school.

I had the best childhood a boy could have, with wide-open spaces to roam, always exploring Henry Ford's property – vast acres of soybeans, corn wheat, tomatoes, even pumpkins and plenty of wooded areas to hone my frontiersman skills.

I was 12 years old when Henry Ford died in April 1947. Little did I know that I would be working for him just six years later at the Rouge Plant. Many years later I realized the influence that this man had on my life. All the many adventures and explorations that he unknowingly provided will never be forgotten, and for that I thank him. Henry, I never knew ya!

Charles R. Dysarz started working at the Ford Rouge engine plant directly out of Fordson in 1953 and quit after two years. He then attended night school at Lawrence Institute of Technology and worked in various job shops around Detroit as a special machine designer. In 1962 he was hired by Ford Advance Engine Department as an engine designer. He retired in 1996 as a senior casting design engineer.

Call the Firehouse

By Leo Early

Many of my memories of attending Dearborn's St. Alphonsus High School in the late '70s are centered on music. From the marching band in the fall to playing Broadway musical scores every spring, perhaps my favorite piece of St. Al's history is of playing the 1978 Sophomore Unity Dance.

By my second year at the high school, I was playing guitar in a four-piece combo called Diamond." With all apologies to Neil, our name had evolved from Black Diamond, a song by popular shock rockers Kiss. Diamond (the band) had a repertoire that was heavy on Kiss material, but the set list was also peppered with tunes by Queen, Peter Frampton, Bruce Springsteen, David Bowie and Sweet.

When the band was booked to play the Sophomore Unity Dance, we decided to go all-out. With Pat Butler and me on guitar, John Ewing on bass and Jeff Bochenek on drums, we rehearsed daily in a basement recreation-room-turned-rehearsal-studio on Neckel Avenue. Kiss' influence was strong enough that our ensemble also attempted to mimic bits of the band's stagecraft. This included "Kiss-esque" lighting, flames, flashes and smoke, though we wisely stopped short of the high heels and makeup. We assembled a loyal road crew that included one kid who was a bit of a firebug and was logically appointed our "pyro-technician."

We built our own speaker cabinets and lights but struggled with the special effects. Amateur chemists, we perilously experimented with the chemicals necessary to create the kind of dramatic flash effects and puffs of smoke that Kiss had employed. Ultimately, we were thwarted by budget and knowledge. We had to settle for paper-match-fueled flaming coffee cans we grudgingly misnamed "flash-pots," an industry term. For in fact, they did not "flash" at all.

In advance of the big gig, our sophomore moderator, Mr. Kwasni, wisely required us to demonstrate our lighting and pyrotechnics in the cafeteria. We lugged in our homemade, multi-color floodlights and our "flash pots" and explained where we would be placing our fog machine, drum riser and amplifiers. Mr. Kwasni's attention immediately focused on the incendiary portion of our act and asked to see just how it worked.

We had brought along a slightly larger load of match heads than previously tested, assuming this amount would produce the desired final effect. We dimmed the lights in the lunch room. We threw the switch on the toy train transformer that electrically ignited hundreds of paper match heads in two Maxwell House cans. Two massive columns of flame shot up illuminating the entire cafeteria! The force of the ignition was so strong that virtually all the match heads struck the 20-foot ceiling and ricocheted, smoldering, back to the floor. "The Kwas" immediately grabbed a fire extinguisher as we hopscotched about the linoleum searching for secondary fires. His eyes were as wide as saucers and he appeared to have broken out in a cold sweat. I don't recall his exact string of expletives, but were all glad there were no nuns within earshot. Fortunately for the sophomores and the band, the extinguisher was not discharged, and the fire department was not dispatched.

After the scene was stabilized, we realized we wouldn't be expelled. To our astonishment, our new co-conspirator, Mr. Kwasni, approved the use of our now re-christened FLAMETHROWERS! The proviso being that we make modifications to contain any flaming match heads.

The Sophomore Unity Dance ultimately went off without a hitch. Mr. Kwasni even sat in with us on piano for an Elton John tune. Our closing number was Kiss' incendiary *Firehouse*, begun by a member of our crew turning the crank on a borrowed World War I mechanical ambulance siren: rrrrrrrrrRRRRRRRRRRRRRRRRR RRRRRRRRrrrrrrrrrr.

I'll never forget the crowd's reaction as our newly modified, faculty-approved flamethrowers went off with a FOOM!! "CALL THE FIREHOUSE!" went the chorus, "CUZ SHE SETS MY SOUL ON FIE-YAH!!" FOOM!! I felt the heat on my forearm and face from standing too close, yet I never missed a note. Diamond really got a lot of mileage out of that gig – St. Al's talked about the show for weeks afterward.

Although none of us ever achieved fame and fortune in the music business, I still enjoy playing and performing music to this day. All thanks to skills that I developed in the sanctified, smokey halls of St. Alphonsus.

Leo Early makes a living in the information technology space. A musician, avid preservationist and author, he is finishing a book on Detroit's historic Grande Ballroom.

Car Keys

By Bill Fader

I was a very lucky kid, I now realize, to grow up in Dearborn in the 1950s. I was an extra lucky kid, I also now know, to have been born in 1941 to the Fader family, where love and trust abounded.

One of the benefits I experienced was that because of the upbringing I had, I learned a sense of responsibility. And so, as a young teen I had a series of jobs, including paper boy, vendor at fairs and bazaars, and grass cutter. So I was able to save for my dream – a car of my own. My parents were willing to allow me this indulgence, and on the very day of my 16th birthday, I became the proud owner of an almost 5-year-old 1953 Pontiac Chieftain Deluxe for which I paid $500, most of my savings.

A black two-door sedan with a three-speed stick on the column and a rather underpowered straight-eight engine, this car was anything but a teen-ager's typically longed-for car. But I loved it! I continued working at part-time jobs while going to Sacred Heart High School in order to keep my Pontiac "healthy," to pay for registration/license plate fees and insurance, and to have spending money for gas and outings.

Of course, I was not the only one at Sacred Heart High who had a car to get around in, though there weren't really very many of us in those days. At some point during the high school years, my pal Glenn O'Kray came to own a much nicer car than mine – a gorgeous black '56 Chevy Bel Air Convertible. I surely did admire his chariot a lot! But still feeling very fortunate to even have my own car as a teen, I truly wasn't jealous.

A discovery occurred a good many months after Glenn got his car. I don't recall what brought it about, but he happened to learn one day that the key to his Chevy would unlock my Pontiac's doors. It would not, however, work in the ignition to start my car. Well, this finding, of course, led me to try my key in his car doors. Yes indeed, I also had access to his car whether or not it was locked. The most unusual thing of all about this phenomenon, though, was that my key would also fire up his Chevy's engine!

Glenn and I both enjoyed relating our tale about the non-uniqueness of car keys produced for some General Motors products in the '50s – to whomever was willing to listen, I'm sure. Strangely, the vehicle belonging to friend Tom, a '54 Pontiac very similar to my '53, was secure from entry by both Glenn and me when it was locked. And as well, our locked cars failed to give Tom access. But other than telling the story over and over, I don't recall that we gave it too much more thought.

But one beautiful, rather warm and sunny late-winter day, Glenn was nowhere to be found at lunchtime, and I thought it would be pretty special to have a short convertible ride. Classmates I was with at the time encouraged the idea, and I charged right into my evil deed. I stole – well, really just borrowed – Glenn's car for a joyride. Six or seven of us piled into the Chevy, I started it, opened up the ragtop to the fresh air and sunshine, and off we went. Up and down Garrison and Morley we drove, delighting in the pleasures of our wicked ways. The ride became even more fun when we spotted Glenn walking along the sidewalk with some other Sacred Heart friends. Horn blaring and voices shouting, we brazenly greeted the convertible's owner. A memory I'll treasure as long as I live is the amazed look on Glenn's face as recognition dawned and he shouted, "THAT'S MY CAR!"

Did I get away with this infraction scot-free? Oh no! Upon entering the classroom just in time for my first afternoon session, I glanced out the window overlooking Garrison Street. What did I see? My shiny old Pontiac had been shoved forward from its legal parking spot into the "No Parking" zone in front of the school. There it sat as ticket bait for the Dearborn Police. I made my apologies to Sister Rose Matthew in the classroom and tore down the stairs, where, of course, the principal, Mother Marie Isabel, stood at her post, clocking in the late returnees from lunch. More apologies and explanations, and then, permission or not, I headed out the front door to rescue my pride and joy. The nuns must have gotten a laugh from my predicament, for nothing ever came of it and no penalties were leveled.

There were additional times, one or two of them anyway, when my Pontiac wound up being moved and steered by boy-power to a place where it should not have been. And there are many more fond memories of my years as a youth in Dearborn, as well, and of my remarkable friends from those days. But this one, the story of the car keys, is one of my special favorites. Indeed, this was but one minor example of the fact that I was a most fortunate boy to have loving parents who had made the decision to make their one and only family home in the beautiful city of Dearborn, Michigan.

Bill Fader is retired and lives in Ferndale after teaching in elementary school classrooms for 33 years. He has a son, a daughter and three young grandchildren.

The Sisterhood
Of the Traveling '49 Ford

By Mary "Meg" Falk

Michigan, 1954. I was 10 years old and living with my family in a small upstairs flat in southwest Detroit. At the beginning of that summer, our parents told us we were moving to Dearborn. I had no idea that this move would set me on a traveling sisterhood journey that continues to this day.

That fall, I started sixth grade at Sacred Heart School with a lot of trepidation and no friends. Soon, however, the girls in my class would become my fast friends. We did everything together. Those were our bike years. At that time, you could call us "The Sisterhood of the Traveling Bike Riders." And did we bike a lot! We were always riding to each other's homes, to different Dearborn swimming pools, sports practices/events, and, of course, to the Sip N Nip on Telegraph Road. We could ride forever, be gone all day, and our parents would never worry. We were just told to be home by dark and not drown in the Rouge River. As I look back, I am in awe of the seeds of sisterhood that were sowed on those bikes then and continue to blossom to this day.

I need to clarify that the sisterhood was never a specific number of girls. Rather it was a large, inclusive group that in big and small subgroups connected at different times for various exploits, slumber parties, sock hops and get-togethers.

The Bike Sisterhood grew older. Eagerly, we took driving lessons and, yes, on our 16th birthday went to Dearborn City

Hall to get that coveted driver's license. Thus, the "biker sisters" graduated to cars, another important chapter in the sisterhood journey.

Since there were three teen-agers in our house, my parents decided to get us an old car to drive ourselves around in. If it got beat up a bit, no problem. It was old. Enter our black, four-door 1949 Ford. What a find! It had a V-8 engine and standard shift, which all kids knew how to drive back then. It also had a spotlight – a really neat feature.

My girlfriends and I had more than a few adventures in that Ford. Where do I start? We did what all the kids did back then: We cruised up and down Michigan Avenue, stopping at drive-ins to look for friends. Probably we were mostly looking for boys. During these rides, we would share our observations, our secrets, our disappointments, our latest heartthrobs and the latest gossip. Our lifelong bonds were getting even stronger in that '49 Ford.

One day when the sisterhood was out '49 Ford cruising, I realized we were low on gas. We pooled our money and drove into the gas station at Michigan Avenue and Howe Street. When the station attendant came out to pump our gas, I said, "We will take 25 cents of gas, please." With a look that read disbelief, he asked, "Where are you going, Chicago?"

One night, we were feeling mischievous. We decided to go to Ford Field, where couples parked to "watch the submarine races" on the Rouge River. (For those of you who do not know the term, it means necking.) Well, thanks to that '49 Ford spotlight, we drove by and shined a beam on all the cars. Of course, the couples thought it was the police, and all of their engines started revving up and they left. We laughed so hard. Now, if anyone reading this was the victim of this prank, I just want you to know that it provided the sisterhood a lot of laughs through the years. Forgive us, but we have no regrets.

Six members of the sisterhood made a memorable trip in that beloved Ford to Tent City at Camp Dearborn the summer of 1960. As it turns out, it was the week of the Democratic National Convention. We all considered ourselves Kennedy girls. In fact, the uncle of one of us served on PT-109 with President Kennedy during World War II. So here we were for a week at Camp Dearborn and we spent a lot of that time on wooden benches in front of one of the communal TVs glued to the convention. There was a lot of celebrating in the sisterhood tent when JFK won the nomination. We talk about that to this day.

Another adventure in our beloved '49er took place on a hot August night in 1962. We were out cruising, feeling hot and uncomfortable. I drove each of the sisters to her home. We each put on our bathing suits and went to a motel on Michigan Avenue. We stealthily made our way to the swimming pool and had a great swim, thoroughly cooling off. We felt quite gutsy in doing this, knowing we could get caught at any moment by the motel management. We didn't. Sadly, that was our final '49 Ford adventure, as we had graduated from high school in June. Soon each of us was off to different colleges and adventures.

The sisterhood Ford "died" sometime when I was in college. It was old, beat up and quietly slipped away. What it left all of us, however, was a treasure trove of memories. The bonds that were forged over 60 years ago on bikes and reinforced with the '49 Ford sisterhood escapades remain to this day – a fine legacy, indeed.

Mary "Meg" Falk lives in Falls Church, Virginia. After over 30 years working at the Department of Defense, she is now happily retired and exploring things to do in our nation's capital that she couldn't do when she was working.

Playmates, Patriots and Picnickers

By Sue Ellen MacDonald-Gay

When I was 2 years old, I moved from Detroit to Dearborn to live with my grandmother, two aunts and my mother. My dad was in the Army in Germany, and it was decided to be the best solution while he was gone. We lived on Vassar Street in west Dearborn. It was a great street to live on as a child, and I had playmates in almost every house on the block. I knew all of the people who lived in all of the houses on the block, whether they had children my age or not.

These were the '40s, and Mayor Hubbard was the mayor. I specifically remember one time when the power had gone off. My aunt called the City Hall (why I don't know), and before long a big black car was in front of the house, and Mayor Hubbard was one of the occupants. The others were men who climbed the poles near the yard, and pretty soon the electricity was on again. My aunt was out there talking with the mayor as I watched from the window. Another time, we had problems with the phone connection. Another call to City Hall and another appearance from the mayor. Even though we had the old-fashioned telephones with party lines, communication was very important. My one aunt was a nurse and she worked a full-time job and then volunteered with the Red Cross during the war. Therefore, a phone was a necessity.

We were taught to be very patriotic as children. Those of us with family members in the service had small silk flags in our windows. Patriotic songs were always played on the radio, and I still have a collection of my aunt's piano music with patriotic themes. We attended every parade that was held in the city, and we supported the war effort. I remember mixing up margarine in some kind of a plastic bag so that it would change to a yellow color. My grandmother would sit me on a chair and let me mix for what seemed to be a very long time.

In August 1945 when the war ended, I had a new baby brother, and I very vividly remember being held by the hand and walked up the steps to Sacred Heart Church as church bells all over the town were pealing in thanksgiving. What I remember most is seeing many soldiers also coming into church on crutches – some of them with missing arms and legs – and my mother telling me not to stare.

By the summer of 1947 my dad was discharged from the service, and he and my mother bought a house on Lincoln Street, only a few blocks away from my grandmother's, and we moved again. I always kept the girlfriends that I had met on Vassar, and our paths crossed for the rest of my school years. My one friend, Sharon, and I are still friends today and e-mail often. A couple of other friends were very close to me while they were alive. In 1948 my sister was born and we filled our house to capacity. We had constant cook-outs, picnics, parties, anything to gather people together. We played kick the can, jump-roped, played tag or whatever every day of the summer. We came in only when my dad whistled or the streetlights came on – whichever happened first.

Back in those days we had a red firebox on the telephone pole on the corner, and that was the way you could summon help for any emergency. I don't remember anyone abusing that source of help.

I can remember a great childhood that began in kindergarten at Whitmore-Bolles and ended with graduation from Sacred Heart High School. There was never a lack of something to do or someone to do it with. We worked hard, both at home and school, and played hard, too, be it paddle-boating at Camp Dearborn or being in the senior play. There must have been 50 or more trips to Greenfield Village and tons to Ford Field. Every year I go back to Dearborn a couple of times and will never tire of seeing the things that have changed and the things that are the same. It was a wonderful city to call home.

Sue Ellen MacDonald-Gay is the mother of six, grandmother of 11. She is still working part time, 50 years after graduating as a nurse.

Life Was a Blast in 1960

By Karl Jenkins

It was a sunny, hot morning July 5, 1960. All the 10-year-old boys on and near Mohawk Drive were out and about on our bikes, but something more was in store today – for it was the day after the 4th of July fireworks, and that meant we were headed over to Levagood Park to gather "sulkur," a name the more wise of us knew well. "Sulkur" was the name given by some unknown sage to the bits of unburned fireworks that rained down from the skies during the fireworks shows – hitting no one – but somehow these boys knew they were there, and now by bright morning sunlight were on the hunt. After all, anything having anything to do with fire always intrigues boys young and old, and we were no different.

As we gathered our treasures (which we'd light later, releasing from each tiny, charred nugget a brief, dazzling flare of red, green, blue or bright white), Tommy always expressed his goal of finding the granddaddy of all "sulkur" – an unexploded "aerial bomb" – the very common firework that, shot high, simply flashed once and a half-second later the "KA-BOOM!" reached your ears. (They're used sparingly or not at all today, probably to spare the dogs' ears, but these were the glory days when nothing seemed dangerous, and thus they were widely used.)

On this day, we hit pay dirt! Bob came running across Levagood's softball field shouting at the top of his lungs, "I FOUND ONE!" And sure enough, we gathered around the holy grail of "sulkur" – a black cylinder approximately the size of a frozen orange juice can. Though we hadn't ever seen one before (had anyone?) five "experts" couldn't be wrong, and we headed over to Freddy's on Drexel, whose mom was the most lenient of everyone's. That made his home a natural for our "blast"

Now, what to use for a fuse? A resourceful bunch we were, quickly figuring that a sparkler would work perfectly. But how to insert it? Of course – a nail! And so there we were, using a NAIL and HAMMER to drive a hole in a can of GUNPOWDER. Perhaps because we were all good Lutherans and Catholics but too misbehaved for heaven, the good Lord spared us, allowing the hole to be made and the fuse inserted without incident.

Now all that remained was to place our masterpiece in the middle of the small back yard, light the sparkler/fuse and take cover, which we did! As we scattered to wait for the sparkler to reach pay dirt, a strange feeling came over me: Maybe I shouldn't be here at the moment of detonation? And so, as we scurried away from our very own "ground zero," I continued over to my bike, jumped on, and started peddling as fast as my legs could go. South on Drexel to Cherry Hill, across and down Mohawk. As I got within three homes of my own, suddenly "KA-BOOM!" and my world seemed to stop. It seemed EVERY front door on the block sprang open and someone came out, searching the sky for the source of the blast. Recall these were the days before air conditioning, so many noises outside were heard by many inside. Guilty as I was, I believed they were ALL staring at me – and so I, too, stopped my bike and pretended to search the skies for this audio Armageddon. To my relief, one by one they all went back into their homes.

Fortunately, my own mother was busy in the basement with the wash (or I would still be grounded) So I turned my bike around and ventured back to the scene of the crime. What I saw amazed me – the boys were all laughing hysterically, Freddy's mom was yelling something about "Why don't you boys do these things at YOUR house?" and in the back yard was a beautiful crater: no grass for 5 feet around, and a hole approximately 12 inches deep!

Amazingly, no police showed up, no windows were broken, no parents were called, no one was hurt, and we all went on to enjoy wonderful lives in Dearborn.

The names in this article have been changed to protect the guilty!

Karl Jenkins lived in Dearborn from 1959 until 1976. He now resides in Phoenix, Arizona.

Underground

Jeffrey V. Kulesus

During winter Michigan temperatures can plummet to 18 to 20 degrees below zero, Fahrenheit. I made snow forts, heaping snow into immense piles in the back yard. In these I carved tunnels and chambers. Foot-long icicles pushed through the walls served as fiber optics, bringing light in from the outside to the dark interior. These snow structures weighed so much that after the spring thaw one could often see large depressions from which it took the better part of the summer for the lawn to rebound.

Some winters were so cold that even the Rouge River froze over. The landscape around it covered in a pure white blanket of fallen snow. Shadows from the trees formed lacelike designs on the snow that wrapped around any landscape relief or drift in the snow. Tree limb shadows fell on the snow like the tracery of old Gothic windows. On moonlit nights the light divided into rainbow colors, like millions of miniature rhinestones. It was magical.

Everything was quieter when it snowed. You could even sense the snow before looking out the window first thing in the morning. It was almost as though snow muffled the forever roar of the city in a quiet, reverential hush. During particularly heavy snowfalls, you could almost hear, or feel, the snow fall. It was then that I loved to explore the Rouge River. The problem was getting to the river more than a mile away without getting frostbite first. So I came up with an ingenious solution.

I discovered a system of underground storm drains starting in Gulley woods a block or two east of Beech Daly Road. These were not sewage or human waste sewers, but rather drains designed to channel water runoff from streets, driveways and sidewalks.

The storm drains ran due west for a considerable way before turning south and ran for several miles. Judging from the direction of the water flow, it appeared as though the tunnels eventually emptied into the Rouge River, so I pried off the heavy cast-iron lid and climbed 20 or so feet down the manhole and into the subterranean drainage world, alone. I was about 12 years old at the time.

There was only a trickle of water at the bottom and, at first, not enough tunnel height to stand completely erect. The sound of every water drop echoed for hundreds of feet. Many of the manholes and all of the tunnels were made from prefabricated reinforced concrete sections. Some of the deeper manholes were extended with brick and concrete work in which cast-iron rungs were imbedded.

At first it took a few moments to conquer my fear and get accustomed to the darkness. My glasses also fogged up quite a bit because of the temperature differential. Then, there was overcoming fear of the unknown. After all, the Saturday afternoon monster movies portrayed giant ants, larvae and other creatures living in such places. Usually I overcame any fear of being alone in the dark before my glasses stopped fogging over. The average temperature below was about 55 degrees, rather toasty after coming in from the 18-degree-below-zero cold outside. The walk through the tunnels became rather pleasant, especially when compared with the severe wind-chill factors up above.

Usually the flashlight illuminated only a couple of concrete tunnel sections at a time. The tunnel seemed to stretch out endlessly in front and behind, but I did find the end where the tunnel near Gulley Road stopped against a face of hard, gray, methane-smelling clay. So I followed the water in the direction that I felt would eventually lead to the Rouge River.

Despite what the Saturday monster movies portrayed, the only astonishing life form I ever found down in the storm drains was a huge crawfish. It looked the size of a lobster but, in reality, was probably less than 5 or 6 inches from one end to the other. I suppose that was a prodigious size for a crawfish. The creature raised its claws up to me in defiance. Actually it was probably more scared of me than I of it. Fortunately the tunnel had gotten wider at that point, and I was able to skirt around the creature by running part way up the tunnel wall and past it to the other side. It was curious that later that day when I returned home through the same tunnel, there was no crayfish to be found.

After I walked through the drains more than two miles without finding the river, curiosity got the best of me. I climbed up one of the manholes, which, at this point, was a good 30 to 40 feet to the top. After forcing the manhole cover open by pushing on its bottom with my back, I peered out, finding myself in the middle of a Dearborn Heights park just north of Avondale Road. Children playing hockey several hundred feet away shouted in shock when they saw me crawl up out of the snow-covered ground. I must have looked like Beelzebub coming up from out of the very depths of the earth. I scurried back down, quickly fitting the cover atop the manhole. I certainly did not want to get apprehended in a place where boys weren't supposed to be.

The end of the drain came several miles after the start. First there was a pale glint of light. As I walked farther, the light became so bright it was possible to see the rest of the way without using the flashlight. The exit, by now wide enough for a car and too high to reach, was barred with a heavy steel grate. The problem was, instead of trying to break in, I was trying to get out. I forced myself beneath the grating only to plunge into the polluted Rouge River.

Now contact with the Rouge River was, back then, a dreadful thing. Urban legend had it that getting any Rouge River containments in your mouth or in an open wound was tantamount to death. I panicked and got out of the water as quickly as possible, vigorously spitting out whatever there was to eject.

Cold and wet as I was, it was possible to shelter myself from the north wind and lie facing southward on the river bank to get maximum solar exposure. There, a strange thing happened. As cold as it was, the sun evaporated moisture from my clothing in visible clouds of steam. It actually felt warm. Parts of the clothing that didn't completely dry became as stiff as boards.

That day I explored miles of the Lower Rouge River, walking east atop its frozen surface or along its banks where the ice became too thin because of the river current. The Rouge River Valley provided shelter from dangerous wind chill, and the sun made it altogether pleasant. The snow glistened in the sun like crystal, casting its little rainbows of light. Sometimes the wind whipped up the snow in little waves like sand in Saharan dunes. I imagined my snow tracks were those of some primeval explorer. It was fun to imagine the exploration of some vast frozen wilderness. At least I was the first person to have ever made those tracks in that particular snow.

Imagination is wonderful. Some adults knock the adventure out of young, inquiring minds, forbidding children flights of imagination or exploration. Perhaps the 1950s and 60s were a more innocent time when young people could experiment with chemicals, electricity, homemade rocketry and fireworks. One could dream about things and actually do something about them. In later years I heard some youths say they wanted to become actuaries, not because they know what an actuary is or does, or even because they have an interest in actuarial science, but because they wanted to make a lot of money. They give up their dreams for a career that perhaps they ended up despising, a pathetic excuse for charting one's destiny. Meanwhile, so many become insensible to the wonders around them, or cast them aside without the least bit of thought – a tremendous ingratitude for God's many wonders, even those that may be found within a grain of sand or at the bottom of a manhole.

That winter I used the storm drain tunnel and frozen river system many times to explore the old Henry Ford Fair Lane property and elsewhere around the Rouge. Protected by watchmen and guards, the heavily wooded property was always something I approached with some measure of stealth.

The old power plant with its fortress-like cut gray limestone walls like those of the mansion was particularly fascinating. The plant contained old toggle switches, electrical gadgets and gauges reminiscent of something out of an old Frankenstein movie. The electrical equipment appeared to be some of the original material installed by Thomas A. Edison for his friend Henry Ford. The power plant used water pressure provided by a dam across the Middle Rouge River. The 8- or 9-foot drop in water level was sufficient to run water turbines Henry Ford installed to power his mansion. Henry Ford was an innovative thinker many years ahead of his time. He used hydroelectric power to power many of his manufacturing facilities in Belleville, Milford, Northville and Ypsilanti. Many of the beautiful lakes in southeastern Michigan were created by Henry Ford's vision of renewable, clean hydroelectric power.

Logs and other debris floating down the Middle Rouge River often got entangled in the dam on the west side of the Fair Lane estate. Once a guard spotted and chased me off the property. I ran westward across the frozen river within a few feet of the dam's crest at the top of the plunging torrent to escape a guard – a foolish stunt that could have easily resulted in drowning beneath the ice downriver from the falls. That manmade waterfall faced with limestone was one of the most exciting spots of the entire Rouge River system.

Fair Lane Manor was a large, multistoried mansion made of cut blocks of gray limestone. It had large overhanging eaves topped with a tiled roof. Inside were large rooms where the Fords once entertained guests including U.S. presidents, Thomas Edison, George Washington Carver and other 1900 luminaries. Henry Ford was particularly fond of square dances, for which he had one large room devoted to that pursuit. The interior of the home, of course, was excluded to the likes of me except when it was open to public tours.

The Ford estate had other fascinating things to see. There was an underground root cellar on the east side of Clara Bryant Ford's old rose gardens to the north of the mansion the size of a well-appointed fallout shelter. The lake north of the home was particularly interesting, because there had been persistent "kid" urban legends about such a lake. It was also said that no kid ever found "Hidden Lake." I set about searching for the lake during the winter exploratory trips. One trip went through the woods immediately south of Ford Road and west of Southfield Road. Eventually I followed the Rouge River south from Ford Road. Not only did I find Hidden Lake, but I also circumnavigated the thing and walked all over its frozen surface. Hidden Lake was actually an old quarry from which clay had been dug for making bricks. The lake drained through a sluice gate and down a manmade stream near its southwest shore. The stream was actually lined with concrete and rocks, and there was even a small, stone-faced, concrete pedestrian bridge near the lake. Henry Ford enjoyed such details. It was as if I discovered the curious, perhaps even whimsical side of Henry Ford.

No doubt Mr. Ford had acquired other curiosities as well. Half a mile or so north of the estate, on the east bank of the river and just north of the Ford Road bridge, was an underground boat garage reputedly built by Mr. Ford for his lover, the wife of one of his executives with a name that sounded something like "Berringer." It is said the two lovers visited each other via boat or canoe on the Rouge River, the shortest distance between the two properties. I enjoyed exploring what was left of the old underground boat garage, which had become so heavily silted up over the years that any boat stored therein would have been completely out of the water. Back in Henry Ford's time the Rouge River had pure water and was said to have teamed with trout. The river was a romantic place, with tall, old trees whose branches arched over the water. In many places, the river looked like a tunnel that wound its way through the trees.

The farthest these explorations went was the lower part of the Middle Rouge River, now part of Edward Hines Park, and the north branch of the Rouge River as far as Detroit's Rouge Park. I found several hollowed-out sycamore trees Indians once used for temporary shelters. There was also a sandy bluff on the east river bank south of Ford Road, next to the Dearborn Country Club golf course, that had a cave-sized hole large enough for a small bear – no doubt in reality it was probably made by a large groundhog.

I used the storm drain tunnels many times that winter. Later I found a smaller drain running parallel to Telegraph Road on its east side and a huge tunnel west of Military emptying into the Lower Rouge from the north. Another time I climbed down a Bell Telephone manhole into a cable tunnel beneath Michigan Avenue and not too far from the Lower Rouge River. Rumor had it that the underground Fairlane Manor bowling alley was connected to the Ford Motor Company Power Plant half a mile or so to the south west via a tunnel that Henry Ford used to visit the Ford Motor Company Engineering Building. Unable to get close enough to the mansion for a good look in the bowling alley, I searched for manhole covers and ventilation shafts between the two sites hoping to find the tunnel. The Bell manhole was on the south bank of the Lower Rouge River about halfway between the two sites. Obviously used for telecommunications, the dusty, dry tunnel was full of cables. Tree root tendrils hung down between pipe section joints like Spanish moss. Fear of causing possible damage or being electrocuted meant discretion ruled the day. I closed the cast-iron lid and went home.

Though now somewhat an unusual and distant memory, back then exploring the unknown provided an exhilarating sense of wonder and adventure. While other neighborhood kids collected baseball cards and talked incessantly about sports, the "underground" provided me excitement and experiences that were quite unique when compared to stereotypical childhood pursuits.

Jeffrey V. Kulesus lived in Dearborn from 1949-1967. He was the president of the Junior Curators in 1963. He entered the U.S. Army in 1967. He graduated from Brigham Young University in 1977 and now works as a consultant for an international actuarial consulting firm. He and his wife, Ami, have five children and now live in a northern Chicago suburb.

ROUGE RIVER
DEARBORN

Gut-Check Time:
The Judo Kid Meets a T. Rex

By Walter Lamb

My dad, Bill Lamb, was a type-A personality with a drive to compete and unquenchable thirst to win in every endeavor in his life, including athletics. Naturally he wanted to instill this trait in his two boys, yours truly and my brother, Billy, who was 15 months older.

Our dad was a special agent in the FBI, and in 1956 he was assigned to the Washington, D.C., field office. There were judo clubs located in the Pentagon, Langley AFB and Bolling Field AFB, to name a few. As soon as our dad caught wind of this fact, it was a given that Billy and I would be enrolled, which we were at 5 and 6 years of age

In 1958 my father was transferred to the Detroit field office, and he purchased a home on the east side of Dearborn. The east side of Dearborn was home to the sprawling Rouge Plant, a magnet drawing migrants from the South and immigrants from what seemed like every country – Italian, Irish, Polish, Armenian, Hispanic, Lebanese, Maltese, Swedish, etc. Most of the kids were second and third generation, and many were tough kids that knew how to fight and liked it.

Upon arrival in Detroit our dad set about locating a judo club to enroll Billy and me and discovered the renowned Detroit Judo Club (DJC) located on Joy Road between Dexter and Grand River Avenues in the heart of Detroit.

In the early '60s the DJC moved to a more spacious location on Livernois. The club hired a legend in John Osako, who was a former grand champion of the United States and the Pan American Games in judo.

Osako was a visionary. He concluded that one option to help secure the interest of young *judoka* would be to make the dangling carrot of rank always seem accessible. He established a rank of junior brown belt, the highest junior rank. The young *judoka* obtaining that rank would wear a brown belt with a purple stripe on the end. When I turned 14, he awarded me the junior brown belt, and I felt special and foresaw no end to my involvement. The judo hook was set.

Our dad purchased a house located at 7740 Miller Road on the east side of Dearborn, one block from Detroit's border, and enrolled us at the local Catholic school, St. Alphonsus.

In the fall of 1963 I was playing on the St. Alphonsus Grade School seventh- and eighth-grade football team. After seven years of judo experience, I had acquired an understanding of base and balance that the coach recognized, so he played me as the starting center and defensive tackle at a hulking 90 pounds.

The St. Alphonsus eighth-grade football team played its home games at Anthony Park, located on the Detroit border. After each home game all the players and cheerleaders would gather at a small Italian restaurant named Chris' Pizzeria. The players would wear all their football equipment sans helmet and spikes. On one occasion there were four "greaser"-looking girls from the neighborhood public school, Lowrey Junior High, occupying a booth.

Before long there were words exchanged between one of the St. Al's cheerleaders sitting with me and the public school girls. One of the greaser girls had a boyfriend known as Rey, who was an eighth-grader at Lowrey but was 15 years of age. Not only was he two years older than all the other kids in his class, but he was also physically mature. I was lucky to even have any peach fuzz, and Rey sported a 5 o'clock shadow at all times. Rey had the same reputation as feared wrestler Shute from the movie *Vision Quest*, that is, if you messed with him, you were a dead man.

When schoolmates observe a small fella chucking a feared bully in the schoolyard with a judo technique, it seems like magic and an aura is gained. It is as if your name gains a tag: "Lamb – he knows judo!" Yet, judo held some exotic magic that boxing and wrestling did not, for aside from throws, pins and submissions, it was cloaked in mystery, having been spawned in Japan. Sometimes, however, having the reputation of knowing how to fight can attract the attention of a Tyrannosaurus rex bully, and such is the case here.

It was the first week of October '63, a few days after the gathering at the pizzeria, when word game down from Lowrey Junior High that Rey "was looking for me" for messing with his girl. Huh? I did think she was a hottie, but I never told her so, nor did I say anything to those girls at the pizzeria that day. On the east side of Dearborn at that time when someone "was looking for you," it meant the same thing as when the Mafia put the word out that so-and-so "is going to get whacked." At least in the minds of guys my age.

Rey was only a few inches taller than me, but probably had 30 or 35 pounds on me. In August a few months back I had seen Rey follow a kid, who sported a pretty sizable reputation himself, for half a city block, kicking him as hard as he could in the rear end over and over again with the "points" he was wearing, as the kid tried to walk away from a fight. It was vicious and scalding to watch. It would not be an overreach to say Rey possessed a myriad of personality issues and was from a broken/dysfunctional home.

On another occasion that summer, he had a dozen or so thin cuts on each forearm that he seemed to be proud of, telling everyone that he was in a knife fight with some guy from southwest Detroit. Everyone knew it was a lot of crap, but none dared tell him so. I don't think Rey ever placed my name with my face, at least not yet. Anyway, now Rey was "looking for me," damn it!

My brother, Billy, advised me not to worry about it and just avoid him. Sage advice. I was successful in following it for about a week. I was with about six buddies in front of Lester's Meat Market near St. Al's on Warren. We snuck over there at lunch hour to hang out and eat Hostess products. Two sixth-graders from Lowrey entered Lester's and proceeded back across Warren. Warren separated the neighborhoods of St. Alphonsus and Lowrey to a certain extent. Afterward I figured that the two sixth-graders must have run back to their school and notified Rey that some of the St. Al's guys were in front of Lester's Meat Market and one of them was me.

One of my buddies had a transistor radio, and I'll always remember the song that came on because we all started singing it. It was *Music, Music, Music* by The Sensations, a very popular song in east Dearborn. Even today I listen to that song and it throws me back to my encounter with Rey.

The music groove was abruptly interrupted by one of my buddies as he released a desperate scream, "Oh, my God!" I followed his gaze and charging across Warren there must have been 30 Lowrey guys screaming with a bead on us. Rey led the charge. The psychological dilemma of "fight or flight" emerged, and four of my six buddies chose flight, but my best friend stood still with a twisted smile on his face. It registered that Rey was wearing his three-quarter-length black leather coat, and at that moment it looked like a *judogi* top to me, and the recognition of this galvanized my spirit.

My dad always drilled it into my head that if you absolutely have to fight, then never, ever allow your opponent to get the first punch in. A couple of things could happen: 1. More than likely observers would break the fight up. 2. He busts up your nose and gains the advantage in the fight.

John Osako always emphasized the use of *kiai* during *shiai* to show fighting spirit.

I combined both my dad's and Osako's advice with a massive war-cry *kiai* and charged the rapidly advancing Rey in the parking lot of Ace Hanses Hardware adjacent to Lester's Meat Market

I launched a football tackle, *morote gari,* double leg or whatever you want to call it and was knocked backward onto my butt. The 25 or 30 Lowrey guys surrounded the action watching Rey make quick work of the little punk. I heard my friend yelling above the din, "Move, move, get him, get him." Jumping to my feet, I knew my boy's strength would be no match for Rey's demonstrated man's strength. But I knew I could use his power against him. I had speed, dexterity and my guardian angel judo on my side. I felt if I did not win, I would be killed.

Rey had assumed a classic boxing stance and was moving forward. He flicked out his leading left foot and nailed me in the groin and followed it with some type of left-handed punch attempt. I cross-gripped his leather and blasted in with a *seoinage* (shoulder throw), but even with the *kuzushi* (having him off balance), I could not execute the throw. The kid was a bull. I switched to right *kouchi makikomi* off of the *seoi* and drove into him, knocking him down and mounting him. I instinctively attempted to pin him, but he powered me off to the side while punching at my face. I had never been in a fight before where the guy was trying to kick me in the family jewels and swinging full-power punches at my face.

The fight continued for about four minutes, with Rey kicking and punching, using brute force, and with me circling, changing angles and levels. Rey landed some great shots that bloodied my nose and bruised my eyes and cheekbones. He also kicked me in the groin a half-dozen times. I was able to finally throw him with my right *seoinage* hard on his face and shoulder onto concrete, and I noticed his chest was heaving when he stood up. He was out of breath and making dry sobs. That made me feel good because I was crying also. We ended up on the ground again and I had his back, but I did not know *shimewaza* (strangling techniques) or *kansetsuwaza* (armlocks) well enough at the time because they were not allowed in 13-year-old competitions. So I attempted a turnover to mount, but this time I punched him in the face before I was tossed off. He was able to get on top of me, and he viciously attempted to smash my head off the concrete with both his hands. I bridged, rolled and escaped.

We stood up and there was vomit all over both of us but it wasn't mine. We stared at each other and Rey did not advance, but threatened between sobs that he would kick my ass if he ever saw me again. He began calling me every street obscenity he could think of. He walked away, but his gang was subdued now. I cried out, "Where you going, Rey? I'm still here!" but he kept walking. My buddy looked at me and said, "That was great! You beat Rey!" I thought to myself, "I did?"

There was no way I could go back to school that afternoon, and I walked home with dry sobs heaving out of my chest all the way. I saw my dad's car in the driveway. I walked in battered, bloodied, covered in vomit and crying. My dad said, "Did you get in a fight?" I said that I had and that I didn't go back to school. He asked, "Did you win?" I said, "Yes." He then asked if I started the fight and if I was able to get the first punch in. I said I did not start the fight and I attacked first. I then told him about the fight and he said, "That's good!" My dad knew that I experienced something that day that touched my essence, and it was something that would be chiseled onto my soul the remainder of my life. I failed to mention to him the fact that my scrotum was black, blue and swollen. I prayed for a week before things were back to normal in that regard.

The following July I entered the second Junior National Judo Championships in Chicago representing the DJC. I was entered in the 14-year-old division, and there were no weight classes, but I lost that concern in the hardware store lot the year before. I beat some Megatrons, getting to the sixth round before losing to Uptown Dojo's Jeff Greene, larger than I for sure but also a slicker *judoka*.

Entering judo tournaments, traveling to cities such as Chicago, Cleveland and Toronto and garnishing medals and trophies are tremendous experiences that my brother and I have treasured all our lives.

Yet, they are not the reason that judo has assumed a position in our essences. Rather it is the social acceptance by peers during those developmental years, the confidence it provided when enrolling in new schools or dealing with bullies. Being a *judoka* is a positive mark on your character and reputation much as a U. S. Marine is positively labeled for life for having been one. "Once a Marine, always a Marine" is congruent with "Once a *judoka,* always a *judoka.*"

I never ran into Rey again, and he can thank his lucky stars for that because he never grew after our confrontation, and I tripled in size, strength and judo skills by the time I was in my early 20's.

Walter Lamb graduated from St. Alphonsus High School and Madonna University. He also attended Michigan State University for two years where he won the 1972 Big Ten Championship and the Midwest Collegiate championship in judo. He is married to Jill and has two daughters, Jody (30) and Brooke (16). He is a private detective.

Forbidden Fruit, Treacherous Ice

By James J. Penn

My father met my mother at a school dance at Sacred Heart School. He married her and built a brick home on Edison, but before they could move in, a doctor bought it, so he built one just like it on Tenny between Cass and Monroe and was able to move in before he sold that one, too.

I was born in 1928 and lived with my parents until my marriage in 1949. I attended Sacred Heart School and graduated in 1946. To this day no one will believe that we had to walk to school, walk home for lunch, walk back to school and finally walk home after school. The rule was if we lived within one mile of school, we had to walk home for lunch, as the cafeteria did not have enough room for all of us.

Well, one of the interesting things while I was growing up was we would wait for the so-called sheeny man to show up, as he would buy scrap copper and aluminum. Our father was in the electrical business. He founded Penn Electric, which operated in Dearborn for over 85 years. He would give us the scrap wire to sell. We would wait for the sheeny man to bring out his big change purse. We got the money, and since I had two sisters, we would split it up three ways. I took mine and headed to the Cozy Corner at Monroe and Military and buy myself a pint of ice cream. I ate it while walking home.

My friend, Walter Frank, lived about five houses down. We

usually walked down the alley. One day while walking the alley, we were hungry and there was a peach tree that had limbs hanging above the alley. We each picked a piece of fruit to eat. That was a "no no." I arrived home a half-hour later, and in the drive was a cop car, and, yes, the owner of the tree had called the police. The police told my father what had happened, and, of course, he told the officer he would give me a good talking to. My father told me to get to my room, and I knew what was coming—a wet wash cloth across my bare butt.

One other thing I remember about Dearborn was we would go to the apartments on Oakwood Boulevard, sit on the stairs and put on our skates. We then would cross Oakwood to the Twin Ponds, where we would all skate. On one of my trips there I was skating and didn't see a small hole in the ice, probably from a fisherman who cut it to do some ice-fishing. I fell on the ice, got up and seemed OK. I walked across the street to the apartments, put on my shoes and walked home. I never felt anything, but that's because it was very cold. I got home, my dad looked at the gash on my forehead, saw the blood running out, so he took me to the emergency room, where I got five stitches, and still today I can see the scar above my right eye.

James J. Penn lives in Lake Placid, Florida. Every summer he visits Dearborn to see if any of his friends are still alive. He continued his father's electrical business until he passed it on to his son, who maintained it until a year ago.

Assault on a Fort

By Lonell Rice

Growing up in Dearborn in the 1950s was a unique experience. Despite being a pretty developed suburb, there was still a great deal of open land. Those were the days when the stretch of Michigan Avenue between east and west Dearborn was still open land, maybe even some farmland. Fairlane Town Center wasn't even a glimmer in Ford Land's eye yet.

Most of the neighborhood kids were boys. My sister and I were two of the few girls. We played what the boys wanted to play—softball, war, cards, building stuff. The boys and we would often go to the back of Daly Furniture's warehouse on Park. Between the building and the railroad tracks was where they'd dump those big furniture boxes. Those boxes made the best forts, and we loved to drag them home to build forts in our back yards. We'd have boxes strung together as tunnels so we could move between forts without being detected, by whom I don't remember.

From Daly's warehouse, we'd sometimes walk along the railroad tracks . As you walked east to the end of west Dearborn, the Rouge River ran along the north side of Michigan Avenue. The area I'm referring to later became the Chicago Road Steak House, now Andiamo. This area was particularly attractive for building forts out of trees, branches and stones because those were everywhere. This area was also out a little farther away from home than I was supposed to go. When I was 8 or 9, one of the neighbor boys, Mike, and I went there frequently to "work" and play.

We'd walk along Michigan until we could find our path, then head toward the river's ravine. There, with the sound of cars buzzing by above us, we'd pull together downed trees and branches for our fort. Building up small walls, we'd pretend those cars held people who were our enemy. Sometimes the darkness of the woods would scare us, and we'd run back to Michigan Avenue and to safety.

Mike and his parents moved from their Dearborn home at the end of that summer so that he could start the school year at his new school. I made one more trip by myself to see our fort. Someone else has been there. It was destroyed. Maybe we weren't so wrong to run back to Michigan Avenue after all.

Lonell Rice is retired and splits her time between Key Largo, Florida, and Harrisville, Michigan.

Polliwogs, Beer Cans and Trolls

By Colleen Ben Stasek

I grew up in Dearborn Heights and attended St. Anselm Elementary School, Fordson High School and Henry Ford Community College, where I got an associate's degree in computer information systems.

My early memories include many trips to Camp Dearborn. I well remember those stone-lined creeks running through the park. They were ALWAYS filled with crayfish, and I remember them as being quite large.

I remember exploring the area where St. Anselm's Church is now located. I loved nature and loved finding pollyiwogs there. As a youth, I collected rocks. I will never forget the day that St. Anselm's Church caught fire.

There were a lot of kids on my block. I remember attaching playing cards to our bikes to make them sound like motorbikes. We were really into digging ditches and large holes. We would then cover the holes with wood. We frequently found beer cans in our forts. (Apparently others enjoyed our forts as much as we kids did.) I remember the Good Humor man, all dressed in his white outfit. I remember the Rotunda at Christmastime.

We spent countless hours roller-skating at the Dearborn Civic Center and very long days at Seashore. Our fingers looked like prunes. I really disliked spreading my hands and toes to show that I showered before being let in. When I was too young to swim past the fence, I would cling onto it while watching the older kids diving off the inside tower.

We lived close to English Gardens. We often would hear the loudspeaker bleat out, "Carry out of peat moss on aisle 2." The neighbors complained, and the city put limitations on the use of the loudspeaker.

We did a lot of tent camping. We took a 14-foot trailer to California, Nova Scotia and King Edward's Island.

I went to the Military Inn many times with my father and LOVED going to Eurich's ice-cream store to get penny candy and seeing a tall wooden Indian and a large pickle barrel. I have fond memories of Sutton's (Outer Drive and Wilson) ice-cream sodas; I well remember the Dairy Queen on Ford and Outer Drive.

My dad drove a DSR bus. He did a lot of filming when the riots were going on.

I worked in the office of the Michigan Humane Society. My husband, Henry, worked in product development for Ford Motor Company. We met where people say you should not go to meet prospective spouses, at a bar, specifically the Schaefer Bar. After my daughters were born, I was a stay-at-home mom.

I enjoy art. If I had to do it over, I most likely would have gone in that direction. My fun activities today include buying and selling trolls on eBay.

My values include politeness, honesty and sincerity. I believe that you should write thank-you notes.

Dearborn has always been home, so that's why we decided to stay and raise our daughters here. I really don't know of any other cities that have such a large Homecoming and block parties. We're a very involved community.

Colleen Ben Stasek is a longtime resident of Dearborn. When you're born in one of the best of cities, why leave home?

My First Friend

By Tom Thomas

I was a very timid child. I never had any friends before I started school, and I didn't really make any in kindergarten either. When I got to first grade (Joshua Howard Elementary), the teacher noticed that I was reading at a much higher level than the other students, so I was given a battery of tests, and it was decided to promote me into the next higher grade. Now I was not only friendless, but I didn't even know anybody in my class.

Walking home from school alone, as usual, I was approached by another kid from the class, who said his name was Jimmy. He invited me over to his house, where I met his parents and we played some games. Jimmy quickly became my best friend, but not my only friend, for it turned out that Jimmy had lots of friends, and pretty soon they were my friends, too. We all played baseball, football and basketball together throughout elementary school. The basketball games were always in Jimmy's driveway, because he had a backboard and basket above his garage door. His older brother taught us all the rules of the game, and we played a lot, because it was Jimmy's favorite game.

We went all through school together and graduated from Dearborn High together in January 1964. Jimmy and I remained friends throughout, but not necessarily best friends. I would guess that the majority of our class would have listed Jimmy as a good friend. Nevertheless, he was always my first friend.

Jimmy had two great goals in life – to play basketball and to fly jets. He achieved both. He became a starter on the Dearborn High varsity, and our team went into the state tournament and finished the year rated sixth in the state. I don't know whether a Dearborn High team has done better since then, but we were pretty psyched about it. Jimmy later joined the Air Force and became a pilot, flying the jets he always dreamed of.

When we heard that he was Missing In Action in Vietnam, we all held the hope that he was actually a POW and would eventually be released. But as the years went by, that hope faded, and eventually his body was found.

I spent almost 40 years of my working life in Cincinnati and lost touch with my high school friends, so I was amazed when I finally returned to Dearborn High and saw that the road in front of the school had been named for Jimmy, and there was a monument in his honor on the front lawn. It made me want to go inside and tell those kids who Jimmy was, and perhaps inspire them to emulate his warmth and courage any time a new kid shows up in their class, knowing nobody.

Tom Thomas graduated from the University of Michigan in 1971, with a degree in psychology. He retired in 2012 after a 40-plus-year career in software development, engineering management and sales. He was married in 1969 to Patty Conway, and they have three children – Andy, Joe and Tracy – as well as three grandchildren – Kent, Carson and Keaton. In 2013 Tom published a book based on his father's service in World War II, called The Honshu Pioneer, *which was also the name of the newspaper published by his father and his Army buddies in Japan, during the American occupation. Tom and Patty moved to Harrisville, Michigan, in 2012.*

A '50s Girl

By Maureen Webster

I excitedly anticipated my first swimming lesson at Seashore that summer. At 5 years old, there were limited forms of transportation besides walking or biking, and my father drove our only car to work. Since my mother had practiced the route to Levagood Park with me, I proudly cruised solo to my summer escape on my stunning red two-wheeler, "purchased" with a filled book of Green Stamps. To this day, I still swim at Seashore, since renamed the Jack Dunworth Pool after the wonderful coach and athlete in Dearborn.

The city of Dearborn also provided other recreational opportunities at various parks, such as arts and crafts, sports and trips to Camp Dearborn. I made some unforgettable gimp key chains, played a ferocious game of zell ball and took regular Tuesday journeys to Camp Dearborn, financing the entire bus trip and activities with one thin silver dime.

The only mayor reigning in Dearborn during my childhood was Orville Hubbard. Although as an adult I would learn of his controversial stance on race, among other things, he was close to perfect in this little girl's eyes. Not only did we enjoy excellent summer recreational activities, but we had outdoor skating rinks and sledding at Ford Field and other smaller parks in the winter. Although Dearborn has an indoor skating rink, the outdoor ones have disappeared. Walk around Levagood Park and you will see the recessed plot of land surrounding the original rink. Two weatherworn benches, a capped water outlet and three poles, which formerly held lights for evening skating, remain holding secrets of my invigorating wintery evenings spent skating with wonderful friends.

During Christmas holidays, Mayor Hubbard provided free tickets to the Dearborn Theater for every child and gifted us with enormous Baby Ruths, far larger than the ones our family customarily bought. We walked to the now-defunct theater and celebrated the generosity of our mayor with all of our friends.

Another fond memory of Orville Hubbard was his appearance at the Camp Dearborn dances. I was a teen-ager, and socializing with friends at the Canteen, where music was playing, when someone announced that the mayor had arrived. He was confined to a wheelchair then, but he mingled comfortably among the crowd of teens, as a lovely aide pushed him around the dance floor. These dances were held regularly for residents staying in Tent Village, the rustic tents with outdoor water pumps and remote bathroom facilities. More modern facilities have since been added.

Those who remember the Civic Center in Dearborn, before the beautiful Ford Community & Performing Arts Center was developed, may recall the roller rink, where you could blissfully roller-skate around the premises, listening to rousing music as you accelerated. Although the Dome, as they now call this area, is used for many other worthwhile events today, I miss that rink.

Dearborn has always prided itself on its rich library system. The current Henry Ford Centennial Library outranks the original main library, but I appreciated the coziness of that first one, the current Clara Bryant Library, which stands on Michigan Avenue and Mason. There was a charming doll house to enchant the imaginations of many young children, and a kind, friendly staff to assist with research projects as our assignments became more challenging. If we lacked transportation to the library, we could obtain a limited supply of books from the Bookmobile, a traveling library parked off Telegraph Road, north of Cherry Hill. On designated days, I could ride my bike there and check out a few books from this fascinating van filled with rich reading opportunities.

Before shopping malls gained prominence, my family would visit the specialty and department stores for men and women on Michigan Avenue. Names like Zolkower, Muirhead, Crowley Milner, Himelhoch, Nanette, Price and Sims would proudly display their wares in their storefronts for everyone driving down the avenue to admire. Farther east, on Michigan and Greenfield, a discount store called Hudson's Basement promised to sell clothing at a cost lower than the flagship Hudson's in downtown Detroit. This may have foreshadowed our discount malls to come. On the opposite pole, Jacobson's sold upscale and luxury wares, often affordable if you patiently waited until the third markdown.

This snapshot of my Dearborn has progressed in many wonderful ways, inviting diversity and change, but it will always hold safe and warm memories for this little girl born exactly in the middle of the 20th century.

Maureen Webster is married to Dan Webster, has three daughters and is a counselor at Henry Ford Community College.

Across Cherry Hill

By Frank Wilhelme

A really important feature of our neighborhood was the Cherry Hill playground. Located just a half a block east of our house at the corner of Reginald, the playground was about five lots wide. Each summer the playground would come alive when the city's Parks Department sent a director to supervise a variety of activities for elementary and junior high kids.

My most vivid memories are of the countless pick-up softball games played on a very "friendly" sandlot field. The field featured numerous mature trees and an incredibly short center-field fence. The challenge was to thread your hits through the trees and over that fence. As we grew bigger and stronger, the game looked more and more like a home-run derby. In our final years of our playground careers, the goal was not only to clear the center-field fence but to have your homer land across Cherry Hill on the fly.

Mom had an interesting way to alert us it was time to come home from the park. We had a bay window on the front of our house and when she wanted to signal us, she would stand in the window. As we appeared at the park entrance, she would come out to the side walk and guide us safely across busy Cherry Hill.

This story is excerpted from an unpublished autobiography. Frank Wilhelme was the executive director of the Historical Society of Michigan. He and his wife, Judy (Jackson), live in Ann Arbor and have two adult children.

Across the Ambassador Bridge

By Frank Wilhelme

As early as age 5 or 6, my neighborhood had expanded a few blocks over from our perch on Cherry Hill. Around that time, my sister, Laura, took me along on one of her visits with her friend, Mary Ann Johnson, who lived on Devonshire, which dead-ended into Cherry Hill a few blocks east of us.

It was on one of those visits that I met John Rumierz. John and I have remained close friends ever since. While we are quite different in many ways, we just seemed to click as friends. John is one of the smartest people I have ever met. Anyone who can pocket a chemical engineering degree plus a master's in chemical physics at the University of Michigan is operating at an entirely different level from yours truly.

One rather amazing memory John and I enjoy recalling was the summer day in the late 1950s that we decided to create an adventure for ourselves. Our great idea was to ride our bikes from Dearborn over the Ambassador Bridge to Windsor. We got pretty excited about this adventure but realized that we could not ask our parents if it was OK because we knew they would not share our enthusiasm.

So one bright and sunny morning we set off down Michigan Avenue into Detroit. We got to the bridge and realized we did not have enough money to pay the two-way toll, so we returned home and repeated the journey the next day and made it to Canada and back to Dearborn without incident.

Can you image making this trip in today's security-conscious world?

This story is excerpted from an unpublished autobiography. Frank Wilhelme was the executive director of the Historical Society of Michigan. He and his wife, Judy (Jackson), live in Ann Arbor and have two adult children.

Chapter 4

family

Steve + Son = Ston

By Pearl Kastran Ahnen

Ston? What? Steve, Son, Ston! That's how the name evolved for my son, whose official name is Stephen Andrew Kastran, raised in Dearborn. When Steve was a youngster, his father would call him Steve or Son, depending on his mood or inclination. More often than not it was Steve, and sometimes Son. One occasion when his father's mind was racing, he'd blurt out a combination of words, thus inventing a new word: "STON." That name was Steve's byword, and whenever he wrote to his family while away at college or off seeing the world, he signed "STON."

Steve, a graduate of Edsel Ford High School and Michigan State University, also earned a juris doctorate degree at the Detroit College of Law, Detroit, and served as assistant prosecuting attorney for Allegan County for several years. He is now a partner in the law firm of Burnett and Kastran in Allegan. But his passion is writing poetry. While in the eighth grade at Stout Junior High, he won a prize for a poem titled *I Am a Man*.

Years ago, when Steve was in high school, he would occasionally visit me while I was working as a reporter/editor for a downriver group of newspapers. I often wasn't there when he arrived, for my job required I go on assignments and interviews. When he found my office empty, he'd sit at my desk, reach out for some newsprint and compose a poem for me. The poem was a pleasant surprise when I returned to my desk.

On one occasion a few years ago, during a sun-soaked afternoon following a morning mist of rain in San Antonio, the temperature rising to the 100-degree mark, he was huddled over a notepad, in a flower-filled garden underneath a colorful canopy, writing. He was working on the last stanza of a poem to honor his younger sister, Deneen, and her fiancé, Curtis, on this August day in 1997, their wedding day.

During his leisure time, he is seen with a yellow legal pad balanced on his knee, chewing on a pencil, waiting for the muse to strike. Then he rapidly scribbles a verse, a stanza, a phrase, and the poem takes form. It's someone's birthday, a couple's anniversary, a graduation, a wedding or just an ordinary fall Saturday, and Michigan State's football team has finished another game. Whether it's a victory or defeat – it really doesn't matter – our poet writes a sonnet about the outcome.

But Steve isn't just an attorney and a poet. As a teen-ager, he starred on his high school basketball team and won many events at swimming meets. He also served as a lifeguard at Camp Dearborn. It was a job he worked at with pride and saved several lives.

On a recent Valentine's Day, I found another poem written by Ston on my desk. This time my desk was at home, since I'm an author and playwright and no longer in the newspaper business.

This poem is called *FIRST LOVE:*

My first cognizant memory is of her warm brown eyes
melting over me.
Next, I remember riding the bus to nursery school
and her work sitting on her lap.
Always a kind word of encouragement
in her reassuring soft toned voice.
Decisions that were required appeared through subtle
persuasion to be my own choice.

Advice and direction given on matters of import
were rational,
well reasoned and of great comfort.
Her arms outstretched, always ready to support and greet,
Whether to clutch a wobbly toddler, or young man swept
off his feet.

As life's lessons and their consequences took their toll,
She contained my anger, soothed the rage,
mended my heart
And healed my soul.
Now as I navigate through the sea of life,
I'm thankful for your worry, consternation and strife.

I am but a lump of clay, fashioned by your hands each day.
The man who stands before you formed from an infant
Molded in your own way.
Such a debt of gratitude will not quench my thirst,
Keeping in mind of all my loves, you were my first.
Love, Ston
Valentine's Day

Yes, Steve is still Ston, and although he loved growing up in Dearborn, he pushed himself to explore the world, Europe first. After his college graduation, he took a year off to explore Europe, working his way through. He worked in an orphanage in Spain, a cobbler's shop in the Netherlands, a residence for foreign students in England, for a fisherman in Greece, and on and on. He came home with a journal filled with notes and poems, and he said the photos were "in his mind."

Since his first journey abroad, he has traveled far and wide, meeting new people and exploring new lands with his wife, Chelle. And his notebook is filled with new poems.

Pearl Kastran Ahnen has written or edited 12 books and 11 plays. Her award-winning plays have been staged at the University of Michigan, Wayne State University and Ohio State University. She grew up in Dearborn and now lives in Glenn, Michigan.

Ston and his father, George Kastran

Notes of Chauvin History

By Jane Knapp Arndt

A bit of history will let you know that the Chauvins have been in Dearborn for several hundred years. It all started in 1636 when the French government sent over Francois Chauvin to survey Michigan land for a claim. He started down the St. Lawrence River after arriving in the New World. He was fortunate to befriend many of the Potawatomi Indians after leaving the Quebec area, and they helped him travel to the Rouge River area. They brought him to the area that they considered very nice. I do not know of any written record of their travels, but the older relatives often repeated what they had been told over the years. Canoe travel was the easiest means to get around, and the trails that the Indians used were worn paths.

When Francois arrived on the Detroit River, he was happy to see that a quiet river stemmed from the larger river. It was along that river that he decided to settle, and he let France know that it would be a good area to send others. He chose what he considered the best spot, and as he measured out the section into farms, he numbered the parcels. His section was number 33, and it was where the river shore stuck out into the river – a good view, too. His family was then brought over, and a farmhouse was built on that section.

The Chauvins and several other families lived along the Rouge. They were farmers and all worked together and had many children. Several of their children had the same name of Francis, and the last name was changed in English to Chovin. Due to diseases there were many children, but not all of them survived to adulthood, and the family set aside land for a cemetery there on the farm. It was many years later, when Henry Ford purchased the land, that he disassembled the cemetery and moved the remains to the private Northview Cemetery. The remains are marked by a tall stone in a line from the water faucet and marked with an "F" – because he paid for it, I guess. None of the names of those who were moved there are listed, but the area is marked as the remains of the Chovin Family Farm Cemetery.

The Michigan Central Railroad purchased right of way from the family in 1869. It was at that time that the family had money. Our great-grandfather passed away soon after. He had built a large new home on what became Michigan Avenue (the Old Sauk Trail). My mother often told of staying at her grandfather's house for Christmas and coming down the open stairway to find that a huge Christmas tree was all aglow with lighted candles. Those were happy times! She was a twin, and she and her sister got into lots of trouble – the two of them would go down to the creek after being all dressed up, and, while the others were getting ready for a party, they played in the muddy shore and were a mess,

Back to Grandpa Chovin. He left each of his surviving children 60 feet of frontage on Michigan Avenue and then parceled out all the land back to the river evenly for pasturage. My mom's mother used her avenue footage to have a home constructed for her five children. My mother told of walking the cows down the lane to fresh pasturage (which is now Charles Street in east Dearborn), and of sitting on the fence to wave to their uncle. He had become an engineer on the trains, and he would blow the whistle for them. They worked together on all the farming chores with all the neighbors – the Laphams, Woodworths, Fords, etc. Everyone went to the one-room Miller School, and Henry Ford was in the class with my grandmother; my mom and sisters even went there, too. When I went to Dearborn Junior College (now Henry Ford Community College) in 1950, I did my teacher observation there in the kindergarten. Miss Ellen Leahey was the principal at Miller School. I told her that my mom had been in her class, and, when I said Esther Miller, she remembered her fondly and was tickled. The very next day I was allowed to be in the class alone with the students, as Miss Leahey had assured the teacher that I was qualified. She knew how well my mom had done, and she could tell that I was the same. That was a real surprise for me, and an honor!

Several homes were built along Michigan Avenue about the same time. With 10 children each given 60 feet of prime property, it was a Chovin section. Some of the daughters had married and sold their land. One had moved to Littleton, Colorado, and another to Orange, California. When my sister and I drove west the first time in 1957, we visited with both of our great-aunts and met their families. The next year when I moved to California to teach, my mom and dad rode with me, and I took them to meet with these aunts. It really tickled all of them when Mom told about how happy the family was to receive boxes of oranges from the aunt when she was little. That made the trip worthwhile!

Whenever we walked to downtown Dearborn, Mom would point out the house beside the Lowrey lumberyard, a low, beige-colored brick bungalow. It was her Uncle John's house, which had been christened "Viroka" when it was built in honor of the Indian woman that had married into our family years before. We really were secure with our Native American neighbors.

My grandmother, Betsy Jane, married Fred Miller and had five girls and one boy who died, as scarlet fever and other diseases took their toll. After she had a new house built on the avenue, her husband passed away after slaughtering a pig in the barn. As a widow with children, she eventually married the hired hand. In 1913 she passed away in childbirth, and the five girls were sent to Detroit to be with relatives.

Our dearest cousin was Charles Chovin, son of Charles

and Mary Chovin and an only child. In 1917 his parents had built a home on the avenue, and so they petitioned the court to take the girls in, but the others, who already had six children of their own, were given the girls. Mom and her sisters had to live in Detroit near Woodmere Cemetery. They had a rough time till the oldest turned 18 and could take over as guardian and get the others out. One by one they got jobs, mostly at the telephone company, and they worked and supported the younger ones.

Cousin Charlie was a lifetime buddy of Henry Ford's nephew, Bob Ford, and so we knew him well. He started the dealership in Uncle Charlie's living room. In 1927 the house was moved onto a city lot on Charles Street, where it is today. My parents were married in January 1927. The renters moved out, so Mom and Dad rented the house from Mom's sisters, and that is where my brother, sister and I were born and lived till 1949, when we sold Grandma's house so that Bob Ford could enlarge his dealership. We moved into Charlie's house there on Charles Street and purchased it from him. So now you know why the house is so important to me.

Mom and Dad both passed away there in the '70s and '80s, and my single sister remained there, but my brother Fred and I both married and had our own homes. Our great-grandfather's tombstone at Woodmere was cracked and replaced, and my youngest son brought the two pieces to our house and placed them behind the garage. So the land is marked by those as the last piece of the original French claim from so many years ago.

Jane Knapp Arndt taught in Dearborn and in San Leandro, California.

A First Mother Brings Her Daughter 'Home' to Meet 'Grandma'

By Lorraine Dusky

Three weeks after I was reunited with the daughter I gave up for adoption, Jane, she flew to Detroit the day after Christmas to meet my mother and my husband. Jane, at 15, bubbling with excitement — her first airplane flight! an adventure of her own! — glided through the gate beaming. Since this was before 9/11, my husband, Tony, my mother and I were there at the gate, and she hugged me enthusiastically and embraced her "new" grandmother too. All three of us were within an inch of each other's height, same coloring, similar hair. No mistaking who the three of us were that day.

I noticed a guy standing a bit to the side, lingering a bit, watching. Jane flashed a big grin and waved, turned to me and said: "I sat next to him and told him the whole story." I nodded to him; he smiled and moved on. A chance encounter, a whole universe he's probably never thought about acknowledged between strangers.

That night, Jane slept on my mother's couch in her apartment; Tony and I took a room at the nearby Dearborn Inn. This way Jane would have the opportunity to get to know my mother a bit without anyone's intrusion, including ours, and we'd be there right after coffee in the morning anyway. Jane was a good sport and had no qualms with this arrangement. Wait till she tells the kids at school! No, wait, they already know! She'd already done a book report on my memoir about relinquishing her, Birthmark, and told the teacher and anybody within earshot that the book was about her, and the writer was her mother. Her birth mother. The teacher was doubtful, but the adoptive parents cleared that up. Yes, she was that girl.

The next day we drove by the red-brick bungalow my father built when I was 5 on Calhoun Street in east Dearborn. We had been living only a half block away down the same street — but across a side street — and Mom let me walk down to the construction site myself, a big deal, I told my husband and my daughter. Once there, Dad always gave me a job, undoubtedly to keep me out of his and harm's way. I was to pick up the nails that had dropped out of the carpenters' aprons — only the straight ones, only the ones we can use, he said. It made me feel as if I were making a big contribution to the whole business. Saving money by not wasting nails! That vision of me — searching for nails, proudly handing them over to Daddy, his thanking me for a job well done — hits me like a fresh wind every time I drive by the house, even now. We did a few other drive-bys of places that meant something to me, my grade school, the motel my parents bought when I was 14, the house on Garrison Street we lived in after we sold the motel — and while I'm living an old movie reel of my life, Jane and Tony joked around. They only saw ordinary structures; I saw my past.

That day after that, Sunday, was the only day that my relatives would have had to meet Tony (most had not come east to our wedding a few months earlier) as well as Jane, and so into the smallish living room in my mother's apartment on Beech Street trooped more than a dozen assorted relatives — my two brothers, Richard and Tom; Uncle Stanley, who had been a radio operator living behind enemy lines during World War II, and his wife, Sylvia; my cousin Beverly; assorted nieces and nephews — Jane's cousins. Relatives. Meeting Grandma was one thing, but all these other people — probably a dozen total — these strangers who are presumably related to her?

Tony to the rescue. He sat side-by-side with her on the couch, making sly remarks about the passing parade to put her at ease, while I chatted with relatives, passed around the cheeses and cookies and cakes, introduced them to Jane and Tony, careful to say, "This is Jane," not, "This is my daughter." They knew who she was; I didn't need to explain.

Adoptees say this kind of reunion experience is overwhelming and uncomfortable — they don't feel like a member of the new family; they already have a family, thank you very much, They feel like they are on display. In truth, they are, just as much as a relative recently returned from India with a new Indian bride would be — but Jane, with Tony's help, took it in stride. And that day, fortunately, everybody was checking out Tony too, deflecting some of the attention from her. My family saw her as a full member of the clan, even if she had been missing. Later Jane told me that the only thing that made her uncomfortable was when someone referred to me as "your mom." Mom was back in Wisconsin.

That evening, Tony, Jane and I headed out to the revolving restaurant on the top of the downtown Renaissance Center, then the crown jewel of the Detroit riverfront and GM's gleaming new headquarters. Detroit might not have been the glorious Motor City of my youth — the automobile industry was already going down the tubes in 1981, Detroit had been through the riots of the '60s, and parts of the downtown had never recovered — but any big city from high enough above still provides a twinkling panorama at night.

To Jane, it must have been simply a big city; to me it was familiar, home. See the Christmas tree in Cadillac Square down there? That's where I used to go Christmas shopping with my mother; the bus from Dearborn stops near there. See that cool white building over there, with the structure on top that looks like a big wedding cake? The windows in the powder room for the restaurant on the top go down to the floor; it's kinda freaky because you're so high up. And the lights on the other side of the river? That's Canada — yes, really it is, a town called Windsor. When Jane stared out the window, I looked at her: My daughter. My daughter, my daughter is here. Have you ever tried escargot? What is that? Snails? Yuk. OK, steak and potatoes it is, with lots of butter. I'm from Wisconsin, the Dairy State, remember? she reminded me. How could I forget? I joked back. I'm still a sucker for revolving restaurants on top of sky scrapers, and it turns out, so was she, as she discovered that night. We both loved heights and revolving restaurants, no matter how corny they seem to the unknowing.

That morning we had all gone to Mass at my old parish, Sacred Heart, where my mother still worshiped. Here is my daughter, Lord. Here is a good husband, Lord. Here is my mother – and the memory of Christmas past when I didn't know where she was whizzed by in a flashback. Now I heard Tony singing in his deep bass, Mother on key, Jane and me decidedly off. Neither one of us could keep a tune more than four notes, and noticing that about her that day gave me a squirt of pleasure. Whether or not I believed in the Catholic God of my youth was not open for discussion that day as my heart repeated: Thank you, God. Thank you for giving me my daughter. Yes, of course, I knew that soon she would fly back to her other life, another mother, another family, in another state, and I would go back east. But now I knew her. Now I would never not know where she was anymore.

It was the Sunday after Christmas, but in my mind it was the first Christmas since I found her. From now on, everything would be counted as before, or after, I found my daughter.

This story was excerpted from Lorraine Dusky's upcoming memoir, Hole in My Heart. *Her controversial 1979 book,* Birthmark, *is considered the first memoir about relinquishing a child to adoption. Her byline has appeared in such national publications as the New York Times, Newsweek, Town & Country and Glamour. She and her husband, the writer Anthony Brandt, make their home in Sag Harbor, New York, a village she likens to Charlevoix.*

His Family Tree Branched Through a Lumber Company

By Richard Fellrath

The first thing I must do is give a disclaimer. This is what I think was told to me or I think I remember. I may have credibility somewhat less than Wikipedia.

The Fellraths came to the Dearborn area in 1848, when Joseph and his children moved from a farm in Sumpter Township to Springwells Township (the exact location is hard to determine, but it appears to have been where the Rouge Plant is now situated). They had come from Wangonbourg in Alsace, France, through New Orleans on June 9, 1845. A cholera epidemic took Joseph in 1854. Joseph's son, Frank (Francois Joseph), my great-grandfather, after several moves bought a 43-acre farm in Dearborn Township (now Inkster) in 1863, the same year as his youngest brother was fighting with the Michigan 24th Infantry (Iron Brigade) at the battle of Gettysburg. Francis died in 1885 and is buried in Mount Kelly Cemetery.

Frank's son, Francis (Frank) Henry, after a stint with the Detroit Fire Department, farmed and started the Fellrath Lumber Company on Inkster Road south of the tracks that ran parallel to Michigan Avenue. Frank was elected superintendent of Dearborn Township in 1913 but not re-elected because he had cooperated with Henry Ford in some of his projects. Francis Henry's health deteriorated, and he went to Miami, where he died in 1925.

The youngest of his four children was Jerome, my father, born in 1915. It is said that there was an argument among the family as to the name, so his mother, Clara June (nee Wiethoff), picked up a Bible, saw that it was translated by St. Jerome and picked that name. Clara died in 1932, leaving my father an orphan. He lived with an aunt, Katherine Schneider, called Kitty, until his older brother, Francis, born 1902, took him in. Sister Cecilia had died in 1920, and his other brother, Richard Thomas, the first to go to college, drowned in Portage Lake (Dexter Township) just after graduation in 1930. It is said that both my brother, Tom, and I were named after Richard, who was a brilliant student and went to the University of Detroit after two years at Sacred Heart High School. Did the brilliance pass on to us? Probably not. Dad and his brother, Francis, ran the lumber company, then called Fellrath Sons.

My dad married Jayne Ayers in 1940, and they started a house in a new subdivision, Dearborn Hills, that same year. Don't try looking up Emerson Street in the 1940 Census—it didn't exist until later in the year. In the interim, they lived in the apartments on Brady Street until it was finished. I was born in November of 1940 (I was conceived on their honeymoon in Cuba). I am the oldest of seven children (one drowned at our cottage in 1951 on that same lake that claimed Richard Thomas). My earliest recollections are of Pensacola, Florida, where my father was stationed as a lieutenant commander in the Naval Air Corps in the latter part of World War II. Santa came in a Jeep into a gigantic hanger. Dad was also stationed in Argentia, Newfoundland, where he said there was a girl behind every tree. (He also said there are no trees in Newfoundland.) He was also stationed in Portsmouth, England, where his unit did anti-submarine duty with the flying boats called PBY's. They were great for finding U-Boats but sitting ducks for the Luftwaffe. Dad did not fly; he was the executive officer. I am told that on VJ Day I tied cans on my tricycle and "separated" the victory.

After the war Dad came home, and we began our ordinary life. I didn't see much of Dad, as he was working in supplying lumber for the new houses in the western suburbs. He said lumber was so scarce that he put a Dodge automobile on a flat car to get back a load of lumber from Oregon. Fellrath's was the first lumber yard to use hi-lo's in the Detroit area. I remember our subdivision still had some wooded areas and the kids in the neighborhood, Tom and Ted Miloch, Jane Ann, Bruce and Kenny Sanborn, Billy Metz.

Tom and I used to run wild in "Vernon Jungles," on the north side of Emerson.

The first TV in the neighborhood was owned by the Metzes, and I was told that I could not watch all that stuff, which would rot my brain. We spent our summers at Portage Lake after 1948, and there was no TV there until the nominating conventions in 1956. I used to sneak out to the car to listen to radio adventures like *The Shadow* and *The FBI in Peace and War.*

Mom was really into the arts and started me in ballroom dancing, which I still enjoy, and took me to the Detroit Institute of Arts to marvel at the armor. She didn't do well with the opera, which I never liked. I started school at Sacred Heart in 1946, and I remember Sister Mary Anthony, whom we all loved. The same could not be said of Sister Matilda; my little brother, Jerry (Jr.), was asked not to return for high school, partly because he circulated a petition calling for her recall. I really do not remember much of grade school except when the new school was built; we took the tunnel to the lunch room in that facility (I am told it still leaks where it did then). I did pick up a love for "toy soldiers," and I would go to Muirhead's to buy my Britains with my lunch money ($2 for five cavalry or eight infantry, hand-painted in England until the U.S. banned imports of lead soldiers). I still have toy soldiers all over the house, some of which I painted.

High school was a good experience. I really don't have a great deal to remember about these times. If you want to get really great stories, you should talk to John McShosh, who, when we took a tour of the building, volunteered that he knew exactly where the "office" was. We had a big problem in high school; the nuns kept kicking out problem students, who were overwhelmingly male. There were 98 girls and 32 boys in our class. Eventually, I am told, the priests stepped in and told the nuns that if they kicked out a boy, they would have to bring in a boy since we hardly had enough boys for the football team. I went out for football for my first two years, but had a hernia in the third and didn't go out in my senior year (Coach Delany was upset with me). I was the sports editor for the yearbook. I had pretty decent grades and enjoyed the humanities (except Latin II, which I had a great deal of trouble with; I loved the stories – it was just that language that got me). Math was a mixed bag. I did well if I could visualize the problem in geometry and solid geometry, but algebra and trig were a mystery. In my senior year I was allowed to purchase a car, a 1953 Chevy, zero to 50 in five minutes flat. It was a "dog" but it was wheels, and I loved to drive around. My little sister, Sue (12 years younger than I), says that if I met a girl to give a ride to, I would put her and Jerry in the trunk.

For one year we got our money's worth in tuition: $200 per family for our six kids.

I loved the dances after the football games. At one such occasion after a game with Wayne St. Mary's, I met Alice Gates, a girl I knew from Portage Lake, and we decided to show the rest of the attendees how the latest steps, including the Chicken, were done. We were doing very well until I had a tap on my shoulder, and the chaperone, I think it was a priest, said "We don't do those kinds of dances here," and I was sent home. I was not always the most popular guy in the school, especially after I suggested to the nun in junior English that we study *War and Peace* as our senior reading project.

After high school graduation in 1959, where someone spiked the punch and things got a little out of hand, it was on to Notre Dame, the University of Detroit Law School and the Army, JAGC. But those are other stories.

Richard Fellrath is a practicing attorney in Troy. He is president of the Sacred Heart Alumni Association. He is a member of the Dearborn Genealogical Society and is president of the Troy Genealogical Society.

The Little Old Lady From Nowlin: Freeda

By Richard Huard

After retiring from Ford Motor Company, Freeda Hoover decided to get a driver's license and buy a car. She settled on a nice white 1967 Comet. Going through a parking lot on Garrison Avenue, she was broadsided by two cars. Can you believe it? She collected insurance claims from both insurance companies.

Her next car was an eight-cylinder Torino. When she returned from a trip to West Virginia, I asked, "What time did you get there?" She replied, "6:30." Then I asked, "What time did you leave Dearborn?" She said, "About 1 o'clock." Thinking about that, the best I ever made that trip was seven hours and five minutes. Then I asked, "How in the world did you drive?" She said, "I don't know."

By now Freeda was about 85 years old and had an early Escort. One morning she called to ask if we could come over to her house and get her car out of the garage. She lived on Nowlin. I asked what was wrong, whether the battery was dead. Her response was "No, it runs well; it is turned in the garage." I said I'd be right there.

I couldn't believe what I was looking at. She had that poor Escort so wedged in the corner of her 1 1/2 -car garage and locked in between the studs so tight. I said, "I will have to go home and get my floor jack. Being on wheels, it will help me get the car out of the corner."

The jack did the job just fine. When we got the car out of the garage, she asked me, "What do you call that jack thing? Maybe I should have one of those things."

Richard Huard is a retired Ford Motor Company technician.

Home to Five Generations

By Carrol Lewis

Would you be surprised to know this is being written by a member of the third of five generations to call Dearborn their hometown? I will tell you about those five generations. It all began in 1926 when my grandfather, O.L. Smith, and his family moved to Dearborn and bought a home on Beech Street. My grandfather never liked his given name (Ora Lynn), so he always went by O.L. He had been an educator in Indiana, but always wanted to be a lawyer. He graduated from the University of Michigan Law School in 1913. He and his family (three sons at that time) moved to Ithaca, Michigan, where he practiced law for several years. During that time he got interested in politics and became a four-term prosecuting attorney for Gratiot County.

The family then moved to Lansing, and he became the assistant attorney general for the state. To continue his devotion to the law, he became a U.S. attorney, then a special assistant attorney for the state. He and Grandma had two other children by then: a daughter and another son.

They moved to Dearborn then so he could become a part of a big Detroit law firm. They had a large home built on River Lane so they could accommodate all the family for special occasions. His background in Republican politics prompted the state party to convince him to run for governor of Michigan in 1940. He answered the call but did not win the election. O.L. Smith died in 1941 after a very successful life and career. In 1944 a new school was to be built in west Dearborn – a junior high school. The school board honored my grandfather by giving it the name O.L. Smith, as he served many, many years on Dearborn's school board and was president of the board when the land was purchased for the new Dearborn high School.

O.L. Smith's first-born son, Arthur, was my father. As a child he often sat in the courtroom with his father and there developed his own love for the law. He graduated in 1926 – also from the U. of M. Law School. He and my mother, Barbara Allan, were married in the afternoon, after their graduation in the morning. After a very short wedding trip, they moved to Chicago, where a job was waiting for him in a patent law firm. During that time, my grandpa hoped that my father, mother and I would move back and settle in Michigan so my grandpa and my father would be able to practice law together. But patent law called my father, so that plan did not work out.

However, moving to Dearborn did work out, and my family became Dearbornites. My father had a position with a Detroit patent law firm, and he and my mother became well known in many areas of Dearborn life. We first lived on North Waverly at the corner of Sheridan, and later they had a home built on Elmwood Court. By then my dad had his own patent law office on Michigan Avenue, near the corner of Telegraph. That firm grew into a most successful venture.

During that time he and my mother moved to a home with some acreage in Dearborn Heights. Then in 1957 he was appointed by President Eisenhower to the U.S. Court of Customs and Patent Appeals. It was a difficult decision for him to accept the appointment because it meant they would have to move from Dearborn to Washington, D.C. However, he was highly honored by the appointment and did accept it. Their time in Washington was extremely eventful, and they enjoyed it very much, but they returned to Dearborn for the summers when the court was not in session and for holidays and special family events. Arthur Smith's untimely death at age 65 occurred in Washington in 1968, and he was returned to Dearborn for burial at Northview Cemetery.

We are now into the third generation of my Dearborn family – mine. I have lived here ever since moving from Chicago with my parents, and I am now 85. Since we lived near Lindbergh School, that's where I attended kindergarten and first grade. When I was in the second grade, I began school in Greenfield Village and graduated from the Edison Institute High School there in 1945.

After my graduation I furthered my education at Michigan State to become an elementary teacher. Where did I begin my teaching career? In Dearborn at Lindbergh School! My high school boyfriend was a Dearborn resident since his birth, and his family home was on Park Street. After marrying, we bought a very small house on Boston Street. He began his higher education thanks to the G.I. Bill. After our two children were born, I became a stay-at-home mom until after Dwight finished law school at Wayne State University in 1954 and began his patent law career in my father's office. Subsequently we moved to North Elizabeth, and I began substitute teaching at Greenfield Village and then taught kindergarten there for a while. When my husband began to practice patent/trademark law with Ford Motor Company, we moved to our home on Rockford, where we lived for 45 years. He died in 2002 and is buried in Northview Cemetery. After a few years, I moved to Chelsea to a retirement complex.

The fourth generation is comprised of our daughter and our late son. Each graduated from Adams Junior High and Dearborn High. Our son continued his education in Washington and then law school at the University of Detroit. He married his high school sweetheart from Dearborn. After law school he accepted a position as attorney for Michigan Indian Legal Services. Several years after that he succumbed to cancer at age 33. Our daughter graduated from Albion College after high school and went on to Garrett Seminary, where she earned her master of divinity degree. She served several churches as pastor and then returned to Garrett, where she earned her doctor of ministry degree. She became the first woman to serve the historic Central United Methodist Church in Detroit as associate pastor. There she met her husband, and they returned to Dearborn, where he served as associate pastor at Dearborn's

First United Methodist Church. They lived on South Silvery Lane in the church parsonage, just a short distance from our home on Rockford. They have a son and two daughters and then moved to Trenton, where her husband was appointed to serve Trenton's First United Methodist Church. During that time, he felt a "call" back to teaching, which he did for several years before attending Yale Divinity School, and that's when they moved to Chelsea, so they were already there when I moved, too. They now live in Royal Oak where he is superintendent of schools, and our daughter has a pastoral psychotherapy appointment.

Now to the fifth generation of the family who have lived in Dearborn. Our grandchildren lived with their parents in the Silvery Lane parsonage, and our greatest joy came from being so close to them. Our grandson began college at Kalamazoo College and then graduated from Wayne State University Law School cum laude. He accepted a position as an assistant prosecuting attorney in Oakland County. He and his wife (also high school sweethearts) are now the owners of my Rockford Street house. When my family moved back to this area, I did, too, and I am now a resident of Oakwood Common, a real homecoming for me. What a fantastic life I have been privileged to lead all through the years and to have known all these family generations. My two granddaughters are in college. One will be graduating from the University of Michigan and will become a music teacher; the other is a junior at Ohio Wesleyan University, studying politics and government.

How happy and proud my grandpa O.L. Smith would be of all this Dearborn family! In reading through all these generations, it is incredible to know that there/has been an attorney in each generation. I end this with a surprise, as I began it. Before this article is published I will become a great-grandmother, so there will be six generations of Dearbornites!

Carrol Lewis is a president at Oakwood Common.

Pop: 'Dot's a Good Vun!'

By Adeline Lienau

My father was a big man, aristocratic, deceptively stern. Underneath he was plain folks. He fixed things, even half-soled shoes, but he insisted on obedience and justice, was never someone to hold his tongue if he disagreed with anyone, be it his congressman or his pastor. He had a deep, rumbling voice and sang bass in the choir. You could feel the vibrations from it in the church pews. He was also a musician, self-taught, playing piano, drums, trombone and cornet.

Christmas was always important to Pop; he was deeply religious. He chose the tree each year and did the trimming; he wanted perfection. He'd drill holes into the trunk and insert extra branches for symmetry, then he used fine piano wire to carefully fasten all the branch tips to the trunk to avoid sagging when the ornaments were added. The large ones went on the bottom and the tiny ones on the top.

Santa always came to our house while the children were at church. The night before, we had an elaborate program climaxing with each child's receiving a large bag of goodies, including fruit, nuts and ribbon candy. It seemed like so much in those times.

When I grew old enough to "help" Santa Claus, I remember trimming the tree with Pop while listening to Madam Schuman Heink sing *Silent Night* on the victrola in Pop's native German. We children (six of us) received just one gift each, but that was a lot, we thought. And we shared. Besides, we were more interested in the variety of cookies Mom had baked. She was a homespun cook, no recipes, but I don't remember any of us ever saying we didn't like something she prepared.

There were some memorable Christmases in my youth, but my favorite one came after I was married and had a family of my own. It was 1947 and Pop was the central character.

As long as I remember, Pop made wine – one 15-gallon keg each Christmas, grape and elderberry usually, and peach brandy once. Each fall Pop would take us into the woods with baskets to gather berries along country roads in Michigan. We'd always get enough for the wine.

But the Christmas I remember he needed a new keg but couldn't find what he wanted, an oak keg charred on the inside. Pop's wine had to be perfect. He took great pride throughout the year in serving it to guests and visitors on special occasions.

That year he shopped everywhere without success. He stopped at my house one afternoon completely disgruntled. "They don't make things like they used to," he grumbled – and I resolved then I'd find him a keg for a Christmas present. He was always a man of simple tastes, so it had always been difficult to give him something he really needed. Now was my chance.

I should have hired a detective. It wasn't easy. I tried every bar supply company in the Detroit phone book, met failure after failure, but everyone was helpful in suggesting other places to call. Finally, just before Christmas, I found one on the city's east side. It was exactly what I was looking for.

On Christmas morning we drove over to Pop's house. He held the door open as the children walked before me up the steps. Then he saw my husband taking the barrel out of the trunk of the car; there was a big red bow around the top of it.

Now Pop's German accent became more pronounced as he grew older. When he saw the keg, he said, "What's that?" And I explained it was his Christmas present. He stood tall, clapped his hands and cried, "Dot's a good vun!"

"Then he didn't leave my side all day. We drove over to my sister Betty's house; hers was the most beautiful, and she was the grand hostess of the family. But all afternoon Pop would have things to tell me. He'd lean over and whisper into my ear, as if it were a conspiracy. How it pleased me. I still experience a glow remembering, and I wrote in recollection:

"Every day of our lives we take our memories;
Whether or not that is what we intend.
Strive to choose just the kind that will stay in your mind,
Give you pleasure when day's at an end.
When old rocking chair has got you and memory's
     all there is to recall,
You'll relax quite content with a life well spent;
You wouldn't have missed it – not any at all.
Especially the Christmas that Pop got the wine keg
he wanted: Dot vas da vun."

Adeline Lienau was born in1915 in a Pennsylvania coal-mining community where she spoke German as a child, moved to Detroit around 1920, then after marriage to Dearborn in 1938. She left Dearborn in 1961 and died in Huntsville, Alabama, in 2011. She enjoyed writing. Her father, Pop, lived on Gulley Road and worked at the Ford Motor Company as a janitor. This piece was originally published in the Birmingham (Alabama) Post Herald circa 1963.

Dad's Deer

By Jeff Lienau

My father didn't like guns and never owned one, but I learned he was very good shot.

When I became interested in a gun and was deemed old enough, he took me to the local Dearborn police station where the YMCA had arranged for the police gun range to be used for instruction; that's where I learned to shoot.

One night the state champion with a rifle was at the range practicing, a young man 20-something years old. He was shooting a custom-balanced 22-caliber target rifle, whereas the YMCA rifles were heavy, Army-surplus bolt-action 22-caliber simulations of the M1 carbine.

At one point the instructors invited the fathers present to try their hand at shooting, and my dad went up there with that clumsy YMCA rifle right next to the state champion. After a round of firing from the off-hand position, dad's score matched the champion. They weren't competing, but I was impressed.

Later on, when he took me deep in the woods, where it was safe to shoot, I fired at whatever I thought I could hit. We came upon a bird in a tree at one point, and he asked me for the gun; it was just a little bird. He said, "I'm not going to hurt it." He fired but not at the bird, rather at the small branch – the branch exploded almost below the bird's feet; the bird defecated and flew off. Dad howled, "Boy I scared the s__t out of him."

Pa was a salesman of large custom manufacturing machinery and participated in "industry" events where he could meet socially with such customers as the Ford management. It was during one of these social activities that his prowess with a gun became apparent to others.

One activity was a deer-hunting expedition that was arranged at a private hunting range north of Detroit. Dad borrowed a gun from his father, a varmint gun, 22-caliber, illegal at the time, regarded as too light for deer hunting, but he wasn't concerned because he didn't expect to shoot anything. The men were transported on chartered train cars. The train had a bar in each one of the cars, which the "guys" took full advantage of. The stories got taller with each drink and each mile, and the bragging about their guns was one of the more common topics. They didn't talk very much to Dad about his gun, though, beyond asking, "What did you bring, Harry? A 22?"

The trip took several hours, and the men in the cars acted as you might expect – loud and drinking heavily, but there was a hitch. While the train had a full bar to service everyone, it only had a small, one-hole bathroom in every other car, and there were lots of full bladders. The train had one scheduled stop before the destination at a very small station. As the train stopped, the men piled out of the cars and began running to the station, but after only a few steps they stopped, realizing the station was very small, could have only a very small bathroom and would never handle such a crowd. The station was next to a grassy field. So, with no other choice, they formed lines, quietly relieved themselves of the booze, then carefully watching where they walked, returned to the train.

When they got to the hunting range, Dad chose his stand location last, trying for the worst location, and expected to sit comfortably with nothing to do. But as fate would have it, after a few hours of waiting he could hear firing in the distance, then a lot more getting closer. In a bit he saw the deer – running as fast as it could. He told me, "I shot it once in the neck so it would stop running, then walked down there close where I could kill it quick."

On the trip home the train car was quiet – the bragging was over. He arrived home proud of himself, more for one-upping his peers than for killing the deer, so he proudly announced, "Hey, everyone, I got a deer."

"Bambi!, You killed Bambi! How could you?" And his daughter ran from the room,

The deer head was mounted; it is a 10-point buck.

After high school, Jeff Lienau moved to Huntsville, Alabama, where he remains. He became an engineer, worked at the Redstone Arsenal, has two children, and retired in 2000.

Dad's Short Career As a Village Guide

By Colleen Murphy

My father, Jim Murphy, had an outgoing personality and was always a persuasive speaker. I believe it was the eloquence conferred on him by his Irish birthright. He never made it to Ireland, but you would have thought he must have kissed the Blarney Stone many times. He had that special gift of gab that one is endowed with after making the pilgrimage to Blarney Castle to kiss the stone. I think it was his gregarious personality that helped him land a summer job at Greenfield Village as a tour guide when he was 16 or 17 years old in 1943 or 1944.

Visitors came from all points of the globe even in those days. Humphrey Bogart and Veronica Lake were very big Hollywood stars, and he recalled their visit well, even though he wasn't their guide.

A guide could be requested to escort a group for their entire visit through the village and the museum. The guide was well versed in all the attractions in the village and the museum. He would escort as few as one person or as many as 20 people. However, weekdays were not as busy as weekends. And sometimes Dad would spend hours in Lovett Hall waiting for someone to request a tour guide.

One afternoon, on a very slow day, Dad had been sitting around the entire morning with not one request to escort anyone. Being a teen-ager and easily bored, he decided the large plantation-style windows with deep sills in Lovett Hall would be a great place to take a nap. The heavy drapes were held back by large rope tiebacks. He climbed up on a sill, unhooked the tiebacks so no one would see him and fell asleep. He never knew how long he slept, but it must have been quite some time because he fell into a deep sleep.

Mrs. Henry Ford, Clara, happened to be in the village that day. As she was passing through Lovett Hall, she spotted the window with the drapes not open. She went to the window, pulled back the drapes and found my dad sound asleep. She shook his shoulder to wake him. Startled, Dad jumped up and shouted, "What?" Mrs. Ford asked him what his name was, and he replied, "Jim Murphy." She said, "Well, Mr. Murphy, you're fired." That ended my dad's career as a tour guide.

I pass by The Henry Ford several times a week, and I always think of this story. Years later, my son Jim (yes, he was named after his grandfather) got a job as a night watchman in the village. He drove a village-owned pickup truck throughout the village on the midnight shift. Like his grandfather, he too was bored one evening and was caught sleeping on the job. Needless to say, just like his namesake, that ended his career at the village as well.

So much has changed over the years at Greenfield Village. It's now called The Henry Ford: America's Greatest History Attraction. Tour guides are now called docents and historical presenters, and the heavy drapes have been replaced with a light-weight fabric without tiebacks. But the one thing that will never change is that people who fall asleep on the job will continue to get fired.

Colleen Murphy is a lifelong resident of Dearborn. She worked 25 years at City Hall in the Department of Public Information, retiring in 2010. She has been a volunteer at the Dearborn Historical Museum since 2012.

Holy Smoke

By Jeanine Deagen Pitrone

It was about 1949, and, as was the custom for the Deagen family, we attended Mass each Sunday at 8 o'clock at St. Alphonsus. Dad Richard and Mother Veretta always made sure that I and my sisters, Janet and Joan, were scrubbed and polished, our hair curled from being bound in socks since Saturday night after our baths.

This Sunday was no different, and the five of us, as usual, arrived early enough to get our regular seats near the front on the left side, the Blessed Mother's side, of the church.

As we knelt and prayed silently, it soon became time for the altar boy to come to the main altar and light the candles. He seemed to have a little trouble lighting the second candle (the 8 o'clock service was a low Mass, so there were only two candles to light instead of the usual six at the high Mass to follow). But after a minute or so, he seemed satisfied and turned to leave the sanctuary. In doing so he failed to notice that the wick from his candle lighter, which he had lengthened to make it easier to light the reluctant candle, had fallen from its holder onto the altar.

In a few seconds there was a small fire as the altar cloth started to burn, and almost immediately it turned into a blaze that brought gasps from the assembling congregation.

My father leaped from his seat and vaulted over the communion rail, removing his prized suit coat as he approached the fire. It didn't take him long to beat out the fire with his jacket, but the coat was ruined.

My father was an hourly worker, a millwright, at Ford Motor Company, so he did not dress up for work. But he dressed impeccably for church, being very particular about the fit of his suit.

No one from the church mentioned anything about the fire that Sunday, but later in the week we got a phone call from the office. It seems someone in the congregation identified my dad to the pastor, and the parish wanted to reimburse Mr. Deagen for his coat. Of course Dad would not take any money from the church.

Soon after the next payday he bought a brand-new replacement suit. Our family continued to sit in that same area for many years, but we never had more excitement than that day so long ago.

Jeanine Deagen Pitrone attended St. Alphonsus School for 12 years. She met her husband, Joe, there. They owned a company called Fun Services, which sold supplies for church fairs. They also ran a retail operation, Fun House. They were married for 50 years before he passed away in June 2013. She splits her year between Sarasota and Michigan.

She Eloped out of Spite, But Her Sons Were Blessed

By Nellie Polidori

My parents lived a difficult life in Italy. My mother had six children, but only two lived. After her babies died, she had a lot of breast milk. In those days Mussolini had a home for unwed mothers who did not want to raise their babies. The government would give these infants to any woman who had milk but no babies and would pay them five liras a month. My mother got two infants. My mom nursed them, grew attached and kept them. Because my parents were poor, they lived with my grandparents. My grandparents had a plot of land in Italy and tried raising sheep and goats. It didn't work. Ultimately my dad came to America but would frequently return to Italy. One day he got caught between a wall and a horse-drawn cart in the mines. He was severely injured and was hospitalized in Colorado for a full year.

In June 1923 my father, mother and I sailed to the United States on a ship named Patria. The trip to America took three weeks. I remember when we saw the Statue of Liberty and everybody was screaming, "Thank God! We're in America!" Everyone had tears in their eyes. We arrived at Ellis Island, which was to close in 1924. We were among the last to go there. We decided to go to Detroit because someone said that there were jobs in the steel mills and assembly plants.

We left New York for Detroit. Before we boarded the train, my father bought some bananas for us to eat on the train. My father knew what they were, but my mom and I didn't. We were hesitant about eating them. My father laughed and said, "Eat them. You will like them." My mom and I both liked them.

When we reached the Michigan Central Station, our relatives picked us up and took us to their home. The very next day, future Dearborn District Judge Vince Fordell's father, who was a superintendent at Great Lakes Steel, came to our house to tell my father that he could begin work immediately for $3.50 a day. My dad borrowed money from relatives to get some work clothes and went to work the very next morning. The few families we knew all had boarders. They called upon my mother to help.

After living with relatives for a while, we got an apartment over a store. I kept crying all night. My father got mad and told my mother to get up and see what the problem was. My mother found me covered with lice. I had slept on a leather couch, and that couch was loaded with bugs. The next day my father went to look for another flat to rent. He got us a place on Solvay Street. The house had an outside toilet, but my parents did not care. It was better than bugs!

In 1924 my dad got a job working at the Ford Motor Company for $5 a day.

A lot of men who had left their wives in Europe came to Detroit to make money and brought their wives to the United States later. Frequently during the days of Prohibition men would come to our house to play boccie in the alley or play cards in the basement. When they played these games, they played for drinks, not money.

Because of the Depression, my father lost his job with Ford and took me and my mom back to Italy. I lived in Italy for four years. At first it was difficult to get used to the different way of life. There was no electricity or heat in the house, no stove, no refrigerator, no cars. My brother had a horse-drawn carriage.

Dominic Polidori courted me for a year. Other young men were interested in me, but because Dominic was his friend, my brother would not let any of them near me. I had my brother's blessing, but not my dad's. He wanted me to marry someone who was educated. My father was very strict. I got fed up with it. I eloped. I did it to spite my father.

We got married in church on October 6, 1932. We went back home after the ceremony, changed clothes and went to work on the farm. What an exciting wedding day! We didn't even have money to take a picture. I regretted what I did, but it was too late. It was done.

Some 16 people, including us, lived in my husband's grandfather's house. When my dad's money ran out, he decided to return to America. My husband and I went with him. Dominic also got his first American job at Great Lakes Steel. He switched from working there at $3.87 to working for Ford Motor for $5 a day.

By the time I was 24, Dominic and I had four sons—Leonard, Tony, Ray and Gino. We purchased our first home for $6,000 in east Dearborn.

My husband died 40 years ago. I had many chances of getting married again, but was never interested. My motto was "Once is enough."

I had always wanted to be a teacher. I'm happy that among my sons, their spouses and children, I have had six teachers in my family. I have missed a lot in life. I never graduated from high school, never attended a prom, except for a few classes, never went to college, never celebrated a communion or confirmation, and did not have a wedding celebration. I never dated anyone in my entire life. But I rejoice in the fact that my children and grandchildren have been so very blessed with not only material gifts but also with loving families and great memories.

Nellie Polidori has lived in Dearborn for over 90 years and counting. She is the proud grandmother of eight and the proud great-grandmother of nine. She worked as Mayor Orville Hubbard's secretary.

The Legend of Hell's Angels

By Donald S. Smock

My father, Donald E. Smock, grew up in Dearborn and died 38 years ago. Like most of the men who saw actual combat in World War II, he did not talk of the war to co-workers or family. He did his duty at a momentous time in history and by the grace of God was able to return to the land of the free and continue his life. He married Teresa Lebert, from another Dearborn family, had four children and lived a good life, providing for his family.

The only war story that I remember was about his Japanese prisoner, a sergeant who didn't speak a word of English, but who, by the time Dad left, was singing *The Star-Spangled Banner.* He went into the Army two weeks after his 19th birthday in 1943, about a year after Pearl Harbor. He mustered out of the Army a few days short of his 22nd birthday, after almost exactly three years of distinguished active-duty service in the legendary 11th Airborne Division (the only airborne division in the Pacific Theater) in World War II. He was awarded not only a couple of campaign medals and ribbons but also a Bronze Star Medal (the fifth-highest combat award in the U.S. military) and a Good Conduct Medal. His unit (the 11th) also received a presidential citation and was highly praised by General Douglas MacArthur and many others for their valorous service in the campaigns against the Japanese in the Philippines.

They were set to be among the first invasion troops of

Japan, and when the Japanese surrendered, MacArthur selected the 11th to be the first of the occupation forces in Japan, in no small part because of their sacrifices and courage in the Philippine campaigns. Thus, the first American flag raised in Japan was raised by men of the 11th. When General Swing, commander of the 11th Airborne, arrived in Japan and was greeted by Japanese generals and other officers wearing swords that indicated their rank, he tersely ordered them to remove their swords and stack them in a pile forthwith. When MacArthur arrived on the USS Missouri for the official Japanese surrender, it was the 11th Airborne Regimental Band that was there on deck to greet his arrival with patriotic tunes, as photos attest to. Legend has it that when the 1st Cavalry Division, whose motto is "1st in Manila, 1st in Tokyo," arrived in Tokyo, it was met by the 11th Airborne Division band. The band played a special song for the cavalry; *The Old Gray Mare She Ain't What She Used To Be*. MacArthur chose men of the 11th for his personal bodyguard, too.

The division was activated early in 1943 (my dad joined less than two months after the 11th was first formed). At that time, it was not clear whether the Army was even going to continue with airborne divisions at all because of disappointment on the part of some of the brass following previous experiences in north Africa and in Sicily. There was talk of perhaps only creating a battalion-strength unit. The deciding factor, according to many historians, was the impeccable performance by men of the 11th at important training exercises, which so impressed Army generals with the well-executed maneuvers that plans went ahead to retain airborne divisions. The 11th consisted of one parachute and two glider infantry regiments (later to also be changed to parachute infantry designation); the division operated at a little more than one-half the size of traditional infantry divisions such as were in Europe, but its assignments did not reflect the smaller size, and it usually operated thus without "backup" troops.

About two years after the creation of the 11th Airborne Division, some 130 paratroopers of the 11th (with Alamo Scouts and Filipino guerrillas) carried out one of the most legendary rescue operations in all of military history at the Los Banos internment camp, some 25 miles behind enemy lines and where there were over 2,000 civilian prisoners, mostly American but including hundreds of other nationalities too. These prisoners included about 500 Maryknoll nuns, priests and Protestant pastors and missionaries, 12 Navy nurses captured at the fall of Corregidor, many women and children, and Frank Buckles, who lived to be the oldest surviving veteran of World War I. This very successful raid was just a few weeks after the somewhat similar U.S. Army Ranger raid at the POW camp of Cabanatuan had successfully freed over 500 American and Allied prisoners of war, an event that was commemorated recently in a film starring Benjamin Bratt, Joseph Fiennes, James Franco and Connie Nielsen.

General Colin Powell, then chairman of the Joint Chiefs of Staff, said, "I doubt that any airborne unit in the world will ever be able to rival the Los Baños prison raid. It is the textbook airborne operation for all ages and all armies."

On February 16, 2005, House Joint Resolution 18, sponsored by U.S. Representative Trent Franks, was passed by the House, commemorating the heroic raid at Los Baños. The resolution also reaffirmed the nation's commitment to a full accounting of prisoners of war and those missing in action. "The truly heroic acts at Los Baños serve not only as examples of the humanitarian compassion of American servicemen and women, but also as an example of our nation's long-standing commitment to leave no soldier, living or dead, in enemy hands. As we have military personnel spread throughout the world today, many of whom are daily risking capture and torture at the hands of brutal terrorists, it is more important than ever to recognize and honor the heroism and willing sacrifice of those soldiers who risk their own safety not to take a strategic objective, but simply to bring a comrade home..."

The 11th Airborne was often referred to as "Hell's Angels" (long before the notorious motorcycle club, which some say was formed by former paratroopers from the 11th). They were later – and more often-known simply as "the Angels," which is an official "special designation" nickname conferred by the U.S. Army as shown on the roster of official names at the Army's Center for Military History.

So with regard to the memory of my late father, like so many other men and women of World War II, he is one of many unsung heroes whose sacrifices make the world safe for democracy and are sometimes forgotten in today's spoiled America. I don't even like to speculate whether those folks who went through so much peril and tribulation in fighting to preserve liberty also opened the way for such things as abortion on demand, gay marriage and so on ad nauseum, or how those who still are with us must view these events in modern America. I much prefer to ponder their great fortitude. And the great debt we owe to them.

Lest we forget ...

Donald S. Smock has been a Dearborn resident for 18 years. He served in the Peace Corps in Senegal, where he worked on development projects for eight years.

Chapter 5

Schools

An Offer from J. Edgar That She Couldn't Refuse

By Michele Denaro Bovich

Here's a salute to the Dearborn schoolteachers of my childhood – and a quick aside about how one of my classes got me into the FBI.

I loved school. We started each day with the Pledge of Allegiance, and an integral part was "One Nation under God."

I attended Oakman School before moving on to Maples. I had a plethora of favorite teachers and will mention a few.

Mr. Orr was our science teacher at Oakman School, and I recall when he had one of the boys in our class stand on his head against the blackboard while chewing a saltine cracker. The student's action demonstrated how he could swallow while upside down because his esophageal contractions forced the food down into his stomach. I guess it was a pretty large box of saltines because each of us in class was given a saltine to chew and chew without swallowing until the saltine, a carbohydrate, eventually turned to a type of sugar.

Mr. Orr must have been one of the earliest "foodies" because we also made ice cream in his science class – you know, salt and ice and LOTS of hand-cranking changed cream, sugar and any fruit into delicious ice cream. I think we had 100 percent attendance that day.

Tiny Miss Miller pounded the piano in music class and taught us the words to Christmas carols and patriotic songs. We sang our hearts out for her.

When our history teacher, Mrs. Augusta Tobin, asked for a volunteer to take our class rubber plant home for the summer, I raised my hand. Imagine my mother's surprised look when two classmates and a red wagon delivered the 5-foot-tall plant to my house for three months of care. It was healthy and 5 ½ feet tall in September with nary as much as a rubber band to show for it.

At Maples School, our math teacher, Mr. Spinelli, often quoted the phrase, "Mathematics is an exact science–there is only one correct answer." You can be certain I repeated that phrase to my children numerous times when they did their homework at the dining room table. My grandchildren have heard that from me as well.

Miss Fish, my English teacher, instilled in me a love of poetry. One assignment was to memorize a rather long poem of our choosing and recite it in class. I chose *So You Want To Go To Morrow,* and I can still recite the first 10 lines or so. Mr. Bloink, sporting his little mustache, was another superb English teacher.

Also at Maples, my ninth-grade civics teacher was Mr. Offenbach, who taught us all we needed to know about the workings (sometimes nonworkings) of our government in Lansing and Washington, D.C. He provided invaluable information, and I loved that class.

Fordson, one of the most beautiful schools in the country, was my high school. It was an extreme delight to walk those beautiful hallways and read in the quiet library with its murals and lovely windows. Hall duty, sitting at the large oak table in the step-up Hall C window, was a pleasure. Seeing class plays in the spacious auditorium and attending assemblies there made me feel so privileged.

During my senior year (1947-48), an FBI agent came to

Miss Hunsicker's shorthand and typing classes and tested us. I was one of two who passed, and I was asked if I wanted to work for the FBI in Detroit. Of course, that was an offer difficult to resist, and I answered a resounding "yes." I didn't hear from the FBI for quite a few weeks because my background was being investigated, but finally a letter signed by J. Edgar Hoover arrived offering me a position.

I worked for the bureau for almost six years.

When a huge case broke in Detroit (I can still remember the case number), one of the assistant directors arrived from Washington. I was fortunate to be chosen to become his secretary while he masterminded the case. When he left, I became the secretary to the assistant special agent in charge.

In 1951 a handsome special agent from New York arrived in Detroit after months of training in Washington, D.C. We knew office romances were risky, but ours jelled, and we spent the next 60 years together, 58 as husband and wife, becoming proud parents of four great children and eight wonderful grandchildren. We lived in Chicago and Pittsburgh before returning to Dearborn in 1959 and have been here ever since.

So, students of today, take advantage of the wonderful opportunity to live and learn in Dearborn. A good education is a golden circumstance denied most of the young people in the world today. Be receptive by enthusiastically reading and studying. A wonderful life awaits you in the great city of Dearborn!

Michele Denaro Bovich's spare-time activities include playing bridge and writing verse for children, but not exclusively for children. Among her writings is a 10-page poem on the O.J. Simpson trial and another 10-pager on a seven-family-member train trip (including two 4-year-old boys) from Chicago to California. Her latest is a poem titled Count Lasagna or How Lasagna Got Its Name.

Unexpected Grace for Social Justice at Sacred Heart

By Father Richard J. "Rick" Cassidy

Sophomore year English class at Sacred Heart High School required every student to write a term paper. The teacher distributed a list of individuals and topics, more than one hundred, in order to give us plenty of latitude for undertaking a task that was so new and challenging.

Near the bottom of the list I came across a name that I had heard my father mention from time to time. I did not know anything at all about this person, Walter Reuther, but somehow I was influenced to make him the focus of my paper.

The small Sacred Heart Library had virtually nothing under the heading of "Reuther," so I headed to the Dearborn Public Library, where I found an extensive number of books about Walter P. Reuther. He was the president of the United Auto Workers Union and a prominent advocate for social justice.

Social Justice. I remember being transfixed when I encountered this term while reading at the library. I was absolutely riveted by this concept. I could not recall that I had ever previously heard anything about it. Yet upon finishing my first book about Walter Reuther, I made a small resolution to keep working for social justice for the rest of my life.

As I progressed in my reading, I learned that Walter Reuther was considered to be a very progressive union leader. His primary concern was to achieve social justice for auto workers through collective bargaining. At the same time, he was strongly committed to achieve social justice for those who were victims of racial prejudice. He also supported initiatives to improve education, housing and health care for people of all backgrounds.

The actual writing of my paper was a challenge. I kept forgetting that the format for footnotes was different from the format for items listed in the bibliography. There was also the task of getting the footnotes properly located in the text and positioned at the bottom of the page.

I received help for the formatting of the paper from an unexpected source: my mother. She did not help me in any manner with content. Yet because of her work as a librarian at the Ford Motor Company's industrial relations library, she was able to assist me with format and typing. Finally, I completed the paper. It was titled: "Walter P. Reuther: Man on a Hill." The title signified that Walter Reuter was striding up a hill whose summit was social justice.

The rest of my high school studies declined after this paper. During the next two years, I languished academically. Even a subsequent term paper failed to generate much interest or energy on my part. I served as sports editor for The Excalibur, the school paper, but nothing in the world of sports could engage my interest as Walter Reuther and social justice had.

When I reached college at Sacred Heart Seminary in Detroit, three things occurred that were closely related to my high school Reuther paper.

First, the U.S. Department of Labor inaugurated a nationwide essay contest on the topic: "Youth's Challenge in the Labor Market of the '60s." I was disappointed not to gain first prize because I felt that I had become an "expert" on workers and unions. However, not a few professors and classmates reflected that national runner-up was still a worthwhile outcome.

Second, during the following year I served as a college observer at Solidarity House, the International Headquarters of the United Autoworkers Union. While I did not have the honor of meeting Mr. Reuther at this time, one of the UAW staff directors appointed me an official youth delegate for the UAW Bi-Annual Convention in Atlantic City.

Third, from far back in the ranks of thousands, I participated in a historic march held in Detroit early in the summer of 1963. This march was the centerpiece of Dr. Martin Luther King, Jr.'s visit to Detroit. Newspapers commemorated it with feature reports and photos. To promote the cause of social and racial justice, Dr. King marched down the center of Woodward Avenue, and Walter Reuther was directly at his side.

When I look back upon these events, it seems astonishing that grace influenced me to select Walter Reuther for my term paper and thus chance upon the concept of social justice. From the time of my initial encounter with Walter Reuther's mission, assisted by grace, I have striven to hold fast to the great ideal of social justice.

Father Richard J. "Rick" Cassidy has treated St. Paul's concept of "Grace" in Paul in Chains: Roman Imprisonment and the Letters of St. Paul *(2001).*

Walter P. Reuther Library, Archives of Labor and Urban Affairs, Wayne State University.

184

For Her First A, It Was the Principal That Mattered

By Russ Gibb

This is a true story. Not a likely story, but a true one that happened to me years ago at Maples Junior High School in Dearborn.

I remember asking my students one day if any of them had never had an A. The only one who raised a hand was a plain little girl we will name Susan. She was a sweet little thing, always ready with a smile, and she always had her homework prepared. But she had raised her hand and said that she had never had an A in any of her classes. So I put that in my mental notebook and promptly forgot about it until it became time to mark her report card. While recalling the incident, I thought, "Well, she has never gotten an A and she has a B+ here, so I'll give her an A!" And that I did.

A few weeks later, after the cards had gone out, I received a call from our principal, Mr. Ray Good. Mr. Good was a very firm, straight-on guy; and he called me and said: "I would like you to come down to my office, Mr. Gibb. I have some parents here that would like to discuss a grade that you gave to their child, Susan." I thought there must be some mistake – I had given Susan an A and maybe, because in those days we did not have the technology there is today and we had to actually write in the grade, I had written in a lower grade.

So I went down there with my book to meet Mr. Good and the parents of little Susan. The father, a rather huge man who looked like he would feel quite comfortable behind the big wheel of a semi-truck; and mother, who also was a very plain, sweet-looking lady like her daughter; and Mr. Good, dressed in his dark suit, firm as ever. And he said, "Mister so-and-so, would you please explain your concern about your daughter's grade?" And of course I didn't say anything because I had all the ammunition that I needed.

The father looked at me and Mr. Good and said: "Mr. Gibb, you have been deceiving my child. You put an A on her card, and she is not an A person. You also said that you think she should consider going to college! Mr. Gibb, that is not your business; that's my business. That is for us to determine, her educational outcome. Therefore, you have been deceiving her. She is not an A student!" Well, shock, shock! I looked over at Mr. Good, and he asked me, "Mr. Gibb what is your comment?" I was stunned! I remember saying: "Well, if I had the power to give a chocolate ice-cream cone to every kid in the world, and if they had never had one before, then I would give them a chocolate ice-cream cone." That's all that I could think of. Not much of an argument, but that was it. Mr. Good looked at me, then looked at the father and said: "Sir, I agree with Mr. Gibb's assessment, and if you would like to carry this on any further, here is the number to the superintendent's office. You may speak to someone there. Please feel free and thank you for coming." And that was Mr. Ray Good, the best principal I ever had.

Russ Gibb is retired but continues to be an active participant in national pop culture activities.

Raymond E. Good

When HFCC Had Rigor: No Grain of Salt Needed

By Janet Lohela Good

At the Henry Ford Community College student union, I remember late afternoons whiling away time with friends. We would spread napkins on the waxed-paper cups with a penny in the center, using cigarettes to burn holes in the napkin. The loser was the one who made the penny drop. Did you know you can balance a salt shaker on a grain of salt? When we were really rowdy, we bounced a Super Ball reverberating among the tables, attempting to reach the very high ceiling.

Now my education at HFCC was much more than this. My intellectual, social and emotional growth flourished in a supportive environment.

My father had been in the military and chose to retire in Dearborn when I was in 11th grade. I graduated from Edsel Ford High School in 1964, but never felt part of the milieu.

At HFCC I had a fresh start. I felt a part of the college adventure. With a car provided by my parents, I could explore the greater Detroit area. This allowed me to work in a variety of venues, including being a guide at Greenfield Village, to engage in friendships from the larger area and to participate in what one might call sophisticated social opportunities.

I loved going downtown on dates, to the Music Hall (I remember seeing *The Sound of Music*), to dine at the Pontchartrain Wine Cellars, to party at the Brass Rail. I fondly remember Darby's late at night with the white tablecloths and tuxedoed waiters serving corned beef sandwiches.

My classes were small enough that the professors knew my name. Bill Hackett (history) and Stewart Gingrich (chemistry) made learning fun. The rigor was uniform. Yes, I did study. You could find me often in the evenings at the University of Michigan-Dearborn library. My home was crowded, and there were no quiet places to be had.

I found being a big fish in a little pond gave me opportunities to practice leadership skills. There was a local sorority, Iota Chi Kappa, of which I was president. This gave me and my sisters a platform to provide charity and to organize social events in the area. I remember having access to the Henry Ford Estate for a tea. A small group of us took food baskets to the Herman Gardens projects.

All of this occurred in two short years. Then I went on to Northern Michigan University with no car and a very different experience.

The beauty of continuing to live in Dearborn is that it allows me to visit Henry Ford Community College on occasion or hear of it. These references always generate fond memories.

Janet Lohela Good retired from the Livonia Public Schools in 2007 after 36 years as a math teacher, counselor and gifted specialist. She continues to live in Dearborn, appreciating the stability of having the same home for 37 years.

A Door Opens, And an 'Average Student' Sees Her Chance

By Adrianna Lypeckyj

One of the most beautiful gifts a person can be given is having someone believe in his or her abilities. Every human has a talent or skill to offer to the world. It's just a matter of getting that one opportunity, that one open door, that one chance in life. I'm thankful that I was given that chance years ago.

I was an average student in high school, struggling to pass my classes. I think what held me back was insecurity and peer pressure. I was envious of all the talented and intelligent students in high school, and I knew I could never compete with them. Even my high school counselor suggested, "You won't amount to anything in life so don't waste your time applying to any colleges or universities. If you really feel like taking some classes after you graduate from high school, you can apply to Henry Ford Community College here in Dearborn because it is about the only educational institution in Michigan that will accept you."

Well, I did apply to Henry Ford Community College and was ecstatic that the admissions office accepted me. They gave me the opportunity I needed, and the rest was up to me. The minute I started my classes at Henry Ford Community College I knew I was at the right place; the instructors were brilliant mentors, the students were hard-working and motivated, the campus was easy to get around, and the classes were small and personable. There were countless activities to get involved with, and I kept busy as a campus tour guide, disc jockey at WHFR (the radio station), a writer for the campus newspaper and a singer in the choir. I was also cast in several plays.

My time at Henry Ford Community College was priceless; it's where I received a quality education, gained wisdom, matured and made lifelong friends. Within two years I received an associate of arts degree and was accepted to several universities throughout Michigan. I obtained a bachelor's degree from Eastern Michigan University and later moved to New York City, where I attended the American Musical Dramatic Academy and New York University.

I've been blessed to work in communications, journalism, hospitality and theater and have enjoyed working in fabulous places like New York, California, Colorado, Florida, Montana, Vermont, Austria and Ireland. None of these accomplishments would have been attainable without the humble beginnings I had. I'm forever thankful to the administration and faculty of Henry Ford Community College for giving an insecure and shy kid that one opportunity I so much needed. They gave me the chance to get a solid education, obtain goals and make something of myself.

Do you have a dream? Do you have a goal? Is there something you really want to do or someplace you really want to go? Don't give up. Believe in yourself and your abilities and before you know it an opportunity will come along. Everyone deserves an opportunity!

Adrianna Lypeckyj is a free-lance journalist and yoga teacher. She hopes to move to Los Angeles in the near future.

Empty Bowls: The Power of the Arts

By Wendy Sample

For graduates of Edsel Ford High School, the English humanities experience provided more than knowledge of art, music and English and how they are integrated. The humanities program taught us the importance of the relationships of all subjects and that it's the creative processes that make us human. And with being human, comes the expectation of being a humanitarian.

John Hartom graduated from Edsel Ford in 1965 in the thick of the English humanities program. After completing a degree in art education, John began teaching high school art with a focus on clay. His school had a service-learning component in its curriculum. In fall 1990, John challenged the students in his clay classes to create enough bowls to serve a soup luncheon to the school staff in exchange for monetary donations for the school food drive. Working as a team, the students built, threw, fired, decorated and glaze-fired 120 bowls.

The meal was a huge success, and participants left with a handmade bowl to remind them of all the empty bowls in the world. Guests were touched by the gesture. Students beamed at the enthusiasm over their work. The moment was magical. That evening John and his wife, Lisa Blackburn, decided that the handmade bowl luncheon experience needed to be introduced to a wider audience to help fight hunger. The Empty Bowls project was born.

The basic premise is simple: Potters and other craftspeople, educators and others work with the community to create handcrafted bowls. Guests are invited to a simple meal of soup and bread. In exchange for a cash donation, guests are asked to keep a bowl as a reminder of all the empty bowls in the world. The money raised is donated to an organization working to end hunger and food insecurity. Now, 20-plus years later, Empty Bowls meals are being held worldwide.

John and I graduated from Edsel Ford several years apart but were introduced to each other in the late '70s by our high school art teacher, Ralph Hashoian. Our professional relationship developed as we worked together on numerous state and national art education conferences, a student art camp, various art-related committees and as members of the national board for Empty Bowls.

As the art resource teacher for the Dearborn Public Schools for 20-some years, I looked for ways to educate the public about the importance and power of the arts. When John and Lisa shared the idea of Empty Bowls, another art teacher and I started planning Dearborn Public Schools' first Empty Bowls event. We were teaching at William Ford and Maples elementary schools in the late '80s, and students from both schools made bowls for our first successful Empty Bowls event. This was an opportunity for students to give back to the community, using art as the conduit for an exemplary service-learning project.

For the next several years we continued to host meals at more schools. Other art teachers had students make bowls so their schools could participate. Soon our events were so well attended that we needed help. We couldn't make enough soup for all the guests, so local restaurants and grocery stores began donating the soup and bread. Eventually we needed to find a location to hold an annual community service event where all the participating art teachers and schools could meet in one place for a large event.

Gary Kuhlmann, owner of Park Place and a pillar of community involvement, came to our rescue. Gary offered to let us use his banquet hall, provided staff to help serve and donated all the soup. The art department was thrilled and grateful. To this day, Park Place continues to support the benefits of Empty Bowls and the efforts of the art department to provide community service opportunities to students.

Over the years the art department has worked diligently to establish relationships that help make this service-learning event a success. Starbucks came on board with coffee. A local business, Bona-Venture, donates all the bread. Local business and individuals donate items for a tin-can raffle. Organizations have donated clay and glazes to the schools. The entire community, young and older, can participate in some way.

Statistics from the Feeding America website indicate that one in eight Americans struggles with the reality of hunger and food insecurities. Young Dearborn artists and their art teachers have raised thousands of dollars to help fight hunger in southeast Michigan hosting Empty Bowls events for the past 22 years. Money has been donated to numerous local food banks, food pantries and soup kitchens. For many years we have partnered with Gleaners Food Bank, donating money and taking students to Gleaners to help pack backpacks for the kids-helping-kids program. In addition to helping pack food, students are provided with knowledge about food insecurities in our community through an excellent interactive education program.

The money and effort to raise awareness in the fight to end hunger through Empty Bowls events are important. In 2015 Empty Bowls will celebrate 25 years of existence, and students in Dearborn will participate in Dearborn's 24th annual Empty Bowls event. Dearborn art teachers look at Empty Bowls as an excellent way to teach students the importance of being an active member of our community working toward a common goal – the joy of giving to others as a humanitarian.

Note: In addition to the annual event, Dearborn art teachers and student artists have helped with Empty Bowls events at the Henry Ford Village Senior Living Community, the Arab American National Museum and several Michigan Art Education Association conferences. You can find more information about Empty Bowls at www.emptybowls.net

Wendy Sample attended Howe Elementary, Stout Junior High and Edsel Ford High School. Her passion for art and education provided her with 36 years of opportunities to work with students from kindergarten through college, and she continues to work with local community organizations on art-related projects.

Chapter 6

Homes

Our Front Porch: A Safe Haven Even Before the Radiator

By Marguerite Assenmacher Baumgardner

The history of our front porch is a long and varied one. During the Great Depression, my grandmother, Magdalene Assenmacher, was widowed and raised four children by herself. Because we lived just two blocks from the old train station, the hobos would jump off the train and look for a safe place to spend the night. Our porch was an ideal haven from the wind and cold. My grandmother, fearing for the safety of her children, had the front porch enclosed with windows and screens. This afforded a degree of safety from the many gentlemen who sought refuge from the elements.

Over the years our porch has been a gathering place for family reunions and the many neighbors who stopped by to visit. As young children we made "camping trips" to the porch and slept there overnight in the summer. We, too, were safe from the elements.

My father had many friendly card games and conversations with neighbors on our porch. In later years he even had a radiator hooked up so he could extend his time outdoors.

Marguerite Assenmacher Baumgardner is a lifelong resident of Dearborn and lives in the family home where she was born and raised. She has been married for 50 years to Walter and is on the staff of the Dearborn Historical Museum. (See page 473 for photo)

A Home on Detroit Street

By Bill Fader

Frank Fader was my uncle, the youngest of eight children in my dad's family. My dad was the oldest. All eight were born in the ocean-cove town of East Dover, 20 miles or so from Halifax, Nova Scotia. Frank and two of his sisters emigrated from there to Dearborn with my grandparents in the 1920s or '30s. Their older siblings had already relocated to the Detroit area. All three of them eventually graduated from Sacred Heart High School, and the family lived on Audrey Street at that time.

Frank may have left the home in Nova Scotia behind, but he did not abandon his affection for a young woman from a community near East Dover whose name was Vera Beck. That intense fondness persisted, and when it was time for Frank to join the armed forces during World War II, he chose to first go back to Nova Scotia to see Vera. While he was there, the two of them were married.

The young couple were separated by many miles and much travel time the first few years of their married life. Frank, of course, moved around wherever the U. S. Navy assigned him. At one point, Vera took a train all the way from Halifax to Seattle to visit her husband. She had a terrible time locating him once she had arrived in the state of Washington. But that adventure undertaken by this very brave young woman is another wonderful story.

In about four years, when Frank had completed his tour of duty in 1945, he and his bride were reunited, and they settled into married life in the beautiful city of Dearborn. At first they lived with Fader relatives. But as it got nearer to the time for their first family addition to arrive, they knew they wanted a place of their own. At that time the well-known builder, Garling, was putting up homes in the neighborhood just off West Outer Drive and Pelham Road. Frank and Vera spotted one on Detroit Street that they really liked, were told they could afford the house, and were promised by a Garling salesman that it would belong to them when all the finishing touches had been completed. Within two weeks of the promised day for taking ownership, Frank and Vera went to the offices of Garling to meet with their salesman and make final arrangements toward the purchase of their first home – a brand-new one, to boot! They were told the home could not be theirs and were given some phony-sounding excuse having to do with payments that would be too high for their budget. That issue had already been thoroughly investigated. They were devastated! To this day, Vera still believes that the salesman had found another purchaser, perhaps a friend or family member. The young couple slumped gloomily in the office, their sad faces accurately reflecting their crushed spirits that day.

While they sat there, young Mr. Garling, the son of the company's owner and president, came in. He was a jovial sort who seemed to enjoy life to the hilt and expected that others should be able to do the same. Seeing the glum expressions worn by Frank and Vera, he wanted to know what was going on that had made them so sad. He listened intently as he was told the story of promises made and broken by the salesman. His response was, almost immediately, a statement to the effect that if they were told that particular house would be theirs, then, by George, it would be theirs! He probably next double-checked that all the papers were in order and told Frank and Vera they would be notified as soon as the house was ready and OK'd for occupancy. He kept his word.

The Faders moved into their new home on Detroit Street soon after, but none TOO soon! They welcomed their first child, a son they named Gary, to his brand-new home within a very few days after.

As the years went by, Gary was joined on Detroit Street by a brother and then four sisters. And as the stories of many families go, eventually Frank and Vera's children's wives and husbands and then their grandchildren came to visit Grandpa and Grandma at their Detroit Street home.

Frank and Vera have called their first house "home" ever since that day in 1947 when they happily stepped over the threshold as the new owners. Frank, sadly, was called away four years back at 95 years of age. But he must behold with great pleasure, from his life beyond this one, that his beloved wife, Vera, still appreciates the comforts afforded by their Dearborn home on Detroit Street – the house that they came to own, partly because a Dearborn businessman named Garling cared enough to make sure that his customers would be very happy with his company's services and products.

Bill Fader lives in Ferndale and is retired after teaching 38 years in elementary school. He has a son, a daughter and three young grandchildren.

Rosebud

By Diane Lienau LaDue

Shortly after Mom and Dad were married, they bought a house on Highland Street near Lindbergh School. In 1944 Dad entered the Navy as an ensign, serving in the Philippines and leaving Mom to cope alone. In 1945 when I was 6, the city decided Lindbergh Elementary needed a larger area for the playground, and our house among others was in the way and was condemned.

The neighborhood was not full as it is now. Rosevere, the street behind our house, had only a few houses on it. The lot behind our house was empty, so the solution the city chose was to move our house to Rosevere—essentially picking it up and turning it around. A new basement was dug on Rosevere, huge wooden beams were placed under the house, and it was turned. The process took all summer.

During the move we did not have a place to live, and the city did not provide one. Mom had a serious medical problem the year before and was still not back to full health, so she and my younger brother went to stay with her parents on Clifton in Detroit, and I went to stay with a friend's family for the summer. Clifton and where I stayed were close to Rosevere, but not so close that we went to watch the house move. So I did not actually see the house move.

This was not an ordinary time, as Dad pointed out in a

letter written during his trip home. Things were scarce. People had plenty of money to buy things; the problem was there was nothing to buy. All manufacturing had been turned to the war effort. If you needed something to fix, you often had to just work it out the best you could.

With the war there also was less police presence than today. The house was locked, but during the move a lock on the back door was broken and the house was vandalized, trashed and was filthy. Some of the childhood movies Dad made were burned, and it was up to Mom to clean much of the mess. The city was liable for some of the damage to the rugs and furniture, but it still was a terrible burden on Mom.

In the fall school was starting, so we moved back into the house, even though the workmen were still finishing up. I can recall walking on the large beams left in the yard that were used for the move. We did not have heat or electricity, so Mom made dinner an "adventure," with my brother and me cooking hot dogs in the fireplace. One day an official came by to tell us the Red Cross enabled Dad to return early to help us cope. Dad arrived home while we were still cooking in the fireplace. I guess Mom always left the fireplace damper open, but when Dad arrived, he would close the fireplace when it was not in use. He told me later that Mom often didn't remember to open the damper when she would start a fire. Then, the house filling with smoke, he would have to open it, losing all the damn hair on his arm in the process.

One of the steps that was not complete by the time we moved into the house was the backfill around the house; the front porch was in place, but there was a hole underneath. The concrete porch formed a nice roof, and I found the hole to be a perfect garage to park a red wagon and my tricycle.

One morning the dirt had been filled in by a plow before I woke, and my red wagon and trike were buried. I guess it was too much effort for the workmen to bend over and retrieve it. My trike! My red wagon! They are still buried under the porch on Rosevere. It may not seem like much, but I didn't have much, and that trike and that red wagon meant a lot to me.

Diane Lienau LaDue was born in Detroit, graduated from Dearborn High School and left in 1958 to go to the University of Michigan. She became a teacher for special students, retired and now alternately resides in Manistee and Las Vegas.

Our 'Forever' House

By Anne McGraw-Mueller

My husband, Mike, and I had been looking for our "forever" house for three years. We had come to the conclusion that because he worked in midtown Detroit and I worked in Southfield, Dearborn was the best location for many reasons. We really didn't want to add to our commutes, we wanted to be close to familiar areas, and Dearborn had diversity and a housing stock that was filled with character. As my youngest daughter put in her 2 cents, she really wanted us to get an "upstairs" house, not a ranch like the one we had.

The first house that really piqued our interest was built in 1880 but moved in the 1930s and had been added onto with a double lot. A large yard for a garden was also on our list of must-haves. But once our inspector found issues that were deal breakers, we moved on.

The second house seemed perfect, built in the 1940s, lots of character, with updates and a beautiful garden. We were so excited that when we couldn't get the deal done, we were heartbroken. (That house was on the market for another year and ended up selling for many thousands of dollars less than what we had offered.)

We were so discouraged, but driving around an area and street that we had never noticed, we found our dream house. The third time really was the charm; from the minute we walked through the front door and saw the fireplace and the window seat in the dining room, we were smitten. It just kept getting better, as we realized there was a beautiful family room off the back that overlooks an amazing yard and garden. The large lot, pond, gazebo and pergola and all the beautiful, mature trees were breathtaking. We had to have it and we got it!

The history of the house is such an all-consuming quest, and so many people have helped us add to what we know. We even found aerial photographs from 1927, when the house was moved from Military as the Dearborn Country Club clubhouse was being built. The story we have heard is the farmer who sold Mr. Ford some of the land for his country club wanted his home not to face the clubhouse, so it was put up on rollers and moved back on a parcel of land that is now Kensington Street. We even found more aerial photos from the 1940s that show our house in the position it is in today.

The photos are in the archives of the Dearborn Historical Museum at the McFadden-Ross House on Brady Street. This wonderful museum is a hidden treasure that everyone in the community should really support and visit frequently.

I want to mention the family names of the people who have lived in our house; it is an honor to thank them for all they did over the years to make this house and property so wonderful to live in. They include the Hebestreit family, the Fercheck family, the Mulcahy family and the Lembree family.

The Dearborn community has been especially welcoming to newcomers, and, as one, I truly appreciate all the information and kindness our neighbors have shown us from day one. Finding this house was what my mom would call serendipity or just good karma.

Anne McGraw-Mueller recently retired from Providence/St. John Hospital of Southfield after 38 years as a patient-care technician. Her husband, Mike, recently retired from the Federal Reserve Bank of Chicago, where he was employed for 18 years as a systems analyst.

My Basement Cocoon

By Martha Stefanec Pearson

In a recent writing seminar, my classmates and I were asked to visit a favorite room in a favorite home from our past. We had four minutes to write about what made the room special. Here's what I wrote about my home at 549 N. Elizabeth.

"My favorite room was the basement. It's where everything happened for my brothers and me. It was our nest. We felt young there, happy, free, creative, and secluded from parents upstairs.

"We had the oak round table on which to put puzzles, Lincoln logs, records, crafts, blocks to build homes, science experiments, and all manner of fun activities. We had a sofa and two chairs and a Helicrafter 1952 TV. Also there were knotty pine cabinets and a fireplace—sacred ground for our records, record player, books, and my parents' memorabilia and awards.

"The other side of the basement housed our bathroom, large bar, washer, dryer, heater, and a very old 1942 GE refrigerator stocked with my dad's beer and all kinds of soft drinks.

"Often between these two compounds that made up our Kidsvillle, we would assemble our long ping-pong table.

"Then we let the fun begin. The TV would be on with volume turned down, 45's would be stacked and playing on the 45 changer ... think Where Are YOU Little Star? We'd each have some drinks, pretzels, and cookies and we'd take turns playing ping-pong or doing some activity at the oak round table. It was heaven - all fun and no worries."

The teacher called "time" after four minutes and gave us our next assignment. We were to go back into this room but, this time, mention the years during which we enjoyed the room and what all was going on in the adult real world that existed outside our childhood.

This time we had only three minutes.

"In my basement cocoon, I was living out my freedom as a preteen and teen-ager. Our neighborhood in Dearborn was filled with young families like ours, with most of the dads employed at Ford Motor Company nearby.

"The years I'm thinking of encompassed 1952-1963, a time of post-World War II growth and peace. Baby boomers ruled the world as our parents focused on giving us children those things they would never afford when young themselves.

"Wartime industry turned to peacetime output, especially in the arena of automobiles. Ford, GM, and by extension, Dearborn itself, was 'on the move.' Cars were King! The family structure was very intact and the focus for our families was continued peace and prosperity ... and YOUTH ... embodied in the Kennedy family's Camelot."

Martha Stefanec Pearson resides in the coastal community of Rockport, Texas. She is a retired teacher of high school students and adults and is now tutoring 5-year-olds.

Chapter 7

Neighborhoods

Caught in the Act!

By Carol Bussa

Mid-February!

Though the snow had been fairly light all winter, I was tired of it. Tired of bundling up. Tired of swinging the broom time after time to clear the walks.

At our house we take turns doing that chore, and I knew that it was my turn. I remembered that I had an early meeting to attend. Worst of all—the weatherman had predicted several inches of fresh snow over an icy base. Grumble!

Instead of rolling over again when I woke early, I got up (Humph!), dressed warmly and grabbed the snow shovel. Glancing out, I could see several inches of snow. This job would be heavy! (I began to feel surly.)

When I opened the front door, I saw a man cleaning the last of the ice from our walk. (Couldn't be my husband—he was sound asleep upstairs.) This stranger's letter jacket said, "Dearborn Swim Team." I waited for him to come collecting, but NO, the athlete swung his shovel over his broad shoulders and headed home.

And now the neighborhood mystery was solved.

For weeks folks had been reporting these two youths who

shoveled walks for free. The 90-year-old offered to pay them, but they refused. The 80-year-old was sure they were the little kids who had moved in at the end of the block. The suspicious neighbor just knew they were casing the area, planning robberies.

At 6 a.m. I had caught one in the very act – of shoveling. And his buddy came along shortly, probably planning more secret kind deeds. How blessed we are to live in a town where neighbors look out for each other and go out of their way to give a lift to people who don't love to rise at 5 a.m. and brave the cold, who perhaps are no longer able to scrape ice and hoist heavy snow. Thanks, Alex. Thanks, August. Thanks, Jim. And thanks to every one of you who makes someone else's day brighter!

Carol Bussa has lived on Morley Court for 40 years. Now that the Bussas' four sons have completed Dearborn schools and moved on, she appreciates the help of other young people in the neighborhood.

A Place for Sharing, Caring

By Michele Featherstone

The city of Dearborn has a spirit that I have not experienced in other communities. When I moved to Dearborn in 1993, I looked for a way to get involved in the community and meet new people. An opportunity came my way when I met the former president of the defunct Pardee Neighborhood Association. She told me that the association disbanded and she was looking for someone to start something new. She referred me to Lois Rinn, who welcomed me to the neighborhood in such a way that I felt I belonged.

Lois and her husband, Bill, owned a historic home at the corner of Madison and Roosevelt streets. They invited me to their home, and I learned many new things about Dearborn. They asked me if I read the book *The Bark Covered House* by John Nowlin and explained to me that their house was owned by the Pardee family, which is mentioned in the book. Their house had many original features and a beautiful staircase with detailed wooden railings. The living room contained a baby grand piano, and Bill and Lois enjoyed entertaining guests with their musical talents.

On one occasion, the Rinns opened their home for an association progressive dinner. We ate at a long dining table, and Lois Rinn served food on her lovely china.

Several years later I met Sue Moran and her husband, Bob, who own another Pardee home at the corner of McKinley and Madison. Like the Rinn home, the Moran home has many original features. Like the Rinns, the Morans strive to preserve the historical character of the home.

It was exciting to read about the history of the neighborhood and see it. The neighborhood does not contain a lot of historical buildings, so these homes are the jewels of the neighborhood.

Sad to say, but another historical home, the Whitmore home, was demolished. Fortunately, Whitmore Bolles Elementary School is maintained and operated by the Dearborn Public Schools.

As I became involved in the community, I met John Wisely and his wife, Roena. They lived in the neighborhood for many years on Harding Street. John was a lifetime Boy Scout and explained how he was invited to many flag-raising ceremonies and school events involving Boy Scouts. It was heartwarming to see John (in his late 80s at the time) raise the flag for a beautification ceremony at Whitmore Bolles School. He wore his uniform with pride and admiration for his community.

I also became acquainted with "George the Barber." He had a small barber shop on Monroe Street between Carlysle and Dartmouth. George Sikora and his wife, Mary, lived in a cute little home on Alice Street. George told me that he had an interest in the community and he liked to talk to residents about neighborhood concerns and the latest news. His barber shop contained assorted memorabilia associated with Dearborn and his favorite sports teams. His barber chairs and other furniture were from days long past. His shop was a true community barber shop because he made you feel welcome.

Another person who was part of the neighborhood was Michael Adray. Adray Appliance was the place where, according to my dad, "Ford employees shop." This was the store where I registered for gifts when I got married, the store where we bought our appliances, cameras and vacuum cleaners. Michael Adray often greeted customers, and he once visited Henry Ford Community College when I was a student. His name was on the back of many shirts because he sponsored numerous sports teams. Everyone knew his name and his family commitment to Dearborn. Although his store closed after his death, his legacy lives on in the form of scholarships and memories.

One thing the residents that I mentioned had in common is that they truly cared about their neighborhood, their community and their families. They were involved at school, their churches and their neighborhood association. Bill and Lois Rinn, John Wisely and George the Barber have moved on to heaven. They raised responsible children and have descendants who are residents of the city of Dearborn. They showed me what it means to be part of a larger family, a community family. They had the true pioneer spirit. They were senior members of the community who took the time to sweep their sidewalks, get to know their neighbors and mentor young people. I always remember the words of Lois Rinn: "People view me as a Pollyanna, but I believe that you have to take time out of your busy schedule to help others. Otherwise life is dull and you become a selfish person."

Since I moved to Dearborn, I learned many things about diversity and culture. Sharing common beliefs is what makes the community strong. Sharing new foods, customs, religious experiences and culture is something that helps people come together. Dearborn is a place that offers the opportunity to learn and grow as a person if you are willing to step forward and work together. It's the people in the neighborhoods who make a difference and make history.

Michele Featherstone moved to Dearborn because she liked the neighborhoods, parks and schools. She has been the president of the Southwest Neighborhood Association. She works in the Student Activities Office at Henry Ford Community College.

Even on Alexandrine, A Magician Never Tells

By Donna Griffin

Growing up in Dearborn meant being part of a great neighborhood. We lived on Alexandrine, one mile away from two elementary schools, one mile from the junior high school and just a few blocks from the high school. Nearly all the kids rode their bikes to school or walked, even in the winter.

In the 1960s, we knew all the families on the block, and lots of them had kids. Our next-door neighbors were the Dulmages, whose family built both their house and ours. I remember fondly the Bierworth, Brett, Giles, Price, Kelley, Hebb, Harrison, Thomas, Carney and Mlot children, along with Mrs. Reith, Dr. Haefele and his family, Pastor Gagern and his family, and the Greenes, who lived next door to the Greens.

When we went trick-or-treating for Halloween, every house passed out treats. Some families gave out apples or homemade brownies, or they popped popcorn and put it into little bags. Some gave out pennies and nickels. Old Mrs. Fournier, who sometimes scared us when we went "thundering down her driveway like a herd of elephants," always passed out sugared doughnuts.

Summers, we spent most of the day outside: inventing games, exploring the woods and sometimes venturing into the storm drain that opened out at the Rouge River. This was a long, scary, very dark tunnel at least 6 or 8 feet across. Once my friend Jennifer and I went so far in that we could see light coming down from a storm drain in the street. We were terrified, but we talked each other into it.

After dinner on summer evenings, we were back outside. Some nights, kids of all ages would gather for a massive game of frozen tag. These games, which I first played when I was perhaps 5 years old, were unusual because boys and girls played together and we got to play with the "big kids." Jennifer's brother even joined in when he came home from college. The rules for frozen tag were simple: There were two teams and one team was "It." If someone from the "It" team tagged you, you had to freeze in place until someone from your team unfroze you. If the "It" team managed to freeze all of the other team, they won. I think the team being frozen could win if someone captured the home base of the "It" team. These games were played over a large area that included the front, back and side yards of several houses. They went on for ages, with team members being frozen and unfrozen again and again. I don't remember if anyone ever actually won a game, but playing frozen tag is one of my favorite childhood memories.

As the evening wore on and the sun set, someone would yell that the streetlights were on. The game would end as kids scattered back to their homes. If we didn't notice the streetlights, we were sure to hear the ringing of a bell. My mother would stand on the front porch and ring "the bell." My father bought this bell when he taught in a one-room schoolhouse in the Upper Peninsula before their marriage. It was an old brass handbell with a clear tone that traveled down the block. This was a signal for all of us to hurry home.

A highlight of the summer was the block party. Alexandrine was blocked off at both ends, tables and chairs were set up in the street, and all the families came out to spend the evening. When we were young, this was very exciting because we were allowed to ride our bikes in the street. We would spend all day decorating our bikes, winding crêpe paper around the frame and between the spokes, taping ribbons to the handlebars and attaching cards to the spokes so they made a snapping sound as we rode. If it didn't rain, we left the decorations on for as long as they lasted and showed them off when we rode downtown or went to the penny-candy store.

For the block party, each family brought its own main dish, plus a dish to share. The dishes were spread out on two or three long tables and always included lots of desserts – another reason the block party was so popular with the kids. We ate on real plates with real silverware and packed it up to take home after the meal. Very few people used paper or plastic back then.

I remember one year when a neighbor was unable to leave his home. Rather than miss the block party, he opened his second-story bedroom window and tossed candy to the kids gathered on his lawn.

At least one year, in the early 1970s, the Kelley family put a projection screen on their lawn and showed a movie. This was before videotapes or DVDs. The Kelleys somehow acquired movie reels and ran the film through a projector set up in the street. I don't remember what movie we saw, but the novelty of it has kept the night in my memory.

Another year some high school boys who had formed a rock band performed in the street. They played Kiss and Aerosmith and J. Geils and Deep Purple. This was a big hit with the teen-agers, but barely tolerated by the parents. The group went on to perform at local dances and even at a festival at Ford Field (the original one, not the one built in Detroit decades later).

That same year, my friend Bill and I occasionally worked as stage magicians, so we brought our most impressive trick to the block party: Cutting a Woman in Six Pieces. This was a large cabinet that Bill had built himself. I stepped inside and he locked each of my wrists to a chain fed through the sides of the cabinet.

He then closed and locked the door and inserted five broad metal blades the width of the cabinet all the way through and out the other side. After removing the blades, he unlocked the door and – Ta Da! – there I was, unharmed. Some of the neighbors asked again and again how we did it, but a magician never reveals his secrets.

For decades after I moved away, I returned to Dearborn each year for the annual block party. My mother still lives on Alexandrine, along with several of my former neighbors and many new friends.

Donna Griffin is the daughter of Don and Laurine Griffin. She grew up in Dearborn with her older brother, Randy, and her younger sister, Laura. Donna developed an inexplicable fondness for physics and is now a science teacher for Oxford Community Schools. She lives in Plymouth with her younger son, Alexander.

Letter to Jenna

By Jon Reed

When we returned to Dearborn Hills from a week's vacation, our mailbox held three sheets of paper. The first said, "To my neighbor (sic) Mr. Reed," and was signed, "From Jenna." A second was a pencil-colored picture of Mickey Mouse traced from a comic book, cute but still just a page from a coloring book.

The last sheet had three questions and went straight to the matter: "Can you paint this picture? Circle YES or NO. Do you like this picture? YES or NO. Can you paint this picture for me? YES or NO. Please answer on another piece of paper. Jenna"

Her questions were charming but startling, and her last, rephrasing the first, was really what it was about. She must have been a little anxious assembling this, her first important submittal to supposed authority. For the past few summers, I've put my oil paintings outside to dry in a hot sun and discovered her peeking at them. Lord help her, she must have caught the bug to become an artist.

I somehow doubted her parents were even aware she left her "submittal package" for me. Why are some children so confounded innocent and direct in their questions, not yet learning the adult practice of obfuscation? "YES or NO?" Only precocious 8-year-olds have the temerity to demand YES and NO's from adult neighbors. What was I to do with this?

How does a sensible adult who doesn't want to get involved respond, without hurting the aspirations of a child? Should I write back, "No, thanks, Jenna; I'm not interested in copying Mickey Mouse in oil, pastel or even water color, because it doesn't interest me?" No, that doesn't work.

Perhaps I should just ignore her request and respond, "Sorry, Jenna; I'm too busy at the moment with a few of my own works to spare any time on this?" That wasn't any good either.

I would have to handle this carefully. Other than her being a friendly kid living next door with her parents and older brother, she is a bright young person whose dreams can still be shattered. It might happen in the future, but I was not the one who would do it if I could help it.

This wasn't a parent's choice like, "NO, you can't go out until you finish your homework!" or "YES, you must finish your meal before you can leave the table." Eight-year-olds can see through most adult bluffs in an instant, so I couldn't work my way out of this so easily. I would have to be honest, but reply in a way that might make a difference in her future; even better if it were inspirational.

Maybe I could I use Francis Church's New York Sun 1897 editorial as a guide: "Yes, Virginia, there is a Santa Claus ... He exists as certainly as love and generosity and devotion exist ... How dreary would be the world if there were no Santa Claus ... no child-like faith then, no poetry, no romance to make tolerable this existence ... The most real things in the world are those that neither children nor men can see."

A "real thing in this world" was Jenna's hope and childlike faith. I called her mother and told her about Jenna's package, and, as expected, she didn't know she had written it or left it in our mailbox. So I wrote a letter and gave it to her for Jenna. Will it make a difference to an 8-year-old? Perhaps or perhaps not. I will probably never know, but it was worth twenty minutes.

Here is my letter to Jenna:

"Jenna:

"I'm so sorry I haven't answered your questions until now, because we were out of town for a week. Your coloring of Mickey is very good and shows you have ability, so I've answered your second question: Yes, I like it. You have the potential to become a great artist. The only difference between your work and a Disney cartoonist is that Disney artists have more expensive equipment, computer graphics, and can paint with solid bright colors on film stock.

"The problem (or opportunity) is that no one can ever do a better version because Disney has already done Mickey. A great artist always seeks to create a new thing; a new way of expressing his or her idea, and that works for anything in the rest of your life.

"The only time it's all right to do another Mickey is when you need to learn the basics, the skills to move forward to new and better creations of your own.

"I already know how to paint Mickey so, to answer your first and last questions, Can I? the answer is Yes, but I've moved on, trying to stretch my skills, like you should.

"If I were you, I would work harder at creating several new cartoon characters that no one has ever seen and put them into trial newspaper-style cartoon strips.

That's exactly how well-recognized cartoonists got their start.

Remember, the greatest artists of all time began with hands just like yours, and the desire to create works of wonder.

Your neighbor,
Jon Reed

"PS. Please keep Mickey's picture so you can compare it with your future paintings."

Jon Reed is a lifelong Dearborn resident and retired after four decades with General Motors.

Chapter 8

Diversity

A Few 'Clinkers' In the Neighborhood

By Joseph Borrajo

"There are a few clinkers."

"Clinker" is a term from the past that dates the person using it. A point I made to the person sharing that thought. However, it also dated me for knowing the meaning of the word and more importantly the context with which it was used, an outdated term used to describe a mindset stuck in the past. Webster's defines "clinker" as a brick that has burned too much, or something of poor quality. It is a spent fuel remnant of a piece of coal. There are other words associated with coal-burning furnaces of yesterday's "banking" the hot embers of coal to keep the fire alive throughout the night, "stoking" the embers in the morning to excite flames that were replenished with new coal shoveled into the furnace bed. A daily exercise before many men like my father went off to work. A far cry from the creature comfort of walking over to a thermostat and dialing up the temperature. Tomorrow's technology may only require a telemetric signal from one's brain to accomplish the same.

The conditioning experience of the Great Depression and the rationing limits imposed during World War II on daily essentials like meat, butter, sugar and tires geared people to make do with what little they had. Waste was unconscionable. Spent coal, clinkers/ashes were shaken through the grating and shoveled out daily and were spread liberally over ice-covered stairways and sidewalks to prevent slips and falls. Squeezing out of a waste product one more practical use. The embodiment of the old saw, "Waste not, want not."

The idea of stoking embers had the function of associating related experiences throughout my life. During the book-signing event of *Best Dearborn Stories Volume II* in 2012 at the Ford Community & Performing Arts Center, I moved among many interesting people and shared stimulating conversation. Sitting across from and engaging in conversation with one lady proved most interesting. After a few words were exchanged, the lady focusing on my name tag suddenly became bright-eyed; she asked if I were the same person who used to write letters to the Dearborn Press & Guide years ago. I responded yes. She then went on to say how my letters would literally incite her mother, who would hurry to paper and pen to respond to my thought-provoking words. I wrote many controversial pieces. The letters her mother would respond to centered on the sensitive issue of race and race relations, challenging a mindset of demeaning intolerance. Giving thought to that chance meeting turned a page to another story that occurred when the city's motto was "Keep Dearborn Clean."

"Keep Dearborn Clean" was a subliminal message for some to keep people who did not fit the racial character of the city out of the city. A letter I submitted to the Press & Guide touching on the issue of race was undersigned with more than my name without my permission. It included my address as well. An unusual act and irregular by all standards. I took the matter to the Press & Guide to protest an action obviously motivated by the content of what I had written. Nothing of any consequence came from it, which spoke volumes of the prevailing culture that would allow something like that to happen. Soon after, I received a hate-filled diatribe drafted on old Sheraton Cadillac stationery. I took my complaint to the Press & Guide again and this time spoke at length to a columnist who wrote a weekly column called "On Target" for the newspaper. He, too, had received similar spiteful mail on the same stationery. After an insightful discussion, we decided to collaborate on a response to the mysterious writer, he in his column and I with an open letter. The two pieces appeared together on the same page. Afterward: silence. Neither of us ever heard again from the person too ashamed to affix his name to his spiteful words of hate.

Another chapter of a vestigial past recently took center stage when an African American family purchased a home in west Dearborn. The man, a professional, is employed in management at Ford Motor Company. Some neighbors did not take kindly to the new face on the block. I shared the story with a friend, who confirmed the shameful point. "There are a few clinkers" was used to describe the people still clinging to an outdated mindset; people who found it difficult to accept others who failed to fit the homogenous makeup of their limited world locked in an antiquated past. For some, the more things change the more "they" stay the same. "Stoking" the embers of "banked" memories and "grating" the clinkers of yesterday and today are a patchwork of experiences good and bad.

Joseph Borrajo is a community activist and organizer, a veteran of the U.S. Army, an alumnus of the University of Michigan-Dearborn and the current vice president of the Dearborn, Dearborn Heights League of Women Voters.

Born in the Ukraine, But Home Is Here

By Adrianna Lypeckyj

My sweet mother, Alexandra Salmaca, who was born in Lviv, Ukraine, never imagined as a child that someday she would become a U.S. citizen. Born just before World War II, she struggled with her parents during and after the war, enduring many challenges. When she was first born, things were running smoothly; her parents owned a store in Lviv and lived in a lovely home just outside the city center, but then the war came and they lost everything. Eventually they lived at a camp for displaced people in Germany, and my mother remembers how tough times were. Meals were scarce and she mostly lived on potatoes and spoiled bananas. There was no money for luxuries like piano lessons or an ice-cream cone, but my mother was still a happy child because her parents loved her dearly.

In the early 1950s her parents had the opportunity to come to the United States to begin a new life. It was a chance they didn't want to miss, so my mother sailed with them across the Atlantic Ocean in an old Army ship that caused many of the passengers to get seasick from the huge waves. Finally after traveling for over a week on the ship, they made it to the New York City harbor and joined the many immigrants who wanted to make the United States their new home. My mother and her parents settled in Rochester, New York, and lived with a host family for a few months until her parents could find work and a place to live.

It took a few years, but through hard work my grandparents were able to open their own supermarket and buy a house. They had more children, and my mother helped raise her brothers and sisters. My mother was finally able to take piano lessons at the famous Eastman School of Music, and by the time she was 13 years old she was an organist at a neighborhood Catholic church. This organist position allowed her to save money for college.

It was after college that my mother was introduced to my father, who was living in Detroit. He too was born in the Ukraine and immigrated with his parents to the United States. My parents fell in love, got married and settled in Dearborn, where my father worked for Ford Motor Company. My parents enjoyed living in Dearborn for many years. Sadly, my father died from cancer when I was only 23, but my mother, who has remained a widow for many years, still resides in Dearborn. She was a church organist at three parishes in Dearborn, directed the senior handbell choir for the city of Dearborn and taught piano to many children who lived in Dearborn.

My mother has spent most of her adult life living in Dearborn, and she considers Dearborn "home sweet home."

Adrianna Lypeckyj is a free-lance journalist and yoga teacher. She hopes to move to Los Angeles in the near future.

Chapter 9

Entertainment

Music, Cars and Girls

By Brent Bachman

I believe the year was 1951, and that June I was 12 years old. That time in my life was very important, as I was moving into junior high school and would soon be a teen-ager. This was a new time in society. I was very much into music, cars and girls. The new music was rhythm and blues, which would eventually become rock and roll. Cars were a few years away, but '49-'50 Fords and '50-'51 Mercurys were the big things, and we dreamed of the day we would have our own cars and what we would do to them.

I was also very much taken with the girls of the day. My old "buddies," who had changed so much over the summer of 1951, had taken on a new look. They smiled a lot, smelled good and brought much confusion to all of us young men. So there were no more frogs or snakes in my pockets; I now enjoyed taking baths or showers, combing my hair, having my clothes look just right, and I know it pleased my mother. I also enjoyed the Friday night dances at the school. They needed me there to help hold up the gym wall.

That Christmas I received one of the greatest gifts ever. It looked like a lunch box and was known as a tube radio, something that is very rare these days.

Although I did not know it at the time, R&B was being promoted by Alan Freed, better known as Moondog in Cleveland. Here in Dearborn, Robin Seymour at WKMH and Frantic Ernie

Durham at WJLB in Inkster played R&B, but many of the songs were considered suggestive by adults and were not played on the radio. We never looked at them this way; it was the beat of the music and the lyrics we liked.

The summer of 1952 our family headed to Blackstone Lake in northern Ontario for vacation, and, of course, I took my radio with me. The lake was 200 miles north of Toronto. We had no electricity in the cottage, so I had to use the battery. My brother Randy and I had our own bedroom, and the radio sat on a chair between our beds. At night I'd turn the radio on, and one night I was totally surprised to hear my R&B music being played by Moondog. Boy, I was in seventh heaven being able to hear my music so far from home, and I listened late into the night, every night.

That radio was my constant companion for a long time. Unfortunately, it's been gone for many years now, but I never forgot it, the pleasure it gave me in bringing my music to me and the way it figured in my life. It was–and still is–a source of a lot of great memories.

Brent Bachman left Dearborn in 1963 when he went to work for the city of Dearborn Heights. He is now a resident of Adrian. He and his wife, Annette Gervais, have been married 52 years and have four daughters and four grandchildren.

Reeling With Movie Memories

By Bill Gutzka

The other day, while browsing the entertainment section of the newspaper in search of a movie the wife and I might like to see, I decided to count the number of screens operating within a 20-minute drive or less from our home here in Hillsboro, Oregon, where my wife and I have lived for more than 30 years. I was astounded when the final tally stood at 60! Everything from modern multiscreen cineplexes with sound systems that will blow your socks off to single-screen venues in restored neighborhood theaters and even theaters that include a brewpub. Needless to say, moviegoing is a favorite pastime here in the rainy Northwest, where we've resided for the past 35 years.

Tallying those screens started me reminiscing about the second-run neighborhood theaters that I attended while I was growing up in Dearborn. There were a half-dozen to choose from, all within walking distance or a short bus ride from our house. World War II was raging, and the family car was up on blocks for lack of tires and spare parts, which were in extremely short supply during the war years. So, like many others, we either walked or took the bus wherever we wanted to go, unless fortunate enough to hitch a ride with a benevolent neighbor who still had a functional car and was going in the same direction at the same time that we were.

My earliest recollection is going to the Alden with my older brother, who, as a condition of getting his weekly allowance, was saddled with having to take me with him to see cartoons and a cowboy flick on Saturdays. As you might suspect, he wasn't thrilled having his little brother tag along with him and his friends. He was elated when I was finally old enough to start going on my own with a group of neighborhood kids who were about my same age.

In case you don't remember, the Alden was that rundown little theater on Ford Road just of east of Chase, within easy walking distance of our house, which was at the north end of Curtis Street near the intersection of Ford and Greenfield. Rumors abounded that it was infested with rats that ran around in the dark eating popcorn and other morsels dropped on the floor while the movie was playing. Most of us kids didn't believe it was true, but as a precaution, all of us, believers and nonbelievers alike, always sat with our legs and feet up on the seat, tucked underneath us, careful never to let them get anywhere near the floor. If I recall correctly, and that isn't always the case anymore, the admission for kids was just 9 cents (or maybe 11 cents), an amount almost every household could spare from the weekly budget if they wanted some peace and quiet for a few hours while the kids were at the Saturday matinee.

Sometimes my mother took me with her to the Alden on Dish Night, an event designed to boost midweek attendance. On Dish Nights the price of admission included a free plate or cup or saucer. If you attended every single week for a year or so, you wound up owning a service for eight, including a sugar bowl, a butter dish and a gravy boat. A dish or two always got dropped on the floor during the course of the movie, usually in the middle of a dramatic scene, shattering both the dish and the concentration of the rapt audience.

When we got a little older, the neighborhood gang and I abandoned the Alden and started attending Saturday matinees at the Midway, located in the heart of east Dearborn's retail center at Michigan and Schaefer. Not only was the screen much bigger, but the bill also always included a half-dozen cartoons (Tom and Jerry, Tweety Bird and the Roadrunner were my favorites), followed by a Three Scrooges short or two and a cliffhanger serial. The main feature was usually an oater starring Gene Autry, Roy Rogers or some other Western hero of that era, though sometimes a Dead End Kids, Abbott and Costello or Charley Chan flick was featured. How much fun we had roaring with laughter at the opening cartoons and comedies and then cheering for the hero in the main feature, while booing the villains and screaming warnings to any character on the screen who was in peril and not aware of it. Moviegoing simply didn't get any better than this, or so I thought at the time. The Midway also had a bigger candy selection, the projector broke down less often than the Alden's, and best of all, there was no mention of rats running loose! The downside was that the admission to the Midway was a whopping 14 cents—a whole nickel more than the Alden. Thus began my first lessons in economics and money management.

If I was fortunate enough to have earned a quarter by the time Saturday rolled around, I had some serious monetary decisions to make. First and foremost was whether to ride the rickety old Colson bus the nearly two miles to and from the theater, or whether to walk in one or both directions and use the money saved on bus fare to buy candy before the movie started, or perhaps a trinket at S. S. Kresge's across the street from the theater when the movie was over. I usually walked in both directions and opted for the candy. Walking wasn't a difficult decision to make when the weather was nice, but quite another matter when the temperature was in the teens, it was snowing and a biting northerly wind was blowing. The best times were when I had extra Christmas or birthday money to spend and could go to the movie, stuff myself with candy, enjoy a 25-cent malt at Cunningham's lunch counter or splurge on a 35-cent hot fudge sundae at Sanders, as well as do a little shopping at Kresge's and ride the bus in both directions. On those days I felt like a millionaire!

The Calvin Theater in west Dearborn is the movie venue that I still remember most fondly because it evokes a very special memory. The first time I saw a movie there was in 1945 when my mom, who loved anything musical, talked dad into taking her to see *Meet Me in St. Louis*. Dad wasn't particularly fond of movies, but knowing Mom needed something to get her mind off the war and worrying about my brother, who was serving in the Marines, he quickly gave in and agreed to take her. He then told me to change my clothes, wash my face and comb my hair because we'd be leaving soon. I was 8 at the time and didn't relish going, preferring instead to stay home and listen to my favorite radio programs. The thought of having to sit through some sappy, boring musical that didn't have a single cowboy or the Three Stooges in it was simply cruel and unusual punishment as far as I was concerned. Worse yet, there would probably be a lot of kissing and stuff. But my pleas to stay home went unheeded, and I went along, pouting and promising myself I'd have a miserable time and hate every minute of that dumb movie.

I was nestled in my seat munching popcorn when Leo roared, the opening credits ran, and much to my surprise I soon found myself fully engrossed in the movie. Little did I realize that something totally unexpected was about to happen to me - something wonderful! I was about to fall head-over-heels in love for the very first time. Her name was Tootie and she stole the show from the likes of Judy Garland, Leon Ames, Tom Drake, Marjorie Main, June Lockhart and the rest of that stellar cast. And she stole my heart. The defining moment came when on a dare she played a Halloween prank and tossed a fistful of flour at Mr. Braukoff and his dog. Being a Halloween prankster myself, how could I not feel an instant bond with that courageous girl! Besides, she was darn cute!

I was walking on air when we left the theater that night, totally smitten, having been struck by Cupid's arrow. A few days later at school, where we had just begun learning library skills, I set about doing some research to find out more about my newfound love. Imagine what a revelation it was when I discovered that my darling Tootie (aka Margaret O'Brien) was not only born in the same month and year that I was - January 1937- but on the very same day! It was a sure sign that the stars and planets had somehow become aligned and our love was meant to be. There was no doubt in my mind that we'd get married, have a dozen kids and live happily ever after - just as soon as I was old enough to go to Hollywood and propose to her. Though that never came to pass, at least my interest in movies other than Westerns and Abbott and Costello flicks had been awakened. I still think of Tootie every Halloween and Margaret on our birthday, January 15.

The Carmen, which opened in 1941, was the newest and without question the nicest of the Dearborn movie houses. Of note was the circular, rotunda-like, glass-enclosed structure at the front of the building that housed the lobby on the lower level and a wide carpeted stairway that led upstairs to a plush soda fountain and candy counter on the high-ceilinged upper level. The admission was a little steep - 30 or 35 cents if memory serves me correctly - but by the time I started attending movies, there I was in my early teens and usually had a few dollars in my wallet, earned by doing odd jobs around the neighborhood, setting pins in a bowling alley on Schaefer Road, or whatever I could do to supplement the allowance I got for helping out at home. So I could afford it and even pay the way for a young lady if I was lucky enough to have a date. The Carmen was where Mayor Hubbard hosted the city of Dearborn's annual Christmas party for the east-side elementary school kids, an event I attended without fail every year. It was also the theater of choice for the junior high set that usually attended in a large group of guys and girls, each hoping to sit next to their latest "crush." Young romance blossomed during those movie-going outings for it was that time of life when young men begin to take serious notice that girls were not only becoming soft and lumpy and curvy in places that they hadn't paid much attention to before, but they smelled good, too! I always enjoyed walking one of the girls home when the movie was over. Brings to mind the old Johnnie Ray tune, *Walkin' My Baby Back Home.*

Reaching high school age and getting a driver's license opened up a whole new world of moviegoing. Sometimes we'd take in a movie at one of the many big, luxurious, first-run theaters that once existed in downtown Detroit: The Adams, Broadway Capital, Madison, Michigan, Palm, United Artist and, of course, the Fox are a few that come to mind. The Michigan and the Fox are my favorites because they were so beautiful. Thank goodness the Fox was saved from the wrecking ball and restored. But usually we stayed pretty close to home: a quick trip to the west end to go to the Calvin or the Dearborn, or the Circle on Warren, or the Melvindale or even the Hollywood on Fort Street. Then, of course, there was that marvelous old passion pit, the Ford-Wyoming Drive In, which has since become America's largest drive-in theater with nine screens, parking for 2,500 cars and is open for viewing year round.

Going to the movies is just one of many fond memories I have of growing up in Dearborn. As the saying goes, you can take the boy out of Dearborn, but you can't take the Dearborn out of the boy.

Bill Gutzka grew up in Dearborn but left to see the world after graduating from Fordson High School in 1955. He and his wife have lived on the West Coast for more than 40 years. He worked for Hewlett-Packard and Intel Corporation before retiring.

The Last Scary Picture Show

By Norma Tino

Years ago, under the Hubbard administration, a free movie for the children was presented at the Calvin Theater on Michigan Avenue shortly before Christmas. Our children always went to this movie and thoroughly enjoyed it. One time the movie was a little scary, so I called the mayor's office to tell them about it. Much to my surprise, Mayor Hubbard got on the phone to talk to me and said they would screen the movies a little more carefully. I was delighted that he would actually take the time to listen to my complaint.

Some years after that, the Calvin Theater caught on fire, and the firemen extinguished it. Then, lo and behold, a few weeks later the Calvin Theater caught on fire AGAIN, and it was again extinguished. However, this time apparently the fire burned enough of the theater to get rid of it forever. And the Calvin Theater was no more.

Was this mystery ever solved? I don't know. I don't know if anyone knows. Maybe that's the scary part.

Norma Tino has lived in Dearborn for 42 years. She and her husband, Dennis, have five children, 16 grandchildren and one great-grandchild.

Chapter 10

Sports

Champs of the Watermelon League

By Len "Buck" Bokuniewicz

During the mid-to-late '50s, there wasn't a better city recreation program in metro Detroit than Dearborn's. For three years (1958-60) I played on the Bullets, a kids-managed baseball team – with absolutely zero parental involvement – in the city's Sub-Midgets, Midgets and Class F leagues. We were never the best team around, but we were always a force to be reckoned with.

In the summer of '57, after the fourth grade, I recalled hearing that there would be a baseball clinic held before the start of the season at Anthony Park in east Dearborn, a two-block-long expanse of open field that ran from Tireman on the north to Diversey on the south, before being covered by a subdivision in the early '70s. I showed up for the clinic on my beat-up, 24-inch Schwinn bicycle.

I stood in amazement when I got to the park. I had never seen so many kids in one place at one time – proof positive that the baby-boom generation had been aptly named.

Nevertheless, after chasing down a few fly balls and making a couple of difficult catches, I managed to attract the eye of a young Dearborn umpire in a white T-shirt with a blue Dearborn logo. He pulled me aside and gave me an "attaboy."

That was the day I became officially hooked on sports.

Several weeks later, my friends Jerry Conflitti and Butchie

Forystek and I learned of a sub-midgets team called the Panthers, being assembled by two classmates of ours at St. Alphonsus School, Dwayne Koscielniak and Craig Castle, and managed by Dwayne's older brother, Walter. I had never thought of Dwayne or Craig as being particularly athletic. And I thought that Walter was a bit of a "hood." Still, we joined the team.

In my very first game, I remember striking out three straight times before hitting a home run over the centerfielder's head on my last at-bat. I also remember that our Panthers team got hammered by practically every other squad that year.

When the summer of '58 rolled around, Jerry, Butchie and I decided to start our own team. I recall the three of us sitting in the den at the back of Jerry's house on Reuter, trying to come up with a suitable team name. We didn't want to be known as the Cubs or the Blue Jays or anything common like that. Such names wouldn't strike fear into the hearts of our opponents.

It was Jerry who came up with "the Bullets." I liked it the moment he suggested it. To my ear it sounded tough, bold, not to be messed with. Besides, the Lone Ranger was my favorite cowboy, and the "Masked Man" was famous for the silver bullets he used in his gun. It was enough of a connection for me. "Let's go with it," I said.

The next job was to find a sponsor. So I was elected to ask my father, the owner of National Marble Company in Detroit, to see if he would consider backing the team.

Frankly I felt embarrassed to approach him because although National Marble sounded like a big-time operation, I knew that it never employed more than five people – usually only four, including my dad.

But with pressure from Jerry and Butch, I asked my father to pony up the money. Much to my amazement he agreed to sponsor the team. So the next day Jerry and I ran to Hanses Hardware on Warren, east of Schaefer, and ordered 12 jerseys out of a catalog. We picked dark blue shirts with scarlet lettering that would say National Marble Company Bullets on the back. Actually it turned out that the red letters were difficult to read against the dark blue background, but the menacing look that the colors of our jerseys produced seemed appropriate for a team of mischief makers like the pack I ran around with in our east Dearborn neighborhood.

The next step was to get our contracts filled out, signed and returned to the Dearborn Recreation Department in the Carmen Theater building on Schaefer, just north of Ford Road. Jerry, our player-manager, took care of all the details and struck up a good relationship with the director of Dearborn Recreation, Mr. Miley – until, that is, the day that Mr. Miley discovered that Jerry was "over age" to play on our team. Butchie and I went with Jerry to a meeting with Mr. Miley, who blew his stack. I had never seen anyone get as angry as Mr. Miley did that afternoon.

Back then we played pickup ball every day at "the island" – a triangular-shaped piece of city-owned property, ringed by giant elm trees and bounded by Esper Boulevard, West Morrow Circle and South Morrow Circle – with our buddies Sam Bitonti, Teddy Fijak, Rick Czapski, Kenny Felix, John Baczyinski, Butchie Krupar and Joe Tomazewski, as well as brothers Tom and Brian Flanigan, who played on the Bullets under assumed names because they actually lived on Ward in Detroit.

That crew of young miscreants was the nucleus of our team for three years, although we picked up Anthony Adams, Mickey Bonkowski, Jan Szymczak, Claude Dameron, Duncan Cameron and Butch Goode before the team folded after the completion of our final season in 1960.

Our big rival was the Pirates, another kids-managed team,

most of whose players attended Lowrey School and lived near Hemlock Park. We often scrimmaged them because we were buds with Noel MacKinnon, their only player from St. Al's.

The Pirates were a good group of guys. I remember two names from that ball team – Ron Terry, who went on to become a three-sport star at Fordson, and John Oliver, who would go on to quarterback the Fordson High football team.

But the team during those halcyon days – the one that won the city championship every year – was the Star Furniture Comets. They had full uniforms in creamy white with red lettering: hats, button-down shirts, genuine baseball pants (not jeans like everyone else in the league) and baseball socks with stirrups. Whereas we showed up at the games on our bikes, with bats balanced atop our handlebars, the Comets showed up in cars, driven by their manager and assistants. When they got out of their vehicles with huge equipment bags – filled with bats, balls, helmets and training tape – the Comets looked like a junior version of the Detroit Tigers.

Talk about intimidating.

I recall that the Comets' star player was a tall, rangy kid named A.J. Vaughn. The very name sounded like a superstar to me. And in fact "Apple Juice" would go on to become an all-around great athlete at Fordson and play both baseball and football at Wayne State. During the 1967 college football season, he set the NCAA individual total offense record with 555 yards.

The Comets' second baseman was Mike Hegyi. A few years later he formed a band at Fordson called the Royal Playboys. The group had fleeting fame when it backed the Dynamics, a Detroit soul group, on the local two-sided hit *Misery/I'm the Man* in the fall of 1963. The record spent 10 weeks in the Billboard Top 100, peaking at number 44.

Other than my memories of competing against the Pirates and Comets and the kids who became Dearborn legends, I remember two things: 1) my only time at bat – a fly out – at Lighted Diamond the year I made the Midgets League all-star team and 2) the time that the Bullets won the Watermelon League championship, in our second year of existence, when we were sponsored by Felix Wine Shop.

The Watermelon League worked like this:

There were a bunch of Midgets divisions, each named after a color. All the teams that failed to reach the .500 mark at the end of the season went into a divisional playoff called the Watermelon League. The city would deliver a load of watermelons to each winning team for a year-end party. We won our division's Watermelon League championship in 1959 and arranged to have the melons delivered to "the island." But after eating just one slice, Butchie fired a piece of watermelon at Sam Bitonti's head. Then Jerry threw one at Joe Tomazewski. And I, in turn, pitched one into Butchie's back. Bedlam broke out in the form of the world's greatest watermelon fight. Picture faces covered with goop consisting of watermelon juice and infield diamond dust.

Throughout those childhood years, Jerry, Butch and I were the three musketeers of our territory around Reuter, from Tireman to Warren. Each of us eventually made our marks playing sports at St. Alphonsus in the Catholic League. Jan Szymczak, who left the neighborhood to attend Orchard Lake St. Mary's and eventually graduated from Detroit Salesian Catholic, was the only one of the Bullets to play college baseball. After two years on the team at Henry Ford Community College, he continued to pursue the game at Eastern Michigan University.

When I reflect on those glorious days of Dearborn recreation baseball, I think of all the valuable lessons we learned as 11- or 12-year-olds by managing our own teams, securing our own sponsors, making out our own lineups and engaging in the amazing pranks and adventures we experienced while riding our bikes to and from the games at Hemlock Park, Ford Woods and Geer Field. My oldest son at the same age, by contrast, played over 40 games of "travel ball" each summer in Oakland County, where his Clarkston team was coached by a former starting catcher for Western Michigan University and an assistant coach who had been a pitcher for the Philadelphia Phillies long enough to have a cup of coffee in the big leagues. In other words, my son had wonderful coaching.

But I think my experience with youth baseball in Dearborn was a better one than my son's in Clarkston. We may not have known enough to hit the cutoff man at that age or the proper way to round first base. We just played baseball every day. I mean every day. Not once, on the other hand, did I ever witness my son and his friends get together on their own, load up their bikes with bats, gloves and spikes dangling from their handlebars to meet somewhere in the middle of a weed-choked field to "play ball." The baseball they played was always organized.

Looking back on it all, I'd take my three years with the Bullets of east Dearborn over my son's time with the Clarkston Riverdawgs any day of the week. Because I guarantee you that we had more fun.

Len "Buck" Bokuniewicz graduated from Dearborn St. Alphonsus in 1965. He attended Michigan State University before becoming a writer for the Auto Club of Michigan (AAA) and Ross Roy. He has four children and retired to Grand Haven with wife Debbie in 2012.

Hemlock

By Emilio DeGrazia

No one dreamed that there might be a basketball gene when I was born in a rented flat at 6327 Calhoun Street, just half a block from Hemlock Park. Though we moved a few blocks north on Calhoun to the house my father built on an empty lot, Hemlock Park was where the action was by the time I was 12. It was a wide space for a city park, with a swimming pool and hill for sleds and king-of-the-hill games. I spent whole half-days at Hemlock Park, cracking open my knuckles playing box hockey with mean-spirited sticks and a black checker piece as the victim puck. Girls wandered through the park by twos and threes, snickering at the depth of our passion for box hockey. But what mattered most to me was the slab of concrete in the middle of the park, the two long basketball courts laid out on them. The basket by the streetlight was the favored spot. That's where the Big Guys came after dinner to pick teams and play until dark.

The Big Guys were famous Fordson High School boys– Johnny McIntyre and Don Greenleaf from Fordson High's 1954 state Class A championship team and the more latter-day sainted varsity players, the Callaway twins, Red Montre and McIntyre's little brother Jimmy. The first time I saw them in Hemlock Park I was born again, gazing at them and expecting one of them to slap me awake. As I sat under a tree watching their moves on the court, my mind narrowed to three thoughts: 1) How could I become a Big Guy too? 2) How could I get into a Big Guy game? and 3) I would make a fool of myself.

I was fool enough as a 14-year-old, not yet having heard of Socrates or the hemlock poison he had to drink to satisfy his thirst for intellectual purity. Nor did I give an owl's hoot about the name of the tree I was sitting under as I watched the Big Guys play until they petered out. The one thing I knew for sure is that I wanted in, and rather immediately I figured out two strategies for getting in: First, I could skip dinner, be the first one to show for the Hemlock Park games, and hope I'd get picked to play as filler until the regulars showed. Or, I could wait it out, hope for a few to get drop-dead tired, then get picked as filler again for the last game. But the math odds were my nemesis. The Big Guys always had to be odd-numbered if I was to have any hope of playing my filler role. If there were six or eight or 10 who hadn't dropped dead-tired, I had to sit on the bench that was the grass under the tree. Even now when I contemplate the long-lasting psychological effects of my strategy, I see that the worry the odds caused is existential: Am I the odd man out, or in? And riding the bench has been so hateful to me that whenever I see even a lovely, well-kept lawn I never want to sit on it.

There was, of course, the old-fashioned way into the Big Guy games: Practice, my boy, practice. If I worked until I dropped and made it hurt, someone would see I needed a break. I tried this and I almost got broken by it. I got in only when the Big Guys were desperate for a proper body count, and if I wanted to touch the ball, I'd have to steal it from someone on my team. To be like them I'd have to be better than all of them.

So by dawn's early light and by the light of the moon I practiced my shot from the top of the key, from the corners, going left and right, off the board and in and mainly off the rim and out. As my T-shirt got wet and my mouth went dry, my sweat glands subbed in for my saliva glands. Yes, it got easier by the year: Four of 10 from any spot, then six, then eight of 10, then one day a lucky 10 of 10. Fluids flowed every time I rang that bell in my mind at the bottom of the net.

Nights I dragged my thighs home behind me from Hemlock Park.

"Where you been?" my papa asked.

"Working out."

"How much you make for the work you do out?"

My rewards were mental. He would never understand something deep like that. "I gotta do it for school," I replied.

"You gotta do something else," my mama broke in. "You gotta change your socks. Your feet stink like something dead."

If only I knew then that one fine day I would entertain an offer to play pro ball, and that I'd eventually spend years wondering if my feet, feeling as numb as the stumps of dead trees, were still alive under me.

I didn't mind the stinky socks until they stiffened up, which they did when I took a time out to sit under a big old Hemlock Park cottonwood tree. There I sat with a few of the younger hotshots jawing about which of the Big Guys we'd choose first, how awesome they were going left, right and to the hoop. Nobody but me seemed to notice the girls who kept passing in front of us by twos or threes, their purring a quiet reminder that we needed to practice our buzzer-beater shots.

One by one I got into the Big Guy games, while fate on rare

occasions conspired with free will to put the ball in my hands so that chance could pit me against great odds to clunk it through the hoop. Chance improved its odds as I practiced longer hours. Now and then, too rarely, Big Guy heads turned, amused. I was a nag who scarfed up the ball no one bothered to chase, my body racing ahead of my common sense to lunge on it. Some of the Big Guys began calling me The Little Shit. I was gaining respect. The next thing I knew, my mind began salivating too, thinking I'm almost there, knocking on the Big Guy door inside of which buzzer-beaters are not just lucky shots but products of free will's hard discipline certain to determine my destiny. I walked home from Hemlock Park thinking–on average more than once a week–that I was fated to be a Fordson High basketball star.

But the stars were making a fool of me. There they were a zillion miles away, like girls, beautiful in a different way. They made no sense, and while the church's windows were beautiful when the sun was out, the bone-white statues of the Virgin Mary made her look sickly and sad, as if deficient in the B-vitamin complex. If she was such a good Christian, why did the Mother of Perpetual Love always have such a miserable expression on her face? What did all that religion mean? There was no tuning that question out of the static in my mind.

One day, as I was in a drug store trying not to stare at some of the magazines smiling at me, I came across a big paperback book, *Philosophy Made Simple.* I looked around before opening it, afraid someone would think I was staring at the cover of a girly magazine right in front of my nose. I found big words inside: "metaphysical idealism," "empirical realism, "predestination," "ontological," "solipsism," "epistemology," "aesthetics." All this for a buck. I dug up a dollar from the loose change I was saving for what I craved most in life at that very moment, a Creamsicle. I then lugged the book home to my room, and it fell asleep like a cat on my chest with me that night. The next morning I ate my eggs and toast, and then it was time to go to Hemlock Park again to work on my shot from the top of the key. My old Wilson rubber basketball was as bald as the top of my father's head. I knew the feel of that ball better than I knew any girl's hand, but the ball never made a fuss about me going to the park the way my father did. I also liked to take along a jug of lemonade, thinking that one of the Big Guys would maybe pass me the ball if I passed the jug to them. But what about my *Philosophy Made Simple*? I could leave it at home under the bed with the socks I didn't want my mother to find, or lug it to the park for a time out. Metaphysical idealism and objectivism–I didn't know what they were. I didn't know what I was. Maybe the book knew what I was.

I left the jug of lemonade behind.

So with my bald-headed old Wilson under my right arm and my incompetent left-hand tuber hanging on tight to my *Philosophy Made Simple*, I walked the five blocks to Hemlock Park. I shot a hundred jumpers going right and a hundred from behind the key and 25 tuber shots from behind the backboard, just to see if that would help. Then I called time out to let *Philosophy Made Simple* figure out if I was a metaphysical idealist or empirical realist.

I left the park still trying to decide, and it only took me a few more years to realize I was double-hooked: basketball and books. During those years I lugged Steinbeck to Hemlock Park, and Rolvaag's *Giants in the Earth* and Salinger's *Catcher in the Rye* and Hawthorne's *The Scarlet Letter.* Poor Hester made the varsity. And *Crime and Punishment* was so interesting I lugged the next book by Dostoevsky I could find to the park. The book was called *The Idiot,* and I was looking forward to spending hours with him after shooting another 200 shots from the top of the key, wondering, as my legs were going numb, what the Athenians had against Socrates and whether they made him sit under a Hemlock tree when they poisoned him.

This is Chapter 9 from an unpublished book manuscript titled Moving Without the Ball.

Emilio DeGrazia, a longtime resident of Winona, Minnesota, grew up in Dearborn. He has had two collections of fiction, two novels, a memoir, a collection of essays and another of poems published. He and his wife Monica also have co-edited Twenty-Six Minnesota Writers *(1995) and* Thirty-Three Minnesota Poets *(2000). His short stories,* Seventeen Grams of Soul *(1995), was winner of a Minnesota Book Award, and his recent collage of creative prose,* Walking on Air in a Field of Greens, *was one of three finalists for a Midwest Book Award as memoir.* Seasonings, *a collection of poetry, is his most recent book. He is currently poet laureate of Winona.*

A Muddy Harbinger To a Magical Season

By Hank Dunick

Early October 1959. A cold, wet afternoon at old Ford Field in west Dearborn. The football field had steep hills in the north end zone and west sideline and a Rouge River forest in the south end zone. A cinder running track wrapped around the field, but there were no lights, no pressbox, no big scoreboard. Nor were there any views or sounds of the surrounding city.

The Sacred Heart High School football team began another day of practice. The school had only 33 boys in the senior class, so the team was made up mostly of juniors, sophomores and freshmen. Coaches Herb Delaney, Harold Popp and Jim Miller didn't know what to expect from such an inexperienced bunch. The Shamrocks had managed to go unbeaten in the first few games of the season despite being outweighed 40 pounds per man on the offensive line in the game with Benedictine High. But, as with all young teams, many questions remained.

The coaches had cooked up a surprise for us on this gray day—an unannounced scrimmage against another team—and, shortly after practice had begun, that team arrived. A large bus pulled into the lot above the field and a blue horde of players streamed down the hill. It was the team from Redford St. Mary High, which had a longtime, powerhouse football program. They had played for the Detroit city championship against the public school champs in the Goodfellows Soup Bowl game in Briggs Stadium. The Rustics had lost only one conference game in four seasons. I think Coach Delaney didn't tell us in advance so we wouldn't get too hyped up.

The ensuing scrimmage was very basic. One running play

after another after another. Occasionally a coach would become so frustrated with his team that he would have them run the same play two or three times in a row, even though the opposing defense knew what was coming. But we had a battering ram of a fullback (Mike Leavey), and no one wanted to tackle him twice in a row. Virtually no passing plays were called, even though the Shamrocks had an outstanding passing game with eight or nine guys who were excellent receivers, a strong offensive line and a quarterback who would eventually play pro ball (the late George Wilson Jr.). I believe there were a few games in which we might have scored 100 points if we had wanted to. But we also had excellent running backs and never had to use our passing to run up the score. And we weren't going to be allowed to let loose in this scrimmage, which evolved into a maze of collisions and whistles and coaches screaming both criticism and encouragement. Somehow there were no serious injuries on either side.

There were about 90 players and coaches present that day, and I would bet only a handful remember the scrimmage. But I remember two tired, muddy teams. I remember the confident look in Coach Delaney's eyes afterward. And I remember the unofficial final score of that scrimmage:

Dearborn Sacred Heart 6
Redford St. Mary   0

Hard to beat a Dearborn team at a place named Ford Field.

The Sacred Heart Shamrocks won all the remaining games on their schedule by an average score of 42-2 and completed the first undefeated season in the school's history.

Hank M. Dunick received his bachelor's degree from the University of Miami. He has his own accident investigation company, handling major accidents for plaintiffs and defense firms. Currently he is the most experienced accident investigator in Florida.

Wrestling With the Pain Of What Might Have Been

By Rami Fakhouri

I walked back into Edsel Ford High School recently, 30 years after my graduation. I headed to the trophy case, excited to see my 1981 All-State wrestling picture that stood there a few years after my graduation – which was the last time I was in my high school building.

Feeling like a ghost from the past as I walked the halls – both comforting memories and much emotion rushed through me, as I was transported back in time. To my surprise, but yet understandably since many years have passed and many other great kids accomplishments have transpired, the only room for pictures left in the trophy cases were of the wrestling state champs – including my teammate Pat Brackett and former neighbor Scotty Wyka, not of the wrestlers who had finished in the top six in the state, which were given the label of "all-state" champs like myself.

As I stared into the trophy case – and past it – as if into space, I whispered to myself, as if talking to my wrestling coach, Pat "The Whizzer" Wyka: "Yes, coach, it still hurts." And, "if only they knew." If only they understood the story, the work, the pain – and why I tried but could not finish first and be state champ my senior year – that last year I would ever wrestle.

There are many sports stories of triumph and pain. Here is another one with a different twist.

I started my senior year in wrestling with high hopes, expecting to be state champ as Pat Bracket was the year before. Pat was a great football player and wrestler – and always would yell as he led the team in drills, "No pain, no gain."

The season of lonely, dark nights continued through winter as I tallied a 30-1 record getting ready to start the run to the state championships. I was in my prime and never felt better. Nothing could stop me now. My goal to become state champ – after 10 years of wrestling, starting in AAU wrestling at the ripe old age of 8 and weight of 62 pounds – was in my grasp. The youth of invincibility, however, was not to be.

It was the week of the wrestling regionals, in which you needed to finish in the top four to qualify for the state championship a couple of weeks later. As I sat on the high school gym floor being yelled at by Coach Wyka, I had understood my wrestling career was over. I had broken my foot. The pain was great, and my foot swelled up to the size of a cantaloupe. Yes, Coach Wyka was yelling at me and disappointed at the same time, as he never yelled at me. I owed all to Coach Wyka – and was sorry to let him down. The Whiz was my neighbor, mentor, coach and friend. He was like a father to me. He kept me out of trouble (the best he could) – both inside and outside of school.

I never would have played any sports if it hadn't been for the Whiz. He taught me how to play baseball, basketball, sort of how to swim, and I tagged along with his son, Ricky – to learn how to play football, and soon the Whiz had recruited me to join him to wrestle on the weekends. Sure, why not. I thought I loved sports, and I loved the opportunity to challenge myself, both mentally and physically.

He boomed with disgust. "What the heck were you thinking, Rami?" Coach Wyka yelled at me while I sat in the gym floor in pain. Yes, parents stop their kids from playing contact sports like football. And after 10 years of football, wrestling and track – having never been seriously injured – I lay on the ground in pain after breaking my foot in three places playing gym volleyball.

Yep, when an athlete competes, he cannot do it halfway, and I had jumped to spike the ball, successfully, I may add, and landed on someone's foot – twist, snap, crackle, pop, went my foot.

With my season done, all I could do was stare back at the Whiz. No words came out. He quickly carried me to the training room and put ice on my foot and then left. I lied back on the trainer's table alone thinking what could have been. There would be no time to put a cast on my foot and heal. Regionals were this weekend, and state was a couple of weeks away. You are not allowed to wrestle with a cast on. There would be no ability to practice, keep in shape, keep my weight down to make weigh-in. The thoughts of any more wrestling vanished.

As time passed that day, the Whiz reentered the training room to take a look at my foot. "Wow, it doesn't look good," he said. "We will get you crutches, and you are not to put any weight on your foot. We are not going to place a hard cast on it right away. Let's ice it and wrap it and see how we are doing in a few days."

"Anything you say, coach," I replied.

The pain was excruciating. Even with crutches my leg throbbed. Ice bucket after ice bucket – the heat generated from my injury melted the ice in no time. A few days later it was hot whirlpool baths and then cold baths in the training room a couple of times of day to accelerate the healing process.

You got to be kidding, I thought to myself. If you knew how bad the pain was without moving – let alone putting any weight on my foot–forget about walking on my foot. How would I wrestle? You sit on your back feet when you wrestle. You push off your foot when you do a takedown. Your competition grabs and twists your legs and feet. Dream on. I did not see any glimmer of hope. But I listened and did as I was told.

The Whiz had a plan. He always had a plan. He talked,

and I listened. The plan was to win enough matches at regionals to qualify for state and then forfeit the rest of the matches – in order to protect my foot. A couple of more weeks of healing, and you would be ready to go for state. Huh? Sounds good, I thought. But I was not wrestling chumps. It would be like boxing with one arm tied behind your back. Good luck.

Regionals arrived. I had a wrap on my foot and some anti-inflammatory medicine to keep the swelling down, and aspirin to help with the pain. I had not eaten much – since I could not work out to keep my weight down. But somehow, after my morning ritual whirlpool for my foot – I made weigh-in.

As I hobbled to the Trenton High School gym floor on crutches to see who I would wrestle first – sshhiitt – great, I thought. My first opponent was the Fordson wrestler I beat only 6-5 a month or so back. Coach Wyka had simple enough instruction as I put my head gear on, threw my crutches down and readied myself to walk (hobble) to the center of the mat to begin the match. He looked me in the eyes and said, "Pin him quick." Huh, I chuckled. Sure, I will do my best. Thirty five seconds later I crawled off the mat in pain, having just pinned my opponent.

Wow. Maybe Coach has something here. Maybe it will work. I pinned my opponent in the next match, qualified for state so then forfeited my next matches and went home. The plan was good for protecting my foot, but it was bad in the sense that I would get a much lower seed and then a tougher draw at state. So be it. I now had two weeks to try to get ready for state.

Two weeks of training ritual of hot and cold for my foot, and daily full-body whirlpool baths to keep my weight down had now passed. There was no wrestling practice, no jogging. I had to compete cold turkey. Time to wrestle had now arrived as I sat quietly in the morning taking a whirlpool for my foot in our Ann Arbor Weber Inn hotel, sgetting ready to go to Crisler Arena, the location for the state championships.

I was the wrestling captain and wrestled at 132 pounds. And this was probably the most competitive weight class at the time, for everyone I wrestled seemed to be the captain of their team. My first opponent was ranked first with only one loss all year. The second-ranked wrestler was state champ the prior year. All I could do was my best – last chance. Give what you got, whatever it is, even though you know it won't be good enough. You give it and then give some more.

As expected, the first match did not go so well. Yes, I lost. The strategy for my opponents was pretty simple and clear – grab my left foot, twist, squeeze and have fun. My strategy was to try to tuck my left foot underneath me and rely on my upper-body strength and speed to compete and deliver some pain back to my opponents. I hobbled my way to winning the next two consolation matches and had qualified for all-state – top six in the state. My final match of my career was against last year's state champion, who was ranked second and who I had never beaten. I was winning through the entire match, and with no ability to train and practice, I just simply ran out of gas. I had no more energy, nothing left to give. I lost by one point in overtime to a fierce competitor who went on to get a college wrestling scholarship at Iowa and do well in the college ranks.

I gave what I could with what I had. I could not ask for any more. There was plenty of pain along the way, but with no pain, there is no gain. I learned to wrestle with the pain – and live with the pain. The pain of my foot and the pain of not being a state champ. Was I content? No. I knew if I had been healthy, I would have been the favorite to be state champ. But I was a winner nonetheless.

After all these years, especially on cold and wet winter days, my left foot still aches.

Rami Fakhouri resides in Florida with his wife, Suzanne, and three children, Yasmin, Dana and Yusuf.

Hockeytown South: The Impossible Dream?

By Vaughn LeClair

Dearborn hockey these days means modern arenas, immaculate ice and kids toting around duffel bags filled with several hundred dollars' worth of equipment. These young players, if they have enough talent and work hard, can realistically think about playing on good college teams, in the pros or maybe even, as Brian Rafalski did, wearing the red-and-white uniform we are all so familiar with.

Sixty years ago things were different. A hockey "facility" was a pond at a local park that had been flooded by the fire department, and "equipment" was a puck, one hockey stick per player and four galoshes used as goal markers. It had been this way forever, but in the1950s the city invested in a few rinks equipped with compressors and in doing so gave birth to Dearborn "Wreck League" Hockey.

Those who took to the ice that first season looked a lot like the pond hockey players they had been the winter before, but there were subtle differences. We wore hockey gloves and shin pads, and goalies used baseball gloves and maybe catcher's equipment. Sophistication had begun. From that point on things improved with every season. We became better players, and thanks to businessmen like Mike Adray and the service clubs, some teams began wearing real uniforms.

Our season actually began in late fall before there was any ice. As we kept an eye on the news from Sonny Eliot and listened to Al Nagler's radio play-by-play of Red Wing games, we also got out our gear and had our skates sharpened, and we went to the hardware store to pick up new sticks and rolls of the sticky black tape that was used to wrap the blades. One thing that set hockey apart from other sports options was the non-participation of the schools. There were no trained coaches or subsidized equipment available, and though the city and a few sponsors provided some of the basics, nearly everything else was looked after by the players. Teams were organized somehow, based on who we went to school with, who our friends were, who we had played with previously, and an informal but relatively efficient pecking order based on a players' ability.

The system worked well enough, but was occasionally short-circuited, like the times some of the players from the elite Detroit leagues decided to play on our teams. One year we had a windfall when a player freshly arrived from Canada joined us. He sailed around the ice like Sonja Henie, carried the puck as if it were glued to his stick and introduced us to something new by uncorking blazing slap shots. Like a group of scientists from Aruba who had stumbled across the formula for building a hydrogen bomb, we began to have illusions of conquest. What we found out, though, was that one player can't carry a whole team, and that while slap shots may be fast, wrist shots are more accurate. Still, it was great to see one of those waist-high missiles come flying in from the blue line, even when they went wide of the net and boomed against the plywood boards.

Any yarn about our Dearborn hockey days would be incomplete without mentioning a few of the people involved: Jack Baker, a little older and the leader of the pack on my block, who motivated us to start playing hockey in the first place. Fred Speier, Frank (Spanky) Lynch and Gary Orthner, some of those who made the phone calls and did the grunt work to get our teams organized. Gordon Haber, who started out as one of the most inept players on the ice, but worked at it and eventually played college hockey at Michigan Tech. The slap-shot artiste was Bill Boyea.

Aside from the players, what I remember more than the

won-lost record of our teams are some of the little things. Good plays and bad plays. Scoring an occasional goal. How cold it was at night waiting for our turn on the ice. Going home to feel the pain that comes when nearly frozen ears begin to thaw. Angrily slamming the heel of my stick on the ice after losing a game we should have won and breaking the blade off a brand-new Northland Special (and not telling my folks the real reason I needed a new stick – what happens at the rink stays at the rink). Getting cut and taking a few stitches, happy to join the ranks of hockey players who have been "sewn up." I also remember the end of the season and the forlorn look of the rinks – the scenes of our epic battles now surrounded by melting piles of dirty snow, with a layer of water on top of what was left of the ice.

The end of winter was the start of the off-season, which to the hard core meant playing street hockey with a tennis ball and driving our neighbors nuts by banging a puck against the back of the garage over and over again as we worked on our shooting. When were a little older, it also meant piling into a few cars and going through the tunnel to the barnlike old Windsor Arena, the only rink that was open in the summer. There we played pickup hockey, at 3 a.m. when ice time was the cheapest, beneath a giant portrait of a young Queen Elizabeth decked out in her crown jewels. I used to think of that portrait years later whenever I saw the queen on television, wearing one of those strange hats and peering at the House of Commons over her bifocals.

Most of my adult life has been spent in California and in Florida, where there were modern, wonderful indoor rinks, but to me, going there never compared to stomping in our skates across a mixture of mud and wood chips at places like Levagood, Crowley or Ford Field, stepping through a battered gate and taking those first few strides out on the ice.

Three years ago, when my wife and I retired and moved to Peru, I figured my goose was cooked as far as hockey was concerned, but a couple of things came along to change that. First, about a year ago somebody brought a hockey rink from a site in California and reassembled it in a Lima suburb. (For some reason they park the Zamboni on the street, and I have thoughts of it being stolen and seeing an O.J. scenario with a swarm of cop cars chasing the lumbering vehicle down the Vía Expresa.)

Also, about the same time the rink opened, I saw something about the National Hockey League being the only major league that has decided against marketing its sport to the 45 million or so Latin Americans now living in the United States. (You can read a statement on this by the league's commissioner by googling "NHL Simply Not Going to Bother"). Also I'd noticed that the National Football League, National Basketball Association, etc. are all over the media down here, but not hockey. Like an old duffer bothering city officials about potholes in the street, I started writing letters (mostly ignored, of course) to some of the league's high rollers suggesting they get the lead out. My biggest triumph so far has been to receive a Fed Ex box containing a complimentary Red Wings hat and a letter from an NHL attorney in New York, and my biggest disappointment has been not hearing from Wings owner Mike Ilitch. Not to worry. I have a new proposal I know he'll like: building a Hockeytown South high in the Andes to sell alpaca Red Wing jerseys for those frosty mountain mornings, goalie sticks for herding goats and llamas, and, of course, pizza. (Pizza Pizza.)

Vaughn LeClair is a 1960 graduate of Dearborn High School.

Life in the Fast Lane

By Edward W. Maurus

I want to be honest and to the point. I never wanted to be an athlete, but in those days in gym class you had to pass a fitness course. On the day that they had the 600-yard run, I thought I would be smart and not wear my gym shoes so I could get out of the run. That didn't really work since Herb Schroeder made me run with my street shoes on. I was so mad that it made me go faster. After the run was over, one of the students told me that Herb Schroeder wanted to see me in his office.

All I could think of was, "He's going to yell at me about the shoes." When I sat down, he tossed me cross-country sweats and told me I was on the team. As I was going, he mentioned that I nearly broke the school record. He also told me to cut my long sideburns.

That first year was a love/hate relationship with the coach. At the end of each race he always told me that I could run faster. At the end of the season I was sitting on the bench when I was told Coach Schroeder wanted to see me in his office. All I could think was "He is going to yell at me about my sideburns again," and really I was hoping that this whole experience was coming to an end. When I got to the office, he threw me my letter saying that I earned it. In those days no one ever got a letter their first year.

Sitting next to him was a small man he introduced as Coach Bridges. He told me he hoped to see me in the spring. As I was going, he yelled to me to cut my sideburns and run faster the next year.

Getting that letter opened a whole new world for me. I

got my new varsity jacket, sweater, and even had orange pants for Varsity Day. In the spring I was going to my geometry class when I saw the name on the door, "Bob Bridges."

I want to be frank with you. I hated math. Even though my great-uncle was the head of the math department for 40 years at Notre Dame, those genes didn't carry over to me. When I realized that was the little man I had met in the fall, I figured out I better hide out in the back of the room. When he came into the room, he yelled out, "Fast Eddy, could you please stand up?" At first I didn't know who he was talking to, and then I realized he was talking to me. When I got up, he had me talk about how I was going to do this spring in track, and that, my friends, is how I passed my geometry class, truth be told.

We were all-region that year, and our mile relay team of Howard Schuman, Gary Scallen, Bob May and me were rated number three in the nation for the fastest times.

I was always scared that I would drop the baton and always had butterflies in my stomach after each race.

I ended up getting five letters in high school and four letters in college. And then it was over, no more 30-mile workouts ever. As we all get older, we tend to look at those people that mentor our lives. For me it was the late Herb Schroeder and Bob Bridges, who still coaches track at Dearborn High.

By the way, I never cut my sideburns, even to this day.

Edward W. Maurus has lived in the same house in Dearborn for over 60 years. He graduated from the last January class at Dearborn High. He is the president of the Dearborn Historical Society and also serves on the board of Friends of the Library, the Dearborn Genealogy Society and the Henry Ford Heritage Society. For 30 years he has been on the board of the Village Community Credit Union and the Laurel and Hardy Society.

Chapter 11

Politics

The Price of Fame

By Joan Dziadzio Boudreau

During my growing-up years my mom demonstrated great concern for her lawn. Mom would not allow anyone else to cut the grass, and God forbid that anyone should walk on it. I believe that she knew every blade of grass on a one-on-one basis because once the mowing was completed – yes, north and south, then east and west along with a few angular indexes on the compass for good measure – she would take her hand clippers and trim any errant blades that might not conform in height to its brethren.

It seemed that she was always outside doing something around her landscape. We lived on Wilson, and in later years it turned out that Mayor Guido lived not too many blocks away. Well, one day while Mom was involved with her ritual cutting and trimming, the good mayor came driving by with a small entourage, as he liked to do, and every so often he was prone to stop and talk to residents who, like my mother, were busy about their properties, "keeping Dearborn beautiful."

That's the background and here's the story: When Mom was about the landscaping tasks, she had a "uniform" that consisted of one of Dad's worn-thin white dress shirts, a pair of faded denim jeans, pant legs rolled to the knees, white nurse shoes and nylons rolled down just below her knees. She presented quite a sight, but to top that off she also wore a hair net to protect her beauty-shop "do."

It so happened that on such a day the mayor came by, stopped in front of the house and proceeded to speak with Mom, telling her how he appreciated how the seniors and residents in general were so dedicated to the upkeep of their properties. My mother, filled with pride, mentally charged this moment in time toward the 15 minutes of fame that we are all due in life. The mayor was on the campaign stump at that time, so he gave Mom a brochure and asked if he could have his picture taken with her. Of course, that only added to her euphoria (secretly hoping that the neighbors were in their windows watching, I'm sure), and she agreed, barely considering her mode of dress.

Well, that campaign came and went, the results of which gave him another term in office. However, for his next campaign, he had a tri-fold brochure made up that included the picture of Mom with the mayor standing in front of the house in all her glory. She was mortified, her reaction being an unprintable quotation that would put the proverbial sailor to shame.

Mom was so mad that she tried to stop distribution of the brochure, but too late. From that day forward, every time she saw the mayor, she would smile, point her finger at him and laughingly say, "I'll get you for that one of these days." They both would laugh, and as time went on, she grew to kind of like her "celeb" status, as that brochure was used in each subsequent campaign. She truly loved Mayor Guido and always felt a kinship of sorts with him.

Joan Dziadzio Boudreau has been married to Cyril (Cy) Boudreau since 1967. She has two children, Chris (married to Tracey Esper) and Amy (married to Sal Gencarelli). Joan has six grandchildren including a set of triplets. She is a graduate of Sacred Heart High School and is a retired Detroit public school teacher.

The Champagne Train To Ann Arbor

By Marie Chapman

The year was 1977. It was nine days before the newly elected mayor, John B. O'Reilly Sr.; the first female City Council president, Marge Powell; and the council were to be sworn into office. They were going to vote on the issue of whether to accept the AMTRAK train station in Dearborn. If they voted the issue down, the station would go to the city of Wayne.

At the same time, my son Tim Chapman, a junior at Kalamazoo College, was doing his English practice-teaching at Cherry Hill High School, a placement he obtained through Dr. Jack Gehm, a former counselor and the principal at Crestwood High School.

While attending Kalamazoo College, Tim had to get a ride to the Detroit train station and later be picked up from there when traveling between Dearborn and Kalamazoo.

So when he learned that the Springwells Home Owners Association, located west of Greenfield and Rotunda, was having a meeting, he attended and told the association why we needed the station in Dearborn – so college students could take the train to the University of Michigan, Western Michigan University, and Kalamazoo College.

One of the residents, Ford Motor Company Vice President

Ed Lundy, stated that he didn't want any bowery bums (author: Damon Runyon) in his back yard. Mayor Pro Tem O'Reilly assured him that he would vote against the train station in Dearborn.

Luckily, my husband and I played bridge with John and Marge Powell, and I felt free to call and apologize for bothering him at such a busy, stressful time; but, could he please do pillow talk and explain to Marge what a boon it would be for college students to get back and forth to their homes and schools using AMTRAK in Dearborn.

Dr. Van Mericas was very enthused. So were other council members. Mike Guido was a student at Henry Ford Community College, where Mrs. Schlaff gave her pupils all the additional reasons why we needed the train station in Dearborn.

Now, how could the mayor be further persuaded to vote for the Dearborn train site? I spoke to Dr. Mericas and asked him to speak to Local 600 and tell the members we needed those union jobs in Dearborn. For years, he told me that that was a neat idea.

And so it came to pass that the station received a majority of votes. The inaugural trip included dignitaries from Washington, D.C., and Dearborn. King Boring from the Dearborn Transportation Department; his assistant, Barbara Bartsch; my husband, Al; and I rode the champagne train to Ann Arbor and had dinner at the Gandy Dancer and then rode back again to Dearborn.

The tracks where the station was to be built were lined with black Austrian pines. I used to watch the workmen daily to keep them from cutting down any pines that were not blocking the station. Over the 30 years, they are succumbing to the pollution and look very scraggly.

I am looking forward to the coming new station, which will be incorporated into the Greenfield Village station. Thanks to Mayor John B. O'Reilly, Marge Powell and all the council members of 1977, we are on the AMTRAK map.

Marie Chapman was a public relations representative for SEMTA for seven years. She spent her early years in Frankenmouth and spoke German at home, giving her a German accent. After she lived in England, she developed an Oxford accent. She is active in several organizations including the League of Women Voters, the Garden Club of Dearborn and the Emmanuel Lutheran Church.

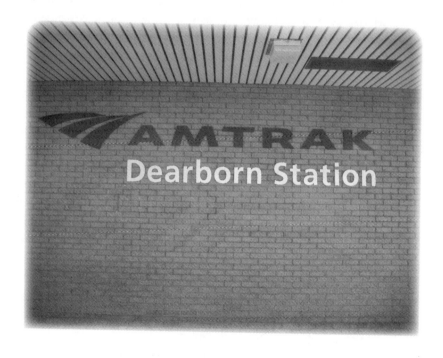

Kay Cushman, Con-Con and Me

By Betsy Cushman

My mother, Kay Cushman, joined the League of Women Voters before I was born; she was elected its Detroit president when I was in kindergarten. She helped found the Dearborn league and worked on a variety of committees that reflected the breadth and depth of her many interests – water and environmental quality, "home rule" and metropolitan government, rewriting city and county charters and the state Constitution, among others. She supported the consolidation of the Dearborn and Dearborn Heights leagues, served as local league president in the early 1970s and as the state league president for two years in 1980.

My father was proud of my mother's achievements and joined the league himself as soon as men were allowed. Growing up, my brother and I were not so supportive, and, indeed, actively turned deaf ears to her involvement. Our attitudes were not entirely unmerited. For example, when my mother edited the league's book, *Dearborn and Its Government,* she insisted that I help proofread it. I was only in junior high, and I found the activity mind-numbingly boring. But the worst part was that she made my friends help too, and they soon refused to come to my house, only returning when the book was published.

Not long afterward, the state League of Women Voters was a key leader in the campaign to convene a Constitutional Convention for the purpose of rewriting the 1908 state Constitution. My mother had studied the issues and wanted to help write the new Constitution. She ran for office. She hired my friends and me to pass out campaign literature door-to-door in a variety of different neighborhoods all over Dearborn. My dad would drop us off and pick us up, treating us to root beer floats at a drive-in afterward. She won the election. I turned 16 the next month.

Other delegates included George Romney, Coleman Young and Richard Austin. It is interesting to note that out of 144 delegates, only 11 were women. "Con-Con" (as it was called) took place from the fall of 1961 to late spring of 1962. It passed the electorate in 1963 and took effect in 1964.

Now it's 50 years later and these "Con-Con Eleven" women delegates are being admitted into the Michigan Women's Hall of Fame. They were each qualified in very different ways and made unique contributions to the concepts and writing of Michigan's Constitution.

Mother loved the political life. I'd never seen her so happy. She lived in a motel room in Lansing from October through May of my junior year at Dearborn High and drove home most weekends. She was an outstanding delegate and earned the respect, if not the favor, of the entire convention. The delegates all got to know each other and formed cliques that reflected their political leanings. In my mother's case, this had little to do with political parties and a lot to do with issues. She had two committee assignments, just the ones she wanted – "local government" and "style and drafting." I knew why she wanted local government, but I asked her why she wanted style and drafting, which sounded pretty lightweight to me. She replied that how things are worded can make all the difference and sometimes overrule the intent of the law.

I visited Mother in Lansing a few times. It was strange to see her living in a motel room and hanging out with her political friends, many of them male. One of them particularly charmed me, the convention's youngest delegate, Jack Faxon. Mother's best female friends were fellow members of the League of Women

Voters, Dorothy Judd from Grand Rapids and Vera Andrus from Port Huron. An October 2010 article in the Grand Rapids Press helps explain why these women made it to the male-dominated Con-Con.

"The conventions opened up opportunities for a whole range of other voices on issues," said Robert Williams, associate director of the Center for State Constitutional Studies at Rutgers University. "A lot of women in those days had gained a good deal of experience in the League of Women Voters and business women clubs. They were sophisticated and well-educated."

"Running for delegate," Williams said, "often doesn't require the same type of party backing as a regular election. The idea of having a one-time impact on the structure of the laws appealed to a lot of women of the era." It certainly appealed to my mother.

I have several memories of going to Lansing to see her. Once Mother wanted me to miss school in order to see former President Dwight D. Eisenhower speak at the convention (December 13, 1961). As soon as Ike entered the arena, I was enthralled. Never before had I experienced charisma, especially charisma that filled the gigantic room. It was magical and I was absolutely stunned. This was a president that had been a total bore on our black-and-white TV set. As soon as his face appeared on the screen, I always wanted to go up and change the channel. I was not looking forward to hearing him speak.

In all honesty, I don't remember a word he said, but I'll never forget his smiling face during his entrance and exit and how I felt the force of his personality all the way to my seat. I suppose it must have been something to experience if you served in the armed forces in World War II, and no wonder so many people loved this man.

As I've said, Mother was in Lansing my junior year in high school, which recalls one of my most embarrassing high school moments. Well, actually there were a lot of them, but here's one:

It took place when the new Constitution was up for voter approval at the ballot box. An educational movie about the convention and what the new Constitution would mean to the state was circulating through the high schools across Michigan, and it was going to be shown in my journalism class. The teacher invited my mother to speak to the class as well. Of course, I was a little nervous and sensitive just in case there was something that my classmates would make fun of.

Well, when the day arrived, Mother did a good job of speaking, and then we watched the movie. She doesn't appear in it until near the end, and then only for a short sentence – but what a sentence! It was just as the movie mentioned "women's issues," and there is my mother saying something like, "It seems to me that this is a case where uniformity of treatment does not necessarily mean equality of treatment, just as you get into it with sex, sometimes." O... My... God. . . . I was shocked and appalled. I believe the earth actually swallowed me because I have no further memory of the incident.

Years later I asked my mother how she could have abandoned her daughter for a school year. My brother was away at college, and my father traveled a lot on business. I had just been issued my driver's license and had complete freedom. What was she thinking? She calmly replied that she wouldn't have done it if I had been a different sort of girl.

That was in 1962 and I'd never have guessed then that 15 years later, I would join the league myself, serve on the boards of four local leagues, the state league board, and now agree to be president of my local league. Today I feel a sense of gratitude to the league and to my mother for the education I received.

Katherine Cushman actively worked for good government

for more than 50 years, right up until her death 20 years ago. People still remember her, and I still hear them say that they want to "get Kay on the phone" to resolve some question regarding good government. She would have known the answer right off the top of her head.

She was one of legions of 20th-century women across this country who served as role models for those who followed. They altruistically believed in – and worked for – good government and an educated electorate. I do know that our local, metropolitan, state and federal governments are all the better because of the League of Women Voters, and I'm so very glad that there is still a league in our communities and that there are people willing to devote their time and talents to keep it going.

Betsy Cushman is a descendant of two prominent Dearborn families, the Snows and the Moores. She is the president of and voter service director for the League of Women Voters, Dearborn-Dearborn Heights.

Hubbard's Closest Call

By Frank (Tom) Jones III

It was 1972 and I had recently returned from Vietnam. I wanted to get involved in politics, something short of being an anti-war protester, so I decided through the urging of a family friend and local politician, Lucille McCullough, to run for precinct delegate in my Dearborn neighborhood. Not only did Lucille convince me, but she also convinced my mother to do the same thing. Always the activist, Lucille thought this would be a good family activity. Her son Patrick McCullough was also involved in local and state politics.

Lucille told my mother and me that hardly anyone ever ran for neighborhood delegate and all you really had to do was get a page full of signatures, your name on the ballot, and it was a done deal. And that was true with my mother: she was unopposed, got about 12 votes, and became a party faithful! Such was not the case with me!

I assumed I was running unopposed but still wanted to let the neighborhood know who I was, so I put together a little newsletter and hand-delivered it to about 100 households. I didn't really have a political position other than a desire to get involved. In the newsletter I talked about the fact that I was a veteran and glad to be home and felt that I wanted to give something back to the community. I talked about our small neighborhood within the city of Dearborn and how good it looked. I had a list of community service numbers, library hours, etc. It was fun! In fact I distributed three updates with different stories and information prior to the election.

Now comes election day.

Not only did I discover that someone else was on the ballot, running for the same position, but my opponent was the longtime mayor of Dearborn, Orville L. Hubbard. Now the mayor, it seems, lived only a block away and had been this precinct's delegate for over 30 years. He never made a big deal out of it. At any rate, the mayor didn't know that someone was contesting his reign until he entered the election booth and saw a second name on the ballot. Mayor Hubbard's response was immediate. He took the day off work and stood in front of the polling place, shaking hands in the rain and letting people see his presence without making his party preference obvious. There were three precincts located at the polling place so only a third of the voters would see his name and then they would see it only if they were registered in his party, which was the minority party in our area. So here was the mayor of Dearborn, the illustrious Orville Hubbard, taking a day off work to fish for maybe 20 votes. I, on the other hand, learning that I backed into Goliath on the battlefield, just wanted to crawl into a hole. I had visions of my car being impounded, getting arrested for jay-walking, who knows? You did know that the mayor was not one to mess with.

Well, the polls closed and Orville Hubbard won his closest election ever, by two votes, 15 to 12. At about 8 p.m. I got a call from the mayor himself, congratulating me on a well-run (ha!) campaign. He relayed to me his utter surprise and shock to see that I had sneaked in through the back door and caught him with his pants down. He couldn't believe that I didn't know what I was doing ... but that is exactly how it happened. Although he was in the twilight of his career as the longest-running mayor of a major city in the United States, he never let his guard down again – and always kept an eye on what I was doing by having me involved in numerous community projects.

That was enough for me!

Busy hands were happy hands!

Frank (Tom) Jones III is a 1965 graduate of Edsel Ford High School. He is retired both from the Ford Motor Company and the United Sates Army as sergeant major (internal/public affairs chief). He splits his residence between Gibraltar, Michigan, and Vero Beach, Florida.

State of the Union

By Trevor Tutro-Anderson

Redford, Michigan, in 2008: I go up to a home whose door is facing the eighth hole of Glenhurst golf course. I knock and an older guy answers the door.

"Hi," I say. "I'm the local organizer for Senator Obama's campaign. I'm knocking on your door today to see if you know who you're supporting for president in November."

Now, everyone is told that if someone is strongly for you or strongly against you, it's a pretty quick conversation at the door. People that are for you need to be asked about volunteering, reminded about voting, and that's about it. People that are strongly against you, you're supposed to thank them for their time and go off to the next door on your list.

The man at the door says, "I'm voting for McCain!"

We pause for a few seconds, staring at each other.

"Want to know why?" he continues.

"Shoot," I reply.

"Well, John McCain was born in America, he's done all kinds of things and service to his country, and Obama isn't from here, and he hasn't done squat."

We pause for a few seconds again, staring at each other some more.

"You do know that Senator McCain was born in Panama, right? Also, last I checked, Hawaii was one of the 50 states."

"Argh," he grumbles, closing the door in my face.

Trevor Tutro-Anderson was a field organizer in the Dearborn office for the 2008 and 2012 Obama campaign.

The Day the Mayor Delivered His Bobblehead

By Maureen Whittaker

I have always had a fondness for Mayor Guido. He was a true servant to the city of Dearborn. My family and I used to run into him all over the city. He was always friendly and would say hello.

Once, in early 2003, we ran into him at the Ford Community & Performing Arts Center. I asked him where I could get a bobblehead figure of him like the one I saw on display in the food court. He laughed and told me that it was from a fund raiser, but if I really wanted one, he would look into getting me one if there were any left. He wrote my name and address on a napkin and put it in his pocket, and we went our separate ways.

Several weeks later, I was at home on a winter afternoon, watching a suspenseful movie by myself when the doorbell rang. I was eight months pregnant at the time and had my pants off because the waistband hurt, so you can imagine I wasn't expecting any visitors. I felt panicked as I went to the front door trying to get my pants back on. When I looked through the small window in the door, who was standing on my porch but Mayor Guido himself! I couldn't believe it!

I answered the door, and he apologized for taking so long in getting the bobblehead to me. He said that he had lost the napkin with my name on it, but remembered my name was Maureen and the name of my street. He went through all of the voter records for people on my street until he found my name. I couldn't believe that he would go so far out of his way to get that bobblehead to me. I thanked him and waved to his wife, who was sitting in the car at the curb. I told him nobody was going to believe that he was at my house. He just laughed.

A few years later, he became ill and passed away. My kids still recall him fondly, and the bobblehead of Mayor Guido is still on display in my dining room. We will always remember the years when he was our mayor and the great things he did for the city of Dearborn.

Maureen Whittaker is a lifelong Dearbornite and the mother of four. She loves community involvement and volunteering. She enjoys volunteering with Habitat for Humanity and the Crowley Park Sustainable Farm.

Chapter 12

Work

Six Summers: A Lifetime of Memories

By Megan Andrus

The year 1998 marked the beginning of my six summers as a lifeguard at Dunworth pool. Since I was a new lifeguard, they wanted to put me at one of the smaller pools, but my need to swim and train with the Dearborn Recreation Dolphins swim team called for me to be at that specific pool. I spent more than half my day, nearly 14 hours a day, at the pool on Monday through Friday. My usual routine was to wake up at 5:30 a.m. for 6 a.m. swim practice, one hour to change and eat between 8-9 a.m., teaching swim lessons starting at 9 a.m., a short break somewhere around 1-2 p.m., guarding from 2-4 p.m., 4-6 p.m. swim practice again, and 6-8 p.m. life guarding again. One of the summers somewhere in the middle, I also coached the Dolphins from 6-8 p.m. This amount of training was necessary for me because I was preparing for, and then actually training for, competing on the varsity swim team at Eastern Michigan University.

I generally taught the older kids who were doing more stroke technique, since I was one of the top swimmers that worked at the pool and had the most knowledge of swimming technique. Guarding the pool was both fun and boring. The schedule usually went 30 minutes on chair, 30 minutes off chair. During the hour, you had to rotate posts with about 15 minutes at each post. The time ticked by so slowly on each chair. There was a lot of yelling at kids for running or diving in the shallow water and throwing each other in the water, stopping people from bringing in oil, and checking to make sure each swimsuit had a lining and wasn't actually just a T-shirt and underwear. I only made two saves during my entire six-summer run at the pool. It was not something you wanted to happen since each time there was a save, you had to do a lot of paperwork immediately afterward.

The days that we guards looked forward to the most were storm days and poop-in-the-pool days. On storm days, you either got sent home early or you stayed most of the time in the guard shack playing cards and waiting for 30 minutes after the last thunder and lightning. Usually after the storm there would be very few kids swimming so it was more likely that you would have more time off chair. Poop in the pool meant that one of the pools (usually the baby pool) got closed for several hours so the maintenance guy could "shock" the pool with chlorine. Sometimes you would get out of sitting on those chairs or get extra time off chair.

Working at the pool was as exciting as some reality shows you see on TV. It had its own soap opera going on, with guards dating each other, late-night pool parties, climbing on the roof, stories of ghosts haunting the "pit," an inside-joke reference to the number 32, guards painting their name in the rafters of the guard shack, and more. It was like being a part of a club where everyone was tan, wore skimpy two-piece swim suits, guys were topless, and this was our typical work day. Dearborn's own *Baywatch* was just as interesting as the TV show itself. My favorite memory was when one of my best guy friends put on my bikini and ran over to jump off the high dive in the dark. I was unsuccessful at snapping a picture of him, but I will never forget the image. I made many lifelong friends in my years working at the pool. I even attended my friends Greg and Shelly's wedding on the pool deck of Dunworth pool. It was a lifetime of memories packed into six summers.

My last year at Dunworth, I worked only part time at the

pool teaching half the day and went on to my graphic design job in the afternoon at the Eastern Echo advertising department in Ypsilanti at Eastern Michigan University.

Megan Andrus lives in Los Angeles. She has a graphic design business, Liquid Red, and an online jewelry sales business, MyAccessoryBusiness. com She also competes for an adult swim team, Southern California Aquatic Masters.

The Joy of Working

By Helen Bandyke

I grew up in a pretty dysfunctional family. I craved order. I found joy in working. I think that it gives order to a person's life and gives one the opportunity to contribute to society.

My first job was at St. Joseph's Retreat at the corner of Michigan and Outer Drive. My sister, May, was a secretary there; my Aunt Frances worked in the kitchen. I was 18 years old. The Sisters of Charity ran the hospital, which served those suffering from alcoholism and psychiatric disorders.

Initially I worked on the Mother Seton ward, where the violent patients lived. Each day was a challenge. Two patients ripped off my clothes. The first time it happened, my aunt asked why I was wearing my coat inside the kitchen. One day I chased a female patient who was so thin that she squeezed through the iron fence surrounding the grounds. My supervisor later asked what I would have done if I had caught her. Good advice! I learned how to cope with incidents such as these. I then got promoted to another ward that was much more inviting. We could even sit down and eat with the patients.

Our workday was from 7 a.m. to 7 p.m. We got two hours off in the middle of the day to rest. Exhausted, I always fell right to sleep during that break. During my first two weeks of employment I lost 14 pounds. At the end of each day, my supervisor would always give me a piece of fruit and say, "Good night, Miss Hogie." Although the work was exhausting, that employment was also the most fulfilling that I have ever had.

I worked as a "Rosie the Riveter" during World War II. I worked there while my husband, Ted, was in San Francisco guarding the Golden Gate Bridge.

Later in life I worked for the optometrist William Fortney, who had his office on Michigan Avenue west of Outer Drive. His son is now in charge of the practice. I walked out the door after Dr. Fortney corrected me twice for the same issue, and I believe his corrections were inappropriate.

Later I worked in the optical department at Montgomery Ward on Michigan and Schaefer. From the large window in front of the store, I could watch the Memorial Day parade go by. When I would go home on the days of the parade, I would always call my brother-in-law, Willie, who was a Marine. I then worked for the optical department at Sears. I worked a total of 35 years for those two optical enterprises.

I found that working not only brought order to my life but also helped keep me going as I went through the stresses of life, including my husband's illness and death. Each of my former employers came to Ted's wake.

After two hip replacements, I finally quit working when I was 85.

Helen Bandyke is 92 years old. She has lived in Dearborn for 61 years. She has three children: Sylvia, Mary Hope and Martin. Her activities include volunteering at the Wayne County Library for the Blind and Physically Handicapped.

Grandpa Bill and Sister Deodata

By Jan Collins

During my high-school years at Sacred Heart School in Dearborn, I sometimes discussed with my favorite teacher what I'd like to do in the future. Although these were the days before the women's movement and I mostly dreamed about getting married and having children (four, I thought), Sister Deodata encouraged me to become a writer, like my mother's father. "You are true to your editorial heritage!" she once scribbled enthusiastically on the top of one of my history papers.

As it turned out, I did become a writer/editor/journalist – just like my grandfather. His name was William S. Mellus, but to me and my siblings, he was always "Grandpa Bill." Grandpa Bill, who dropped out of high school in the 10th or 11th grade, was an entrepreneur who loved the news business. After working for a few years at the Detroit News and another group of newspapers, in 1933 at the height of the Great Depression, he purchased a group of four weekly papers that served the downriver area. He was 30 years old.

Nicknamed "Wild Bill" and "Battling Bill," he loved to expose corrupt politicians and other bad guys. One of his most dangerous battles was against the Black Legion, a Ku Klux Klan-type of organization that in 1935 had an estimated 100,000 members in Michigan. Grandpa Bill exposed this cult of "hooded avengers and killers" and published the names of many of the local members (some of whom were prominent businessmen and attorneys, appointed officials and even police officers) on the front page. The Black Legion retaliated by putting out a contract on his life – twice. But the police chief, who was a friend of my grandfather's, thwarted the first plot; the second one went awry.

The Mellus Newspapers, with Grandpa Bill at the helm, won hundreds of local, state and national awards for editorial excellence over the years. I got to see the operation first-hand beginning in 1958 when I was 13 years old and needed a summer job. Happily, Grandpa Bill had one for me.

I worked in the Women's Department at first, where I wrote engagement, wedding and "society" stories. (Some years later, I even wrote up my own wedding.) Later I wrote for the Features Department and was a proof-reader, too. I spent many happy summers in the Mellus Newspapers building (a marvelous art deco edifice built in 1941) on Fort Street in Lincoln Park until I finished college and graduate school and moved to Ann Arbor with my new husband. And therein lies another Grandpa Bill story.

Soon after moving to Ann Arbor in 1967, I walked into the Ann Arbor News building and applied to be a reporter, giving my grandfather's name as a reference. After my interview, I rushed home and called Grandpa Bill, telling him he would probably hear soon from the Ann Arbor News editor. "Please give me a good reference, Grandpa," I implored, "and please don't tell him that I'm your granddaughter." Grandpa Bill did as he was requested, I was hired, and the editor was never the wiser.

Grandpa Bill sold his newspapers in 1969 and died 10 years later, a month before my second child was born. I worked as a reporter and columnist for daily newspapers in Michigan, South Carolina and North Carolina for 16 years until I became a writer and editor at the University of South Carolina. I retired from full-time work a few years ago, but still free-lance regularly for newspapers, magazines and other publications.

A painting of Grandpa Bill, his perpetual cigar clamped between his teeth as he taps on his typewriter, now hangs above the desk in my home office, where I write and remember Grandpa Bill – and Sister Deodata.

Jan Collins graduated from Sacred Heart High School in 1962. She lives in Columbia, South Carolina.

Are We the Worst Class You Ever Had?

By Patricia Gee

My career as an English teacher began at Lansing Sexton High School. Later I taught at Poughkeepsie High in New York. However, in the late 1960s, our family relocated to Michigan. For a time, I was a stay-at-home mom with three sons. After a while, I missed the students and applied for a substitute teaching position in Dearborn. Before long I was back in the classroom.

Upon seeing a sub, many students viewed my presence as a "day off" and sometimes asked, "Are we the worst class you ever had?"

My most memorable experience took place in Virginia Bissig's classroom at Edison Junior High. It was a lovely spring afternoon and all went well until the last period. Earlier, the sixth hour science class enjoyed an outdoor activity at a nearby pond. Students conducted scientific experiments with water samples and selected flora and fauna, too. The warm weather and freedom exhilarated the class.

The seventh-hour bell rang and the exuberant group entered the room. With them were 50 or more baby frogs. Students carried the amphibians in paper cups, purses, tin cans and even in their cupped hands. On the top floor our classroom windows raised up. Just in time, I looked to see the little frogs lined up on the wide sill. A couple of boys "flicked" them off—into oblivion. As one leaned out, the other asked, "Did they hit yet?" Frogs hopped everywhere! Following a brief lecture on animal cruelty, two volunteers gathered the survivors into a cardboard box and took them to the science lab.

Decorum ruled as we tackled the lesson plan. For about 15 minutes all went well. Suddenly a large black bird flew in the window. Low-hanging pendulum lights offered perfect swooping places for the bird. Chaos began immediately. The girls shrieked, "I'm not staying by that thing!" and ran for the door. As the intruder dived, flapped and squawked, the boys played "catch the bird." Finally the feathered friend retreated to a small interior room and managed to escape.

Again we returned to the work at hand. In a few minutes a gentle buzz sounded near the windows. Soon three or four sweat bees moved into the room. Screeching girls fled to the safety zone near the door. Other students swatted with their notebooks. In a minute, I turned out the lights and admonished the class, "Don't bother the bees and they won't bother you. They'll go to the outside light and be gone."

Before long, I heard an ominous buzzing near my ear. I pirouetted slowly and hoped the bee would find another spot. However, when I moved, it moved. A student sounded the alarm, "Teacher, there's another one," as he pointed to a bee flitting near my hemline. Without warning, the boy smacked my knee with the biggest binder imaginable and proclaimed, "I got him!"

All these years later, the memory of that day remains. The kids were great, but the frogs, the bird and the bees turned out to be unforgettable and maybe ... the worst class I ever had!

Patricia Gee is a retired Fordson High School English teacher. She is a longtime member of the Dearborn Genealogical Society.

The Denizens of the Deep

By William Hackett

There is an unwritten history of most institutions known and enjoyed by insiders. In the 1950s, when Henry Ford Community College was located on the upper floors of the Miller School on Lois Avenue in east Dearborn, there was time for great teaching, staff camaraderie and a little hilarity. The staff was a mixture of World War II GI Bill veterans and younger teachers. Some came from the high schools and some directly from colleges and universities. Hilarity and a little rebellion would be the description of the Denizens of the Deep. This story plays out with different personalities.

One of the players was Dean Eshleman, who was a very serious and excellent leader of the college. He worked under the leadership of the superintendent of schools and was a part of his cabinet. Other players were the smokers on the staff. They would regularly take their puffs in the basement furnace room. This was forbidden, but since smoking was so common, school officials looked the other way. It is the way of institutional bureaucracy to count things in the form of survey and forms to be filled out.

These missives came with increasing frequency from the dean's office. Some of these in their earnestness caused the denizens of the furnace room much merriment. They often filled out these forms anonymously and with silly answers. They further constructed a set of their own surveys, reports and forms and distributed them unsigned to faculty mail boxes. While this perplexed some faculty members, others were very amused. The dean was not amused and put out a bulletin stating that all transmissions to the faculty must be signed. Thus was born the Denizens of the Deep, which became the signature line of future bulletins emanating from the furnace room. Many of these, lost to the wastebasket, were very creative but caused the dean more consternation. Fortunately he let this tomfoolery run its course.

When the college moved to the Evergreen campus in the spring of 1962, the Denizens left their furnace room environs and varied their mischief to include awards such as the Golden Shovel Award – pile it higher and deeper – presented to new Ph.D.'s. A Rube Goldberg-type C-machine was a protest against grade inflation. It took a D grade, ran it though bells and whistles variously entitled "nice person" and "lots of potential" and out popped a C- grade.

The ultimate fun was the Arthur D. Thomas award. Thomas, one of the most revered faculty members, made a gaffe at a dedication ceremony, introducing the superintendent of schools, Dr. Stuart Openlander, as Dr. Stupid Openlander. The incident was institutionalized by the appearance in the College Catalogue 1973-75 under the title: Faculty Award, given to the faculty member "who has, during the course of the academic year, demonstrated to the satisfaction of his colleagues the qualities of daring, courage, and/or clarity of perception as evidenced in his public pronouncements." To the uninitiated the nice words hid the real intent, which was to announce the latest gaffe. A statue of a person with tongue hanging out and hand clenched at the throat was for a few years presented to honorees.

William Hackett is a retired Dearborn teacher of history at Edison Junior High School, Edsel Ford High School and for 30 years at Henry Ford Community College. He is a former member and chair of the Dearborn Historical Commission,

That's Life

By Bob Hansen

It was July 23, 1967, and I was 22 and in the Army National Guard. My unit was at the armory at Eight Mile Road and Evergreen. We were bored. We had lots of freedom. A group of guys and I told our commanding officer that we were going to get our 2 ¼-ton truck (aka Deuce and a Quarter) washed. Instead we went to my buddy's house, sat on the porch and drank beer. I often wonder what the neighbors thought about the Army truck on a residential street.

Eventually we meandered back to the armory. We saw all kinds of cop cars speeding down Eight Mile Road. When we arrived at the base, our commanding officer asked where we had been – there was a riot going on in Detroit. We mumbled our response.

Our commanding officer asked for volunteers to go to the center of the riot to protect the firefighters doing their job. There were no volunteers.

Ultimately, we went into Detroit. There were all kinds of shooting going on. It was like being in a war zone. I spent more time on the ground than on my feet. It was a scary time. Some of my buddies in the National Guard were cops, and they were eager to shoot. However, shooting was not possible – we had no bullets! And we could not shoot without the permission of our commanding officer.

For a while we were posted on Tireman. Mayor Hubbard, the old Marine, carried a shotgun and was ordering us to protect Dearborn.

The Red Cross was selling food to the National Guard at unreal costs. The Salvation Army gave it away. I don't make donations to the Red Cross.

Life Magazine published my picture during those riotous days. It took the editors three years to find out my name. There has to be a better way to get your picture in Life!

Bob Hansen retired from a tool-making career at General Motors. He now lives in Myrtle Beach, South Carolina, and spends his summers in Dearborn.

Fat Farm

By Gretchen Ackermann Moss

Sitting at my editorial desk opening mail, I read a request for a story from a business called the Fat Farm. What is a Fat Farm? Why did I receive this letter in Dearborn from a business in Illinois? It didn't take long to figure out. I was an editor of lifestyles pages, and the Fat Farm people were seeking publicity to no doubt build their business.

Why call it a Fat Farm? Time spent at a farm could mean indulging in rich food, lots of creamy meals and no worry or concern about the number of calories consumed. What popped into my mind was cousin Earl's appetite on the farm. He liked rich food and his mother-in-law's cooking on the family farm in Davison, Michigan. He could devour a cake for dessert all by himself, topped with loads of whipped cream.

I read on and became more interested. Many business and professional women took time off to spend a week at the Fat Farm to indulge in exercise and eat fat-free meals to both get in shape and lose weight. Many of the women enrolled at the farm were business women from the Chicago area. The Fat Farm was located about 80 miles directly south of the windy city in Gilman, Illinois. The Fat Farm coordinator suggested that I invite a Dearborn woman to attend a free four-day retreat. The candidate did not necessarily have to be overweight, but be energetic and someone who would welcome the experience.

I thought immediately of Dearborn resident Pat Meredith, a good sport who would allow me to write about her and join me in exploring a Fat Farm.

Mrs. Meredith said yes. So we packed our leotards, bathing suits and warm clothes for our outdoor hikes in the early morning. I volunteered to drive to Gilman, found it on the map and accepted the invitation.

It has been several years since our visit to the Fat Farm, but it was one experience we will never forget. It was a cold November day when we arrived at the farm. It was an old white frame farm house on a country road. Not much else around but snow-covered corn fields.

We checked in and found our room on the second floor. It was a small, simply decorated room with two beds; we quickly noticed the absence of a telephone, radio or television. We changed into our leotards and headed for the exercise class already in progress. All the participants were wearing pale pink leotards issued to them when they checked in at the beginning of the week. We were latecomers taking advantage of our four-day stay. We stood out in the crowd, Pat in bright green and yellow and me in black-and-red stripes. Many of the participants must have wondered who we were and why were we there.

We spent the next three days trying to enjoy all of the classes. Our meals consisted of very small portions–all very bland, but definitely nutritional. I took a picture for future reference: Three or four bits of food the size of walnuts comprised the evening entree. We were weighed and measured from head to toe and told that we were on a special diet to lose weight and firm up our muscles. Not a truer word was spoken. OK, it sounded good, but could we both survive the test? Pat was close to becoming ill after the first 10 hours. I tried to comfort her. I even raided the refrigerator one night to please her and made sure she drank plenty of liquid. I didn't get caught late at night surveying the huge refrigerator. I tiptoed down the steps.

We overslept the first morning, and by the time we dressed for the brisk morning walk and were ready to go on a hike, we met the class members returning to the farmhouse. We did better at keeping in step with the other exercises and swim classes. Every evening we attended lectures on keeping fit.

We both agreed it was a unique challenging experience and perhaps worth our time and effort. On the way home, we stopped in Benton Harbor at Schuler's restaurant to reward ourselves with a big meal. We were seated at a table for two next to a roaring fireplace. We ordered from the menu, something mouthwatering. When the food arrived, we glanced down at our plates and found a complete meal, unlike we had seen in four days. Neither of us could eat the normal portions. We had shrunk our stomachs!

It was a stormy ride home on snowy I-94, but we both felt good about losing weight. Pat could again fit into her size 6 dresses and me in size 10. That was our earned reward.

We now know what a Fat Farm is and how it is run, similar to a boot camp with regulations and strict time schedules.

Gretchen Ackermann Moss is a member of the Dearborn Historical Commission. She has three sons. Brian Ackermann is a chiropractor. Bradley Ackermann is a fellow at Eli Lilly. Jeffrey Ackermann is the director of energy for the state of Colorado.

Odd Jobs

By L. Glenn O'Kray

My first job was selling eggs to our neighbors with my older brother, Dan. Unfortunately, Florence West, a neighbor, found a dead chick smiling at her when she cracked open one of our eggs. My mom told us that we had to examine each egg with a candle to make sure that no baby chick was inside. (Serve no eggs after their time.) I remember being excited as Easter approached – we could then sell a ton of eggs for our customers to decorate. The egg distributor gave us nothing but brown eggs that week! My interest in private enterprise faltered a bit.

Dan and I then had a Detroit Shopping News route. I had a rough time handling all the papers on my bike, so Dan delivered the papers. I didn't know how to fold the papers. Darned if I remember what I did in that partnership!

The Detroit News route with Dan came next. It was a pretty good time. Christmas showed the generosity of our customers. On my collecting from my first customer in the third week of December, I was offered a $1 tip. I refused to accept it – I thought that was too darned much. Fat chance of that happening today!

Ultimately, I bought my own route. It grew from 35 customers to about 100. I delivered papers on the first three streets of the northeast quadrant of Ford and Outer Drive. There was a chicken farm on Outer Drive. I well remember having to hold my breath as I rode my bike by the feces-laden chicken coops. In retrospect, I think that I learned a lot about myself. I found out that I was in the business less for the money than for the social aspects of my route. Lonely housewives would frequently bring me into their kitchens to have a cookie or two and chat. And not only were there feathered chicks, there were also teen-aged chicks that I had on my route as well!

I worked for the Detroit News station manager, Dale Yokum. I was a station captain and got to hand out papers to news carriers. I made much less than I had as a paper boy. But the idea of being "part of management" had to be a misguided turn-on. I remember Yokum's taking me and a couple of other station captains out to dinner one night. He told us how good the management experience was. I am embarrassed to say that I couldn't stop laughing like a hyena on nitrous oxide.

I worked as an usher at the Fox Theater in the summer of 1960. I think my shift began at 4:30. That was the end of my social life. I got paid 65 cents an hour. If I forgot my lunch, whatever I earned paid for my meal. I had to take a bus down to Washington Boulevard and walk to the "Ox"; as a snotty nosed teen-ager, I thought that this moniker was much more appropriate for a place that provided me with the most boring job in the history of mankind.

When I was attending the University of Detroit, I was a breakfast cook, a dishwasher and then a head waiter at Marygrove College. One day the boss of the food service that ran the operation told me that I was spending too much time cleaning greasy cookie sheets. "Just rinse them off," he ordered. A couple of weeks later a group of Marygrove coeds stole a cookie sheet weighed down with cherry cobbler. They ate all of the baked goods and came down with a good case of the runs.

My other jobs included being a telephone operator for a health club (where I had to cover for a guy running around on his wife), being a cashier at Federal's (cut into my social life), driving a cab (loved it), loading box cars (midnights–wrong time of day), typing up sports stats for the University of Detroit (loved it).

I had a love-hate with the experiences of the many crazy jobs I had during my youth. They had so many terrible aspects to them that I told myself, "I can't do this all my life. I have to finish college," and I did.

L. Glenn O'Kray is the vice chair of the Dearborn Historical Commission. For 30 years he was the director of financial aid at Henry Ford Community College and is currently an adjunct instructor. He and his wife, Jane, have been married for 47 years.

His Dream Job Was Only the Start

By Lutz Reiter

I was born in Berlin during World War II. After our apartment was bombed out in 1943, we were evacuated toward the eastern border of Germany. In 1945 we were evacuated toward the Dutch border. Finally my family ended up in Cologne.

In 1959 I attained my apprenticeship in electrical engineering. To further my education, I took advantage of an opportunity as a maintenance electrician with Ford Motor Company Cologne in industrial electronics.

Ford educated its best electricians in a special course to learn power electronic repair. After working at Ford, I studied full time for my associate degree in industrial electronics.

In 1966 the Braun Company in Frankfurt offered me a position on a development team designing and building optical pyrometers for industrial use.

My goal was always to work in the United States, Canada or Australia in my profession. To accomplish this I needed to have a good understanding and working knowledge of technical English. Frankfurt and Birmingham, England, offered a six-month exchange program for people to work in their profession in England. Because of high unemployment in England in 1968, participants' incomes were very limited. In my case, that meant I would earn 60 percent less than my salary at Braun. People said I was crazy to consider this, but in my mind, it was worth it to learn technical English.

The University of Birmingham in England needed a

technician to implement ideas into practical solutions for electrical arch controls. The professor leading a team of four Ph.D. students made it possible for me to work an additional six months. Three months later he said, "I will become department head at the University of Windsor in Canada. These four Ph.D. students can't finish here, so they will have to come with me. You have solved several of our practical problems, and therefore I invite you to come with us to Windsor." That was my dream.

The University of Windsor sent me a contract and paid for my trip. In New York harbor I was fittingly greeted by the Statue of Liberty. I celebrated the Fourth of July 1969 in New York, then took a Greyhound bus to Niagara Falls and to Windsor. On this bus trip I met Dorothy Wolfe, a Dearborn High School teacher. She was to eventually introduce me to my future wife.

The University of Windsor employed me as a senior technician in the electrical engineering department, repairing general and sophisticated instruments used in teaching and research. Also I was in charge of the operation and safety of the high voltage lab, which had a million-volt electronic generator.

Shortly after my arrival in Windsor, machine shop owners noticed my ability to repair their German and other European precision machines. This side job grew steadily due to word of mouth. After many years working at the university, I established my own company in Dearborn, Industrial Electronic Services, in which I worked for 29 years.

In 1974 my wife and I bought a home in Dearborn, where we raised two girls and two boys. All attended Dearborn High School, and then all were college-educated.

They will continue my dream.

Lutz Reiter has two daughters who are teachers, one in Northville and the other in Bloomfield Hills. He has a son who is a buyer for a large automotive company and another who is a Dearborn firefighter.

Tales From Hitsville U.S.A.: The Honkie and the Diva

By Douglas A. Warren

In late 1963 I received a call from a friend who had been working for Barry Gordy at Motown Records/Hitsville U.S.A. He was moving up to disc recording engineer, cutting the master discs from which the vinyls would be pressed. He asked me, "How'd you like to work here as purchasing agent?" Of course I said, "Yes!"

What a unique phenomenon it was. When I began, employees were about 50-50 black/white. We all got along extremely well, and it was truly a Motown Family. We all even called it that!

My favorite at Motown was Marvin Gaye, definitely the most kind, thoughtful and affable individual there. The second would have to be Smokey Robinson, as he also was always most humble and kind to everyone. Virtually everyone realized their unique and fascinating capacities at the fast-growing, high-potential organization that Motown was. I should not leave out Barry Gordy himself. Even though he ruled the roost with whipsaw determination, he was always well respected, as well as feared.

A short time after beginning my employment there, I was asked, "How would you like to go out with Diana Ross?" Being a "honkie" from Dearborn, I had some reservations about the matter. You must realize that in '64 the racial climate (at least as far as I could determine at a very inexperienced 21) did not seem to be nearly as open as it is today. Therefore I declined and of course could kick myself today for not taking advantage of that opportunity. Also at that time the Supremes were just beginning their illustrious singing careers, and the word "diva" was virtually unheard.

One thing that I did do though (as the Motown Family reverently always pushed black/white interactions) was attend a "purchasing event" with Mary Wilson, also then a Supreme, for those who are not Motown aficionados. We both visited a Dodge dealership on West Grand Boulevard, just down the road a piece from Hitsville U.S.A. We purchased a white '63 Dodge 330 station wagon for the Temptations to travel to their various gigs in and around Detroit. Mary Wilson was surely the most affable of the Supremes.

I invited my friend Dave Gorden to the '63 Motown Christmas party, which he still remembers better than I do.

Stevie Wonder, as you would no doubt imagine, was quite a unique and talented individual, but he was also surprisingly happy. He's probably the only Motown person who might still remember me from those golden days. He had an excellent memory, but in addition I used to do (and still do) a quasi-accurate, quasi-memorable Bela Lugosi imitation: "My name is Count Dracula, and I'm going to bite your neck!" Stevie loved it! I used to spend lots of time with him around Hitsville. In between his recording sessions, he'd often come into my office. I was not exactly babysitting (as he was 13 years old then), but kind of watching over him.

Not overly empathetic to his blindness, some of his fellow entertainers used to place objects directly in front of him so he would bump into them! He had an uncanny (almost radar/echo-sounding) way of sizing up a room, so they'd purposely change the room around in an attempt to fake him out. I found little humor in this, but he'd just laugh it off and have a great old time.

I left the Motown Family in '64 for reasons upon which I will not elaborate. After that, the city of Dearborn continued to play a significant role in my life.

Even though I moved many times in Dearborn between 1958 and 1975, I appreciated the fine living conditions and environment, friendships made, secondary educational experiences and of course all the fond memories. Go for it, gang!

Douglas A. Warren retired from teaching in the Livonia Public Schools. After years of surfing, Doug had his knees replaced. He and his wife, Lynda, reside in Commerce Township.

The Price of Safe Streets

By Karen Wisniewski

About 1920, the villages of Springwells and Dearborn had a combined population of 5,000. But thanks to Henry Ford's building of the Rouge Steel plant, the combined number of people living in these two communities soared to 50,000.

Springwells and Dearborn each hired a police chief and several police officers. In Springwells, so close to Detroit, and especially because this was during Prohibition, trafficking in illegal liquor was rampant. It seemed everyone was getting a piece of the moonshine profits, from little old ladies making booze in their bathtubs to entire families brewing it in their attics and in the backs of their family-run storefronts. With the constant hustle of workers coming in and out of the city for every shift at the steel plant, the Springwells police had their work cut out for them. The steel plant wasn't the only huge industry in the area, as other auto factories and brickyards employed thousands of workers as well. Large, two and three generational families lived in homes built on narrow lots, and the larger farms were subdivided and built on. The Springwells Police Department had over 60 guys handling crimes involving pickpockets, prostitutes, armed robbers, burglars and drunk-and-disorderly arrests.

Over in the quiet town of Dearborn, where there were only about 14 officers, it was mostly traffic problems, petty theft calls, domestic troubles, vagrants, escapees from Eloise Hospital and criminals on the lam from Springwells that kept these officers busy.

When the two towns merged in 1929, the police departments merged as well. In no small measure due to Henry Ford, the two parts of the unified new city were booming. But after Prohibition came the Depression, and the hard times seemed endless. Dearborn recovered as the nation recovered. The police department ranks swelled as the population swelled. Dearborn was a desirable place to live, work and visit.

From Dearborn's beginnings in 1920, safe streets and secure neighborhoods come with a price. Four officers made the ultimate sacrifice. Here are their stories. Within the borders of Dearborn are four very special locations where these officers fell. I think people should always remember them.

From 1926 to 1928, Springwells was named Fordson. In August 1928, Fordson Patrolman Cecil Spencer was in pursuit of a tire thief on Warren Avenue. He maneuvered his motorcycle to pass a slow-moving truck on the left when that truck suddenly turned left and Spencer crashed into it. He lay dying on Warren Avenue near Kingsley as citizens came to his aid and moved him from the street to the grassy boulevard. Two hours later he was pronounced dead at the hospital. Spencer was 28 years old, married with two children.

Patrolman Andrew Cain was directing traffic on Schaefer Road in December 1939. Traffic was heavy as last-minute Christmas shoppers were pouring in and out of Montgomery Ward. A speeding car struck Cain as he stood in the roadway. He never stood a chance of getting out of the way. Fire and Police Department personnel rushed to his aid from City Hall, but he was dead before he reached the hospital. Cain, 42, was married with six children.

Police Lieutenant Lou Hinkel was shot to death on Robertson Street in August 1974. Callers reported an enraged man waving a rifle around. Hinkel convinced the man to come out of the house, but he came with his gun. Hinkel felt he could talk to the man and get him to put his gun down, but when Hinkel stepped from cover, the gunman shot him down. Hinkel, 51 years old, was married with one child.

Corporal Norbert Szczygiel was working undercover in August 1977, and with his partner had responded to a bar on Schaefer Road. There were calls of a man with a gun inside the bar, but then the man walked out on his own and began indiscriminately firing at responding officers. As the uniform officers scrambled for cover and returned fire, the gunman also took cover and continued firing sporadically. Szczygiel stayed in his unmarked vehicle in communication with the dispatcher, warning other officers who may be approaching. When the gunman was finally apprehended, a tragic discovery was made in all the commotion–Szczygiel had taken a shot to the head and lay unconscious in the car. He died three days later. Norbert Szczygiel was 29 years old, married with two children.

I was born and raised in Dearborn and was proud to be a Dearborn police officer, but nothing made me more proud of my department's history than the legacy of these four special men who gave their lives in the performance of their duties.

Karen Wisniewski is married to Michael Ball. She has a daughter, Caroline Mrowka. She retired after 25 years with the police department. Her final rank was detective sergeant. She spends as much time with family as possible, connecting with nieces and nephews and making many visits to cousins in Poland. She loves volunteering and doing research at the Dearborn Historical Museum.

Chapter 13

Businesses

Latte in Hand, Hooked on Michigan Avenue

By Cornelia T. Bradford

There are clearly two equally valid opinions about $3.50 lattes: It is insane to spend that much money on what is, after all, just coffee; or having one's cappuccinos, lattes and chai frappuccinos boosts the economy, fends off isolation by socialization and thus makes the soul feel good. I, for one, a self-proclaimed street café addict, got hooked on stopping at the Starbucks on Michigan Avenue in west Dearborn, getting my latte and watching the world go by.

The 20-year-olds among the patrons may not remember that some Dearborn ladies used to have their coffee in fine china cups in the restaurant of the elegant Jacobson's department store, once, before changing times and demands gave Michigan Avenue a more modern, outdoor facelift. I wish that there had been room for both—room for the old-world charm, service and quality Jacobson's seemed to provide and room for the equally, yet, differently attractive, contemporary "internet café" and other chains.

The death of the little bookshops was analyzed and portrayed in movies, books and papers by people more qualified to do so than I. Mourning the closing of the Little Professor on Michigan Avenue, its owner's and employees' friendly advice and the convenient access to the variety of international papers and magazines the store had in stock made me realize that the losses of my generation are comparable to the losses of the generation who wondered if they could afford keeping their horses when they ordered their first Tin Lizzy.

I will not be around when Dearbornites, who have been known around the world as proud Ford people for a century, will have to decide whether they can keep the car and still afford the recommended use of the public transit/people mover ticket. I hope God will allow me to watch from above, latte in my hand.

Cornelia T. Bradford has lived in Dearborn since 1993. She took up writing as a hobby when teaching had become too strenuous.

Cloudy Weather For the Fairlane Club

By Bruce Chambers

Although Dearborn had a wonderful public parks program, including Camp Dearborn, the increasingly popular sport of tennis was confined to the school or public courts or the YMCA's courts, weather permitting, but definitely not in the winter.

In about 1967 a group of 50 players put up $1,000 each and approached the city of Inkster with a plan to build a tennis complex. Their proposal was denied, and the monies were returned.

At this time the Ford Motor Company owned a considerable amount of undeveloped land in Dearborn. The company was approached and agreed to lease the necessary property, recognizing the future value of an upscale tennis-swim-social club. It was to be named the Fairlane Club after Henry Ford's home.

Through the shrewd business acumen and contacts of Walter Roney and others, the necessary funding was procured and the elegant upscale tennis-athletic-social club was completed in 1976.

It originally included 10 outdoor clay and eight indoor tennis courts, four indoor racquet/handball courts, one large, sunken, L-shaped outdoor pool with adjacent bar and grill and one indoor lap pool with whirlpool and sauna, two bowling alleys and a billiard parlor.

Complementing facilities included massage, barber and

beauty shops, laundry service, ample male and female locker rooms.

In keeping with the changing times, two indoor tennis courts, the billiards room and bowling alley were replaced with a basketball court and a large, extensive, weight equipment room with a circular track and separate rooms for classes such as yoga.

Food and social areas included and remain today: several meeting rooms, a library, a beautiful large ballroom off the attractive entrance lounge plus the Oak Room initially overlooking the indoor tennis courts. They have all been used by the club and as rentals.

For years the Fairlane Club was the outstanding social/racquet facility in the lower Detroit area. The courts were filled day and night in every season. Male and female tennis teams competed with other tennis clubs. There was an interactive club swim team. Friday night couples tennis/bridge was so popular that it was difficult getting in.

The facilities attracted notables such as comedian Bill Cosby, tennis pros Billie Jean King and Jimmy Conners, Detroit Mayor Dave Bing and Ford Motor CEO Alan Mulally.

When the auto industry declined, so did the membership. Also, numerous "successful" members have emigrated from the Dearborn area; others have succumbed to the aging factor. Currently the new ownership is working very hard to restore the club to its former "glory" days. It remains a beautiful facility.

For us remaining originals, it continues to be a significant part of our lives. Come and join us.

Bruce Chambers is a retired Fordson High School teacher and supervisor.

Yesterday's Downtown

By Georgia Terns Clark

The summer that I was 10 years old, my dad decided it was time for me to do the weekly grocery shopping. I was the oldest of seven children, and my dad worked two jobs. He had taken me grocery shopping with him in the past, and I knew the people at the A&P store on Michigan Avenue. There was John the butcher and Julie and Irene, who were cashiers, as well as Kathy, who worked in the meat department and other areas of the store.

My dad taught me how to check the hams for the ones that had the least amount of fat and how to find out if a chicken was a young fryer or an old stewing hen. My dad was paid every two weeks, and I would take his check over to the A&P and get it cashed. I would then do the shopping, using the list that my mother and I made up for the trip.

When I was finished, we would load the groceries into the wagon that my brother Woody and his friend (and our neighbor) Doug Baker brought to the store. The wagon belonged to Doug, but, as with a lot of Doug's toys, it somehow found a home in our garage. The weekly shopping was always supplemented by bicycle trips to the A&P for more milk, bread, meat, etc. during the week. If I didn't have enough cash to cover the purchases, then Julie or Irene would let me bring the difference in the next time I was in the store.

For shampoo, aspirin, birthday cards, make-up and other items, we shopped at the M&M Drug Store on the corner of

Michigan and Military right next to the A&P. The pharmacist (and he may have been the owner) was named John. M&M's also sold candy, ice cream, comic books and had a lunch counter where one could get a light meal or just a Coke or Vernors. The small drinks cost 5 cents, and for a penny more, one could have a cherry or lemon or chocolate flavoring added. When I was in either seventh or eighth grade, there was a special once a week when one could get an ice-cream soda for 10 cents; they were normally 20 cents. A couple of people who frequented the lunch counter on a regular basis were Randy, who worked at the barber shop on Military, and Jerry, who delivered newspapers he kept in a large bag with a strap that went over his shoulder.

Next to A&P on the west side was Zolkower's Department Store, which carried clothing and yard goods. There was an open field and then the Wrigley's Supermarket, where my girlfriend's family shopped. I remember going there on Fridays with my friend Betty Nichols when there were samples of foodstuffs and not being able to eat most of them because they were meat products and we couldn't eat meat on Friday.

In later years the A&P moved south of its location to Mechanic Street, now Newman. M&M would become the Otis Jones Drug Store, then a florist shop where my sister Peggy worked and later a bridal shop where I bought my wedding gown. The last time I was in the area, the building, as well as the barbershop, had been demolished and a new structure put in place.

Across Michigan was Sacred Heart Church, the priests' rectory and the school our family attended. West of Sacred Heart was the Howe-Peterson Funeral Home, where most of the funerals that I attended were held, including my mother's and my father's.

For pizza, there was Angelo's on the southwest corner of Michigan Avenue and Haigh. I cannot remember if there was any seating in the place, but you could see the cook making pizzas.

Later Angelo's would move down the street to a larger building, and the old store would become Bill's Party Store, which sold pop and beer.

Across from Angelo's was what we called the Haigh mansion, which was situated on a large parcel of land. It was later sold, with the IBM building occupying the southeast corner of the lot. Mr. Haigh would walk through our neighborhood with his collies, one of which got in a fight with our cocker spaniel.

Past the Haigh place was St. Joseph's Retreat, a mental hospital run by the Daughters of Charity. Their habit included a large winged headpiece somewhat like the one worn by Sally Field in *The Flying Nun* TV series. The nuns would walk through our neighborhood, and we became friends with Sister Agnes. We would visit her at the hospital, and she would show us around, generally offering us ice cream, which was kept in a large freezer with a lock on it.

On the northeast corner of Michigan and Military, I seem to remember a gas station kitty-corner from M&M's next to Muirhead's. We would ride our bikes up there and stop to get a Coke out of the dispenser for a nickel.

Going east on the north side of Michigan Avenue past Muirhead's, there was a car dealership, which sold either Kaiser-Frazer or Hudson cars, the ballet school where my sister Teri would take dance lessons for years and the Dearborn Music Shop, which later would move to the old Kinsel Drug Store on Michigan at Monroe. In the glass windows of the music store would be displayed the new records–I remember mainly looking for the latest Elvis Presley or Ricky Nelson release.

Across the street was Lim's Gardens, where one could get Chinese food as well as American food. Frutchey's Dry Cleaners, where we would get our wool school uniforms dry-cleaned, and the

Daly Furniture store were east of Lim's.

Going further east on Michigan Avenue, at the corner of Howard, was another drugstore that had two large apothecary jars, one filled with a red liquid and the other with a green liquid. I remember the Calvin Theater having a sign on the front saying something like, "It's cool inside," since it was one of the few air-conditioned businesses in the area. At the Calvin, one could go to the movies on a Saturday afternoon for 25 cents, see two movies and a lot of cartoons. During the summer, it also had a Wednesday afternoon matinee.

The main Dearborn library at that time was on the corner of Michigan Avenue and Mason, where I spent a lot of time. It was divided into two sections on the main floor–books for children and then the adult section. I remember wondering if I would be challenged about going into the adult section when I finally did about age 13 or 14. Upstairs was the reference department. In front of the library was a drinking fountain.

Between Mason and Monroe were quite a few shops including two dime stores, Neisner's and Kresge's, which were side by side; Kinsel and Cunningham drug stores, which faced each other on the north and south corners of Michigan and Monroe; and several clothing stores, Albert's, Zuiebach's, Winkelman's, Price's.

We lived two blocks north of Michigan Avenue, and so, within an area of less than a mile walking distance each way, there were many places to shop and just hang out with one's friends.

Sometimes we would take a bus to east Dearborn to shop at Montgomery Ward's, aka Monkey Wards, and the Federal Department Store at Michigan and Schaefer Road. Buses seemed to run every 10-20 minutes on Michigan Avenue.

Most of these memories are from when I was young and

did not have a driver's license. Once I reached 16 and got a license, I did not walk as much. I miss the fact that I now live in Livonia, a city that does not have a downtown area, and that my kids did not have the same experiences that I did. With the exception of the school bus, they have never taken a bus anywhere or had the option of walking to a variety of stores; instead, they pretty much had to be driven everywhere.

Georgia Terns Clark and her husband, Bruce, have lived in Livonia for 34 years. They have two children and are expecting their second grandchild.

Smoke Gets in Your Eyes

By Jim Clark

Back in the 1950s and early 1960s, independent neighborhood grocery and drug stores were the norm. West Dearbornites might recall Jason's, Sutton's and Rooney's/Greco's drug stores and markets such as Lane's, Toit's and the Dearborn Public Market.

One of the lesser-remembered markets was Koze-Kold-Kuts, a small, cinderblock outfit located on Telegraph between Wilson and Sheridan, really more of a party store than a grocery. (This was well before Telegraph was made into a divided roadway.) But for those of us in that neck of the woods, it was the perfect place to go for an impressive selection of penny candy and a quarter-pound of garlic baloney.

The owner of the place was a large, gruff man who usually sported a week's worth of stubble on his face. He was always there, behind the counter in a wrinkled and stained white apron, keeping an eye on the legions of kids who entered and stood before the candy counter, trying to decide if they wanted some of those gummy green spearmint leaves or a roll of licorice, the black kind with the little red ball of candy in the middle.

I don't ever recall seeing "Mr. Koze" without a big, fat cigar in his mouth. As a kid, it was an imposing sight, and the pungent cigar smoke was, at the same time, somehow exotic and repulsive. He seemed to always blow the smoke into your face as you conducted business at the cash register.

Of course, all of this was seen through the eyes of an impressionable little kid, with things seeming bigger and more dramatic than they really were. That said, the fact remains that the guy's cigar smoke was intentionally expelled into the faces of many customers. There was no malice intended, I'm sure, probably just a way for the guy to have a little fun. We chuckled about it more than anything.

But one day, as the story goes, one of the older teen-agers in the area had had enough of the smoke-in-the-face routine. What happened next is good old Dearborn lore, but I expect it's true, knowing how irascible some of the kids could be. Ripping off the cover of his own pack of matches, the kid placed it on his palm to protect his skin, and then proceeded to take his hand and crush the cigar right back into the store owner's face, running out of the store after the audacious act.

Word around town was that the store owner just laughed off the "attack" and then immediately fired up another stogie.

I don't know if the teen's stand of defiance ended the rude smoke-blowing behavior for others, but I recall being subjected again the next time I went to the store for a Mason's root beer and a bag of New Era potato chips. The store owner also tossed a couple free Mary Jane's into my bag, so maybe he was an OK guy after all. Maybe.

Jim Clark was born and raised in Dearborn. He attended Clark Elementary, Bryant Junior High and Dearborn High School. He graduated from Eastern Michigan University. He is retired from a writing career and now lives in northern Michigan, where he continues to do periodic free-lance writing.

The Last Nail

By Hank Czerwick

By the time this gets published, the old girl will have been razed, and the bulldozer and wrecking ball will have moved on to their next victim. I'm writing about the business fronts and residence at 4850 and 4854 Greenfield. This was the location of my Aunt Gene's ladies store and my Uncle Joe's real estate and builder's office. In the back, and an integral part of this building, was their home, a two-family affair. No one had lived there since their respective deaths in the 1970s, but their son, Joe Jr., used the place as a warehouse for his electrician's business until his passing a few years ago.

Not many passers-by realize that the stretch along Greenfield from Michigan Avenue north to Mr. Ford's farm (now the Henry Ford Village retirement community) was predominantly residential. It consisted of many free-standing homes mixed in with those having business fronts similar to my aunt and uncle's. Most of them are gone and only two or three remain to be seen. One by one they have been replaced by the business-only establishments that line Greenfield today.

The buildings, a tall hedge and fruit trees shielded the wonders of the private space behind 4854/4850 Greenfield, as I'm sure it did at other addresses along the way. Here there was a huge garden, burgeoning each fall, with fresh vegetables to be picked and shared with family. I was told that my cousin Joe sold some of its surplus on the sidewalk out in front. There were the aforementioned fruit trees and their bountiful harvest that was surely added to the sidewalk sale. A variety of out-buildings provided for much exploration during family visits. There were rabbit hutches and a chicken coop. There were storage buildings, as well as my cousin's hobby shop, where he built models of ships, race cars and a variety of World War II vehicles – he let me play with most of them. There were flower beds and arbors and rhubarb (allegedly from Mr. Ford's farm) and rustic furniture upon which to sit and observe this tranquil and private space.

In the huge three-stall garage, my uncle kept his car, a 1941 Pontiac, and his 1946 three-quarter-ton Ford pickup truck. It was one of the first delivered after the war and was black with a cream-colored grille, matching wheels and pin-striping. He kept it under a cover when he was not out inspecting his various building sites. It continued to look very new for many years after.

In the back was also a small pool for summer dipping. One winter, as a child, I forgot that the pool was there and decided to run over its slightly frozen, snow-covered surface. The results were predictable – and I fell in! That resulted in one of my worst memories at 4854/4850 Greenfield. My Aunt Gene put me in a tub of hot water and made me drink hot milk with butter melted in it. Yuuuukkkhh!!! To this day I cannot stand hot milk or the smell of melting butter.

The business fronts are collapsing, but the garage still stands, as do the rotting, tilted out-buildings. The cement pool is still there. And the infamous tub is still in its place. I have salvaged two of the doors and installed them in my own home as a memento of the soon-to-be-demolished site of these memories. The first nail to be driven in the construction of 4854/4850 Greenfield will soon become its last.

Hank Czerwick is a longtime resident of Dearborn. He is a retired Ford engineer as well as a retired Henry Ford Community College instructor. He is a former member of the Dearborn Historical Commission.

From 'Honeymoon Salad' To a Meat Market Marriage

By Karen Faaleolea

The smell of a meat market is something you never forget. It wasn't a bad smell, just one you'd expect in a market that sold lots of meat. It was four long counters filled with everything you could think of when it comes to the protein part of a meal.

In the back room, where the meat cutters worked, saws buzzed over a wooden floor that was covered with sawdust. This helped to keep the floor from getting too slippery. There was a large walk-in cooler where sides of beef with purple inspection stamps were aged to tenderness. Every item was trimmed by hand, catering to the customers that lived nearby in Dearborn Hills. Accounts were kept and deliveries brought right to people's homes.

This store of the 1950s and 1960s was located at the northeast corner of Michigan Avenue and Telegraph. The alley ran behind the building and still connects to the ramp to northbound Telegraph. Apartments, now condos, stand behind that on the hill, and beyond those is the Rouge River. I have to mention the river because it was the home to some really colossal rats that benefited from the fact that dumpsters hadn't been invented yet. Anyone in the alley during the quiet hours of the day or night would have been astounded at the size of those well-fed rodents.

I bring all this up because I often look around Dearborn and think about how the city was when I was growing up and how different it is now. History just seems to ooze out of the corners without being asked.

With the passing decades, the entrance to that market has morphed into the green-awning-covered entrance to a German restaurant. The restaurant, once called Hoppe's, occupied just the building on the west side of the market, seating only about 50 patrons.

Both Mr. Zalman and Mr. Hoppe were hard-working businessmen. Today I think the word "workaholic" would apply to each man. Long hours were spent at their respective stores, and both men prospered. Mr. Hoppe got some of the meats he needed from Zalman's market. In turn, Mr. Zalman would stop in the restaurant for a quick bite. The "honeymoon salad," he would say with a laugh, "lettuce alone."

Early in the 1970s both men passed away. Each made his exit in a memorable way. Mr. Zalman personally drove himself to Oakwood Hospital while suffering a heart attack. He survived the attack, recovered somewhat, but did not live long after that. It is said that Mr. Hoppe died on an airplane while going home to his native Austria for a visit.

As far as the business is concerned, a new owner bought Hoppe's and continues to operate it as a German restaurant named Richter's. He was able to expand into the space that was once Zalman's Prime Meats. Today's customers enter the German restaurant through that very same door. All this leaves me wondering why the places of the past just won't "lettuce alone."

Karen Faaleolea is a lifelong Dearborn resident who is a historical presenter at Greenfield Village.

Our Prescription for Success

By John Krasity

I was born in New Jersey but moved to the east side of Detroit when I was a child. I was 18 when I was drafted in 1945. I was shipped to Yokohama, Japan. Initially I was with the 142nd Ordnance Battalion, which dealt with automotive maintenance. My most significant memory of Japan was seeing Hiroshima. There was almost nothing left there.

When I returned to the United States, I was assigned to a cavalry unit in Ft. Riley, Kansas. I suspect that was because I knew how to ride a horse. I was a noncommissioned officer and worked as a radio operator.

When I left the service, I attended Wayne University, later to become Wayne State University. I enrolled in the pharmacy program. I was the editor of Pharmic, a magazine for pharmacy students. That's where I met my wife, who was also a pharmacy student.

Initially we didn't hit it off all that well. We were always having arguments about the content of the magazine. Our first date was to discuss the budget. On that date we had an argument about the finances of the publication. While we were funded by the university, the money was never adequate. I thought that we should sell more magazines. I won the argument because I was the editor. However, she won the long-term argument after we got married. She decided everything – where we were going to live, our furniture – just everything! We had an argument over buying a grandfather clock. Ultimately we bought one that I still have today, and we bought one for each of our four children.

Our first house was near Whitmore-Bolles School. When we bought our first home, my parents decided to move to Florida and open a restaurant. Well, the business went belly up. One day my dad knocked on my door and asked if he and my mom could stay with us for a while. Of course I agreed to that. My 4- year-old daughter objected when it became apparent that she would lose her bedroom. She was and is quite stubborn. My parents ended up staying some three years. There was a 1942 movie entitled *The Man Who Came to Dinner* that pretty much summed up our situation. My family and I joke about that to this day.

My folks ended up buying a house near ours. We had a swimming pool, and my parents seemed pleased to sit by it and watch our kids while my wife and I worked.

After that we moved to Dearborn Heights. My wife and I raised our four kids there. Kathy was the oldest; she is a retired school teacher. Then came Joan, who got a degree in business but decided to stay at home. Then came Eric, who manages our pharmaceutical equipment business. Then came Kenneth, who is an attorney.

My wife and I started the Fordson Pharmacy on Michigan Avenue. When we set up the business, we didn't have much money. My wife's parents helped us get going. I built the furnishings for the shop. They are still in use today. One day my dad sat in the pharmacy and counted the number of customers we had per hour, and that was seven. He said that we would not be successful. However, we proved him wrong. We sold the business after 10 years and made a hefty profit.

My wife and I set up a business to sell to doctors, then hospitals. We started that business on Grindley Park. We outgrew that and moved to 2020 N. Telegraph. We now have a 17,000-square-foot facility. The magazine that my wife and I worked on for Wayne University turned out to be a great apprenticeship for developing a catalog for our business. While my older son now runs the business, I still am active in it.

I have been active in the Kiwanis Club. I have been heavily involved in the athletic booster club at Wayne State University. I have volunteered in scouting.

The saddest day of my life is when my wife died with Alzheimer's. We had a wonderful marriage. We were very close. Though she has been gone for three years, I still miss her.

When I am gone, I want people to say that I was honest and hard-working and that I helped a lot of young people become pharmacists and other professionals.

John Krasity is a resident in Oakwood Common.

He Doesn't Wash The Dishes Anymore

By Samir "Sam" Leon

I came to the United States from Syria in 1977. I came as an engineering student. I began my studies at Oakland Community College and got a job washing dishes at the Big Boy restaurant. One day early in my employment I could not get my car into "drive." I drove to the restaurant in reverse – for seven miles!

After two years, I became a cook and forgot about engineering. By 1983 my brothers, Walid and Moufid, and I saved up enough money for a down payment on a restaurant in Novi. In 1986 we started another restaurant in Livonia.

In 1987 we opened Leon's in Dearborn. We had three bad years. In 1990 we almost lost it. My wife, who is a very religious person, had a dream that we should restructure our building. We all agreed to go ahead with her plan. We put $30,000 into renovations, and we never looked back.

We began to host free Thanksgiving dinners in 1991. We decided to make this a tradition for as long as we were in business. My employees donate their time. I figure that we have given out at least 17,000 dinners. I believe in giving back to the community. Some people leave tips, which we give to charities. I estimate that we have given away $80,000 through the years.

We have had up to 12 restaurants at one time but now have eight. I think that we are successful because we work hard. I work at least 10 hours but usually 14 hours per day, seven days a week. We have good help. Six employees have been with me between 19 and 22 years. They are like family. Whenever they need help, I give it to them. We take care of our customers. The customer is always right.

We use 180 dozen eggs each day during the week and 360 dozen on Saturday and Sunday. We use 80 pounds of coffee a day. We make our own hash brown potatoes and use 1,200 pounds a week.

I was close friends with Mayor Guido. One day he wanted me to go to an event, and I was running late. He took me to his home and outfitted me in his clothes. Then we went off together. I went with Mr. Guido to the U.S. Conference of Mayors' meeting in 2006. Through him I sat with President Clinton three times. I was also "adopted" by John Nichols, the former Oakland County executive.

I still have family in Syria. I call home and talk for about 25 minutes every day.

God bless America. It is truly a land of opportunity. My family came from Syria with nothing and now look at us!

Samir "Sam" Leon and his wife, Maryann, live in Plymouth. They have four children.

Food for Thought

By Patti Mack

All of us have had experiences where something triggers a memory – be it a good memory or sometimes an unpleasant one. Perhaps a song you hear on the radio reminds you of a time in your life when you were a teen-ager. Or maybe the smell of baking bread reminds you of your grandmother's kitchen and how safe and warm and loved you felt. Well, I too have experienced these flashbacks. Yet none are as real to me as when I fondly remember restaurants that have now closed in my dear city of Dearborn.

For instance, there was the Sun Dog on Michigan Avenue and Telegraph. It was so quaint and eclectic for its time. The menu was actually painted on a shovel they gave you to order from. I was not 21 years old at the time but was working full time as a secretary in human resources for Ford Motor Company. Being in the department that hired interns for the Ford College Graduate Program (FCGP's), I had an opportunity for many dates with eligible young men. My first recollection of Sun Dog was going on a date with this extremely handsome fellow, and although I was not 21years old and was not ordering a drink, the establishment wouldn't let him order one either. I could tell he was extremely bummed out. I ordered a steak, baked potato and whole artichoke for dinner. For those of you who don't eat whole artichokes, you take the steamed vegetable one leaf at a time and peel it away and dip it into butter and slide your teeth off the end to get a teeny little bit of artichoke – until you can get to the artichoke heart. Well,

I was peeling my artichoke, and a few layers down there was the BIGGEST beetle you have ever seen just clinging to my vegetable. Of course he wasn't alive, as he had been steamed, but I screamed and the waitress came running over. Needless to say, my date had to pay for only one meal, did not have a glass of wine, plus I never heard from him again.

Then I met my husband-to-be, and of course we dated and visited many restaurants around the city. Picos Tacos (though not in Dearborn, but on Telegraph and Joy Road) was my first try at Mexican food. Then Jack-n-the-Box on Outer Drive and Michigan Avenue moved in. They too touted a "taco" that was some type of mystery food that they would throw down into a vat of grease, but those "tacos" have not been deliciously duplicated to this day. But maybe then maybe it's for the best.

Some classier restaurants that my guy would take me to if he had a little extra money were Howard Johnson's on Telegraph for a root beer float; Crabby Joes on Michigan Avenue, where I experienced my first steamed mussels and clams; and the highlight was the Hyatt and its revolving restaurant, Top of the Hyatt. That was the most romantic, except I always needed to be facing the way it was revolving for fear of becoming nauseated. But the view was magnificent and I felt like a princess.

In 1970 my guy finally popped the question, and our wedding date was set for April 30, 1971. My soon-to-be in-laws made reservations for the wedding rehearsal dinner at Doug's Body Shop on Michigan Avenue. My memory is not too clear on how the place looked – or even what we had to eat – but I do remember that one of the mothers of one of our groomsmen was at the rehearsal at church for some reason, all decked out in her snow boots and winter hat with a pheasant feather sticking from it, and somehow she was brought along with the wedding party as someone's date.

Don't get me wrong, I loved her dearly, but the boots and skirt and fancy hat dressed on a lady who looked as if she lived on a farm weren't fitting into my idealistic wedding plans. It was there that I was introduced to a Golden Cadillac drink, and I remember that they were extremely expensive and the whole wedding party started drinking them and never stopped. They were made with vanilla vodka, white chocolate liqueur, Galliano herbal liqueur, white crème de cacao, cream and sugar syrup. Mixed with ice and then strained into a large champagne flute garnished with shaved dark chocolate, they were a drink fit for royalty. I have to admit I have NEVER had another one of these drinks in the last 42 years since marriage, but, yes, at least the wedding did still take place.

So many restaurants have come and gone during the years I've lived in Dearborn: Bill Knapp's and its marvelous au gratin potatoes; Paisano's with its fall-off-the-bone ribs and luscious Italian dishes; Chambertain at the Holiday Inn for so many birthday dinners and anniversaries; 4-Vees Lounge in east Dearborn, which had the best cheeseburgers around and was a great place to have lunch while working at Ford Motor Company. And who doesn't remember Angelo's? Never will I find chicken cacciatore or antipasto salad made like Angelo's used to do. Mama Angelo would sit at the end of the counter and make sure that all her customers were treated well and having a good time.

And one final restaurant that is dear to me in my memory was The Egg and I, now called Leon's Restaurant. Hubby and I got married and said we would not have children, would be free-spirited, not own a home and travel the world. Well, we ended up buying our starter home in 1973, still live in it today, but continued to seek our dream of travel and free-spiritedness – although it's getting harder and harder to do with a mortgage, credit card bills and lawn and home maintenance to contend with. It was in 1975 when my biological clock was ticking real loud. We were eating at

The Egg and I (they had the best, fluffiest omelets I've ever eaten), and I looked my sweetheart in the eye and said, "You know, I've been thinking that maybe it would be nice to have a baby." He grabbed my hand and looked into my eyes and said, "So have I, but I didn't want to bring it up." So, right there in the middle of The Egg and I, we made our decision to become an average American family with children, dogs and cats, mortgage, bills, crabgrass, and live in our little love nest on Monroe, all cozied within the great city of Dearborn, Michigan.

Patti Mack retired from Ford Motor Company in 2002 after 35 years. Volunteerism has become her main interest. She was recently elected president of the Garden Club of Dearborn. She is also a board member of the Friends for the Dearborn Symphony as well as Toll Gate Questers and a director of communications for the League of Women Voters, Dearborn/Dearborn Heights. She also enjoys membership in the New Colony Club of Dearborn, Women's Division for Project Hope, Project Hope League and is the chaplain for the Historic Memorials Society of Detroit.

The Perfect Fish Fry:
A Lifelong Quest

By Jon Reed

Lenten season, 40 days from Ash Wednesday to Easter, means Catholics abstaining from eating meat on Fridays. This tradition has created Lenten Friday fish fries at church halls, bars and local restaurants all over the world. A lot of Dearbornites have been on lifelong searches for the perfect fish-fry experience. Raised Protestant in Dearborn, I was alone in looking forward to Lent and fish on Friday. I thought fish was a great treat rather than a restriction or requirement like many of my childhood friends. Most of my Catholic friends had to give up something during Lent, and they all thought fish on Friday was more of a duty than a treasure.

There was no fresh seafood market in east Dearborn when I was growing up, so I happily ate fish sticks at home, blocks of mysterious, fishlike paste covered with brownish, crunchy coatings. They tasted great. We were only vaguely aware of other strange things in the world like tasty fried-fish paste: having our gums wiped at school with fluoride to prevent tooth decay, eating sugar cubes with blue medicine dots to prevent something called polio, having to duck and cover under school desks in case an atomic bomb went off nearby. Cigarette ads had doctors certifying tobacco as harmless, and we had yet to learn about asbestos, DDT and ultraviolet rays. But we never questioned what exactly fish sticks were made of; they just tasted great.

I much preferred fish sticks to macaroni and cheese, but I felt lucky. Downriver friends complained about having to eat baked muskrat on Lenten Fridays – large, ratlike animals requiring lots of ketchup to kill the taste. It was never clear why muskrats weren't meat, but they fell into a fish category, according to most Catholic parents at the time. In warmer weather, Dad rented a rowboat and took us fishing for bass and pike, or cane-pole fishing for perch and bluegill. Fresh-caught fish tasted wonderful. But in Dearborn, if we didn't want macaroni and cheese, we had fish sticks on Friday because there were no fishing trips during Lent.

If we didn't have any frozen fish sticks in the house, our parents took us out to dinner on Fridays to Shore's Fish Fry. Shore's was an old Warren Avenue bank that never made it through the Depression, converted into a family-friendly neighborhood saloon. Entering patrons were greeted by the largest collection of multicolored liquor bottles ever seen behind a bar. A big sign hung over the hundreds of colorful bottles listing more drinks and prices than anybody could count.

As kids, we wondered what all these adult drinks like martinis and manhattans were. What exactly was fish house punch, a margarita or a Tom Collins? What did the mysterious sloe gin fizz actually taste like? Alas the future was so far away. The place had vinyl-topped chrome tables and chairs, but it served the best all-you-can-eat, lightly battered, deep-fried Great Lakes fresh whitefish on Fridays.

The fish was perfect, hot and crunchy, with lathers of tangy tartar sauce. The only problem was that I could never admit to my friends on Monday that I actually liked fish, Shore's or not. No ordinances kept children out of saloons back then, so our family wolfed down fried fish and Faygo and Vernors pop, all the while inhaling strange wafts of stale beer and cigarette smoke. We always finished before the atmosphere became too loud and crazy, but what childhood adventures!

Years later, when I was married with my own family, Shore's was long closed, and the best substitute was Brown's Fish and Chips on Ford Road. Brown's served really good fried fish during Lent, but it wasn't the same as Shore's. For one thing, everyone had to stand outside in a line to get in, wafts of frying fish escaping every time the door opened. Inside there was no bar, only a cacophony of noise, frying fish and cigarette smoke, with a large roomful of people eating beer-battered cod. Somehow East Coast frozen cod had replaced fresh Michigan whitefish without anyone knowing when or how it happened. I began to yearn for Shore's.

Brown's on Ford Road moved over to Greenfield but closed after several years. The search for a great alternative Lenten fish fry began in earnest, but nothing satisfied. Friends commiserated, offering advice like "You have to try a place only we know about." Others would cluck and recommend "a place out west we know about." Even pizzerias began holding Friday fish fries. How good can Italian pizzeria fish be? Do they serve pepperoni with it? Knights of Columbus, American Legion and local saloon Lenten fish specials failed to beckon with their sodden, lukewarm offerings. Nothing came close to Shore's. The search continued.

Later, other friends advised us to try a place on Joy Road, but it was just like Brown's before it closed: a line of waiting people, crowds munching on three pieces of over-battered, somewhat warm and smelly cod, and piles of French fries. The owner sat nearby, smoking, counting receipts, watching that no one took too many plastic containers of tartar sauce. Nope, this wasn't the place.

Every year, we tried different Catholic parish fish fries trying to find a good experience and perhaps rekindle memories of Shore's, but no. How great can it be trying to enjoy fried fish in a disinfected school gym with folding chairs, teetering tables and plastic-foam plates? How to put up with the commotion and dozens of willing Cub Scouts clearing tables? What chance could there be that we might find someone who knew how to fry fish in a parish kitchen?

Advertisements for Catholic parish fish fries in Dearborn's local paper listed "Transfiguration Fish Fry," which made me wonder whether the fish was transfigured by frying or did eating the fish transfigure the diner? "St. Nick's Fish Fry" brought to mind Santa Claus behind a deep fryer, ho-ho-ing. What to make of an ad, "Our Lady Queen of Angels Soup Days Are Back?" Angels in my soup? What about Blessed Sacrament's "Catfish Dinner $8, Whiting Dinner $7, Perch Dinner $8?" How did they keep them straight if they're all battered and fried in the same fryer, and how can catfish be a dollar better than whiting, whatever that was?

With dozens of questionable choices and only 40 days to work with, what were hungry people to do? About to forget the whole thing and just find a nice seafood restaurant, we agreed to give it one more try. There was a parish near us, Saint Albert's, with an all-you-can-eat fish fry. We drove over, depressed to find a typical gym filled with noisy kids and old people seated at folding tables. At least it was all-you-can-eat.

Our plastic plates were filled with fresh fried fish and, to our amazement, the deep-fried cod was lightly battered, hot and crunchy, and every bit as good as Shore's. I went back for more, not sure what I had just experienced. And then just a little more. Someone in this place knew how to cook fish, frying small batches, using good fresh fish. Except for a lack of Faygo and Vernors, a neon-lit bar and the smell of booze and cigarette smoke, I was transported back to childhood heaven in east Dearborn.

Jon Reed is a lifelong Dearborn resident and retired after four decades with General Motors.

Chapter 14

History

A Guided Tour of the Rouge Before the Rotunda Fire

By Robert Bierman

Here is a typical, abridged narration I gave a few thousand times when I was a tour guide at the Ford Rotunda from October 1953 until November 1962. Early 1954 is the date for this tour.

Good morning ladies and gentlemen:

My name is Bob Bierman. I will be your tour guide this morning on your two-hour tour of the Rouge Steel Operations Building and the Final Assembly Plant. As we depart the Rotunda and proceed on Schaefer Road, you will see the Rouge Plant off to your left. It is located on land purchased by Henry Ford in 1915 and today is the largest industrial complex in the world, covering some 1,200 acres, about two square miles. Employment stands at 65,000 with a daily payroll of one-and-a-quarter million dollars. Back in 1929 employment here stood at 103,000.

We are now entering the plant grounds through Gate 10. On both sides of the road are two of several plant parking lots that can accommodate 20,000 vehicles. Coming up on your left is the Dearborn Engine Plant. During the Second World War the Pratt and Whitney aircraft engine was built here. Across from the plant is the Tool and Die Plant. Directly ahead of us is the Steel Operations Building. This building is one mile long and one-quarter of a mile wide at its widest point. We are now driving under the Stamping Plant, a facility we will visit at the end of the Steel Operations tour. As we emerge, the Glass Plant is on your left and beyond that is the medical facility and the fire department. Next on your left is the Assembly Plant, built in 1918; it was first used to build Eagle Boats for the U.S. Navy. Those boats were launched from the boat slip off to your right. Today lake freighters, like the Henry Ford II and Benson Ford, bring raw materials into the plant, including iron ore from Minnesota and limestone from Rogers City, Michigan. The plant consumes 4,500 tons of iron ore, 200 tons of limestone and 7,000 tons of coal every day. Today Ford and Mercury passenger cars are produced in the Assembly Plant at the rate of one every 52 seconds. Assembly from start to finish takes 90 minutes.

(This narration resumes as we leave the Rouge Plant and return to the Rotunda.)

Coming up on your right is the Ford Administration Building, which was built in 1928. Henry Ford ll and other top company officials have their offices here in a wing of the building referred to as Mahogany Row. (This was actually Ford World Headquarters until the Central Office Building, as it was called originally, was built on Michigan Avenue in September 1956.) The Rotunda on your left was built in 1934 as the Ford exhibit at Chicago's Century of Progress World's Fair. It was dismantled, transported here, rebuilt and opened to the public in 1936. It was closed during World War II and recently reopened on June 16, 1953.

(End of narration)

The Rotunda was destroyed by fire on November 9, 1962. Visitors to the building since it opened in 1936 topped 18 million. Rouge tours resumed on November 12 from the Lincoln-Mercury building across the street. At that time there were a few interesting things about the building. Among them was a sign in the men's room for many years that read: "PLEASE ADJUST APPAREL BEFORE LEAVING." This reminder became necessary when the building, which for years had been staffed exclusively by men, became coed.

Henry Ford II and other top company executives occupied

the building in the early '50s and would have lunch in the private executive dining room located in the Rotunda. They often would get there by an underground tunnel that ran between the Rotunda and the Administration Building. So it was not uncommon to meet Mr. Ford in the tunnel as he would be heading to the Rotunda for lunch and we were heading the other way to the cafeteria in his building.

While my starting pay at the Rotunda was only $260 a month, working there had many benefits. We would be fitted every spring and fall at Detroit clothier Kilgore and Hurd for a suit and topcoat. Every Wednesday after work we would leave our suits hanging outside our locker. They would be cleaned, pressed and returned the next morning. There were about 20 guys, no women, who worked in the Rotunda as special-events representatives taking tours or working the floor. As tour guides we would be assigned the hourly tours, taking two or three a day, or "special tours" for important individuals or school groups. In 1962 I was having lunch in the Lincoln-Mercury cafeteria with a seventh-grade school group as I watched the Rotunda burn. Working the floor, we could be a narrator on a turntable; working the information desk, announcing movies, tours, etc.; keeping an eye on rowdy kids; or working with Frenchy, who operated a plastic injection molding machine. The machine would spit out quarter-size plastic medallions with the Rotunda pictured on one side and profiles of Henry, Edsel and Henry II on the other side. They were given to visitors as souvenir key chains.

It was just a few days after the Rotunda fire in 1962 that I was allowed to return to a part of the Rotunda where my locker was located. After cleaning out my locker, I left the building and never conducted another tour. Seven months later I graduated from Wayne State University. I was directing public relations activities for Ford in the 13-state Western Region when I retired in January 1995.

Robert Bierman was born and raised in Dearborn. He has authored a book, The Gang on Kendal Street.

A Haigh and Both His Houses

By Patricia Ibbotson

Haigh Elementary, named after Henry Allyn Haigh, a noted citizen and early Dearborn resident, was my first school in Dearborn.

When I was a teen-ager back in the 1950s, I used to visit the old Haigh mansion. It was in a wooded area on the northwest corner of Michigan and Haigh, with a street address of 22734 Michigan Avenue. There was a lane through the trees to what appeared to me to be a Southern-style, white mansion with pillars and a long porch across the front. When I discovered it, the front door was open and anyone could walk in – which is what I did. It had probably been vacant for some time, but it felt as if the previous occupants had just left. They even left toothpaste in the medicine cabinet in the bathroom. I expected them to come back at any moment.

Back then I didn't know much about the mansion's history.

Time will play tricks with one's memory after 60 years, so I decided to do some research. I discovered that the first Haigh mansion was built around 1831 by Colonel Joshua Howard, who lived in it while he was supervising the building of the Detroit Arsenal in Dearbornville. The same bricks that were used to build the arsenal were used to build the house. The mansion was three stories high, with spacious rooms that opened onto a wide hall and had huge fireplaces that warmed the rooms.

The mansion was purchased about 1850 by Richard Haigh, Sr., who lived there with his wife, Lucy Billings Allyn Haigh, and servants. Their son, Henry, was born on March 13, 1854. It was called Maplewood because of the acres of maple trees that stretched from the back of the house all the way to the Rouge River. There was also a sugar maple grove and an orchard with hundreds of apple trees. The mansion sat on 20 acres of land reaching beyond the Rouge River to the north and Military to the east. The outbuildings included a large barn. The barn was the scene of a murder, according to the diaries of Haigh's son, Henry. The diaries claim that a "victim's roaming ghost returned and wandered wearily around on dread and darksome nights."

The house caught fire the night of March 21, 1901, and the building was destroyed. Only the outside walls were left standing. Richard Haigh, then 90, and his wife, 83, were alone in the house and managed to escape with their lives and little else. The fire started in a shed adjoining the house. Henry Haigh had married Caroline S. Comstock, and they had two sons, Andrew Comstock and Richard Allyn. Henry, who was living in Detroit at the time, rebuilt the house in 1902, but he could not replace the priceless volumes in the library, the oak paneling, the carved fireplaces or the mahogany chests of rare designs. The second mansion was also a slightly different style from the original.

Henry died May 16, 1942, and Caroline followed him on October 8, 1946. Their final resting place is Northview Cemetery, which was founded in 1883 by Henry Haigh

Photos dated 1954 in the Burton Historical Collection of the Detroit Public Library showed the grand mansion I remembered. It seems a shame that such a historic building should be razed. The Dearborn Historical Museum archives indicated that the mansion was put up for sale in July 1955 by Richard Allyn Haigh and his wife, who had moved to Farmington. They had donated dishes and books to the Dearborn Historical Museum; the rest of the furnishings were sold at auction in August.

The mansion was razed over several days in late May 1956, and the area where the mansion stood is now the site of an office building facing Michigan Avenue with some green space between it and the Dearborn Towers condominiums in the back. To paraphrase Henry Haigh's nostalgic comment in his diaries about his youthful days, the enchantment of those Maplewood days in Dearborn is forever gone.

Patricia Ibbotson is an author with an avid interest in local history. She lived in Dearborn for 50 years and currently resides in Westland.

Planting Seeds Of the Henry Ford Story

By Patricia Long

I was born in Pennsylvania, and, when I moved to Dearborn in 1965 with my Dearborn-born husband and four children, Michelle, Jim, Dave and Brad, I knew little about auto pioneers. I had met Al and Rose Chevrolet as their dance teacher. Al was the only son of Louis Chevrolet, and we developed a friendship. The Ford name did not stand out. That was about to change, starting with one memorable conversation.

It was in the spring of 1966 when an elderly gentleman knocked on my door. He was a Ford retiree and told me he had permission to plant a garden across the street from my historic Park Street home. He needed access to water and asked if he could use my water. He was willing to pay, but who needed pay when the water bill was $3?

I had a tremendous amount of respect for older people, and I wanted to tap into what this person who would have been born at the turn of the last century could tell me. Two conversations stand out. In the first talk he proceeded to tell me what the Ford Motor Company did for his hometown. I knew about the swimming pools and other amenities, but not what made most of what I saw possible. While telling me about the amenities and gifts to the city, he looked at my 1963 Plymouth station wagon and said he thought that anyone who was receiving the benefits of this city should certainly be driving a Ford.

I had to know what was the most remarkable memory the

man had in a time period that brought millions to America. When I put the question to the gentleman, he pondered a while, but emphatically said, "The $5 day." He described the greatest Business History Moment that had ever existed. It boiled down to making it possible for the working man who was building the car to own one. Details of the $5 day can't be fit into this short story, but I did indeed research it one day.

It came to be that I joined the Dearborn Historical Society at about the age of 40. It was a graduation present to myself to engage in historical activities after receiving a degree in secondary education from the University of Michigan. I found myself as the vice president of the Dearborn Historical Society when I was asked to deliver a short speech at the dedication of the historical marker during the 75th anniversary celebration of the founding of the Ford Motor Company.

A few years later I became a guide at Fair Lane, the Henry Ford estate. When the Model T was placed in the garage, it was the perfect setting for me to pass on the essence of gratitude to the hundreds on my tours. My training manual did not mention the $5 day—but I did. Later it was placed into the training manual. I felt that I had witnessed and learned enough to claim that the seeds of the middle class were ushered in due to the $5 day and other events in automotive history. Indeed, my interest in Henry Ford started during that long-ago talk on my Park Street porch.

Patricia Long has had three careers: first as an Arthur Murray dance instructor, then as a high school teacher and finally as a disabilities examiner. Pat is active in volunteer work, having served both in the Dearborn and Detroit historical museums. She has been an officer in the following organizations: the Society of Education at the University of Michigan-Dearborn, the University of Michigan Club of Dearborn, the Juvenile Diabetes Foundation Club in Dearborn, the Dearborn Hills Civic Association and the Henry Ford Heritage Association.

Police Lights, a Cloud of Hay And a Hearty 'Hi-yo, Tractor'

By John Malone

In 1963 I was employed at the Dearborn Historical Museum as a general handyman/maintenance worker. I usually helped with anything that came up at the Museum. For the Fourth of July the Junior Historians decided that they would like to have representation in the parade that Dearborn held every year. After several weeks of arguing about what form their representation should take, it was decided that they would decorate a flatbed trailer and ride on it during the parade. Mary MacDonald, who was the Museum's artist and also doubled as the leader of the Junior Historians, made arrangements with one of the city departments, and we soon had a very large tractor and flatbed trailer sitting at the back of the McFadden–Ross House.

The Junior Historians usually met at the McFadden-Ross House on Saturdays, and when the Saturday before the Fourth of July rolled around, the kids arrived very excited, and their excitement soared when they saw the tractor and trailer. Mary MacDonald got them organized with the idea of getting the trailer and tractor cleaned up enough to decorate. The rest of the day was spent spraying, throwing buckets of water and scrubbing away at a very dirty tractor. Extra bales of hay were requested and costumes were planned.

It was decided that since I was employed by the Museum and therefore insured, I would be in charge of the tractor and trailer. Another reason I was to drive was that I was raised on a farm. (I was between the ages of 7 and 11 when we lived on the farm.) I got to the Museum early on the Fourth and was sent off down Michigan Avenue to east Dearborn with cries of "Be careful not to plow anybody under," and "Don't drive too fast," and "Don't drive too slow because you have to be there to pick up the kids."

With these cries following me, I pulled on to Michigan Avenue. I have often wondered what people thought when they saw a young, red-bearded man dressed in boots, coveralls, a plaid shirt and a large straw hat driving slowly down one of the busiest streets around. The word "slowly" should be emphasized, as every time I tried to speed up, the trailer wobbled back and forth, and a cloud of hay filled the air behind us.

I was stopped by the Dearborn Police, who were interested in what I was doing. They called the station and got permission to escort me. It was probably the first time in history that a tractor doing no more than 10 miles per hour was escorted through Dearborn.

The police escort was great. They got me to the kids on time and escorted us through west Dearborn with lights and siren. The kids thought it was great and the people lining the streets seemed to enjoy the entire parade. The kids' costumes were great, and a good time was had by all.

John Malone is retired and living in the Upper Peninsula town of Laurium. It, like Dearborn, is a friendly town of many nationalities. It has more than 200 inches of snow each year.

From New York Westward, Father Pat Left a Trail

By Father John Rocus

It's a little hard to imagine how things must have been way back then. This area was a wilderness, but with the westward migration of our pioneering ancestors on trails, rails, roads, canals, rivers and lakes, small groups of Catholics from different ethnic backgrounds began to put down roots and establish faith communities throughout the Midwest, including here in Dearborn. They were courageous, hard-working and faithful as they built their churches, as well as rectories to house their priests. And as for those early pastors, they too were a tough breed. One of them was Father Patrick O'Kelley. He was the pastor of my home parish, Sacred Heart, at the corner of Michigan and Military, where he died on October 8, 1859.

As a young boy, exploring the west end on my bike, I one day came across a graveyard on Cherry Hill and there discovered his chapel-like tomb on a small hill in the center of the cemetery named Mount Kelly in his honor. At that time I didn't attach too much importance to my discovery, but in subsequent years, as I migrated westward, I would find his name on many historical markers outside the Dearborn area, such as in Ann Arbor, where I settled at St. Thomas the Apostle. Father O'Kelley was the founding pastor there, saying his first Masses in the farmhouses of local Irish settlers. In my travels throughout the area, I found that his work carried him north and west to the new Irish communities that continued to spring up.

At a certain point I, too, found myself called to the priesthood. I went to the seminary in Hales Corners, Wisconsin, and one Sunday I visited a local parish where I was shocked to find Father O'Kelley's name on a historical marker. I was to learn that at that time, Milwaukee was part of the Archdiocese of Detroit. My first summer assignment as a seminarian was at St. Mary in Pinckney – again, founded by Father Pat.

In time I would return to Michigan to be ordained and to begin my work as a priest. My first assignment was at St. Joseph Church in Howell, founded by Father Pat. After that I would eventually be assigned at my current parish, Holy Spirit near Hamburg in Green Oak Township. I soon discovered that for a while this was actually his home base where he occupied a log cabin at old McCabe Cemetery, from which he served the community that would eventually become St. Patrick Church in Brighton. In time, as the Irish community of St. Patrick began to grow, new communities necessarily came into existence. One of those parishes would be my own here at Holy Spirit as St. Patrick parishioners who had moved southward were asked to form a new parish. And so, I'm prepared to claim the good father as the founder of Holy Spirit, once removed.

Over the years since that first visit to his tomb, I've grown to be quite impressed with the work of this seemingly tireless priest, especially since I have found myself in so many places where his legacy still exists. And I thought that perhaps I had seen the last of him, but last summer, he made yet one more appearance. I was on a boating trip on the Erie Canal in western New York, that waterway on which many of the early Dearbornites traveled on their way here. While on my journey, I found evidence that he had passed that way, too. As a matter of fact, he was one of those first Irish immigrants who sailed west and stopped to say Mass for his people near Rochester, where he founded his very first church, before moving on to Detroit.

I only wonder where I might encounter him next.

Father John Rocus was a late vocation to the Catholic priesthood. He was ordained in 2001 at the age of 51. He was a woodworker in Ann Arbor for many years before answering the call.

A Member of the Village

By Michelle Saad

Front-porch communities were on their last few years of existence when I was a child. I remember when we played for hours in the front yard and up and down the block. Mrs. Ester on the corner was watching over her lawn and us, in her own way, ready to tell on me or my siblings for the slightest infraction, but sometimes I heard her laughing at our silly games. Then there were Mrs. Owen and Mrs. Grover and even Mr. Phillips at the end of the street. He would give me a dollar every time I came around helping my brother on his paper route. Someone was always watching and we knew they would inform on any suspicious characters. Not that any ever did come slinking along.

This utopian impression of the good old days has left me fumbling to enjoy the current state of community where front drapes stay closed so daylight doesn't cause a reflection on the television screen. I wondered how and where to connect with people living in the present when I yearned for the past.

Greenfield Village – it is a place and an answer to my question. Historically significant buildings, some even resting on the original earth of their foundations, are like a sanity-recapturing sanctuary. Ever the forward thinker, Henry Ford put it all together, and it draws in numbers rivaling the Smithsonian. People come from all over the world to see it, and it is seven minutes from my house.

Having a membership card is like my second form of identification; it says I belong to The Village and the community that loves it. With my imagination and shade hat, I wander from one era to the next. From the blacksmith shop to the machine shop I watch American life unfold. The Presenters, dedicated caretakers, are all dressed in period costume, perfectly tailored. They complete the spell, adding their motions to the history of the wood, iron and sweat. We can see them working a farm as they did in the 1800s, year round with period tools and machinery, every post attended and all doing their part. A hypnotizing aroma guides us like noses on leashes to the farmhouse wafting with smoldering coals and a Dutch-oven lunch. I disappear into the value of their hard work and their ability to transport me and my family into other times and places. I see how much of the "simpler times" was full of sun-up-to sundown work, simple enough.

One of my favorite places is the Cotswold Cottage. I have always wanted to live in a place that had its own name and not the numbers on a grid we find so convenient today. The stone floor has been worn down through the centuries, and I softly shake my head in awe about it every time I see it. My children have their favorites as well, and I get a sense of pride when they ask to "go to the Village." My son likes the Wright Brothers bicycle shop, and we stop there every time. He has also developed a taste for pocket watches, a timeless classic. My daughter loves the school houses and the McGuffey Readers set on the table in Henry Ford's childhood home. Then there is Edison's laboratory, Menlo Park. More than a doorway into another time, it is a whole block. I could go on and on, but you either know what I'm talking about or you need to go experience The Village.

Michelle Saad is a wife and mom.

The Canoe That Stopped Traffic

By Bob Schuelke

It had to be 1973 or '74 when the Army Corp of Engineers straightened out the Rouge River and concretized the banks of the river crossing Rotunda Drive. When we were kids, my brother Bill Schuelke, now deceased; our friend Jack Tate, now the Dearborn Historical Museum's acting chief curator; and I used to play up and down that area. So we wanted to take a trip down the old part of the river before it was converted into a concrete river.

We were now in our mid-20s and had served in the military. So the three of us put Jack's canoe into the river at the Ford Field bridge and planned on calling for a ride back, somewhere around the Ford Rouge Plant. GOOD PLAN!

We sure enjoyed canoeing past the Brady Street bridge, and when we got to the middle branch of the river, we turned left and paddled up river to Ford Fair Lane and to the waterfall. We had a good look around and saw a lot of fish and wildlife. We turned around and headed back downriver under the Michigan Avenue bridge, and under the railroad bridge we crossed Rotunda, enjoying the sights. When we got within sight of the Ford Rouge Plant, we saw a 55-gallon drum swirling in the river. The water seemed to end at that point and went down a 48-inch concrete pipe.

We pulled the canoe out of the water and had to portage about 100 yards or so and get back in the river. As we paddled past the rest of the Ford plant and under the Dix bridge, we approached the Fort Street drawbridge. We could see the bridge operator in the tower waving and laughing at us. Believe it or not, the guy raised the bridge for us and stopped traffic. What a nice salute to us and our canoe.

After that great moment, we soon realized that the riverbank was too high for us to get out of water. Soon we were past Zug Island and in the Detroit River. As the freighters passed, they all gave a tug on the horns and waved. The water was very deep and rough for a canoe, with the waves from the freighters. Needless to say, we were scared that something might go wrong. But all went well, and we finally got out at the public launch at the foot of Southfield and Jefferson near the old Carter's hamburger joint.

We called for a ride and got picked up with a station wagon, a canoe on the top and three happy and relieved guys inside.

We never intended to go that far, but we had no choice. When the trip was over, we were glad we did go that far. The map showed we had canoed about 16 miles, and it was a good day, remembering when we were kids and creating new memories to tell about today.

Bob Schuelke is a lifetime resident of Dearborn (DHS '65). He is married to Edwardine and has three children and seven grandchildren. He is a retired electrical inspector from Canton Township. He is a master electrician and contractor.

To Antarctica and Beyond

By Erwin Spencer

I was greatly influenced by my parents. They were great people. While I grew up in Dearborn, my parents ultimately bought a farm between Northville and South Lyon. They bought 123 acres from a 95-year-old farmer who developed a tree on which three different types of apples grew. I came from a very religious family. I had two uncles who were pastors at what is now Good Shepherd United Methodist Church.

There were two segments of my life that were especially interesting. The first was going to the Greenfield Village Schools. The second was my career in the U.S. Navy.

The Greenfield Village Schools were a great place for me. They were really interesting. The school was developed by Henry Ford, who believed in a hands-on way to learn. Our chapel services, frequently attended by Henry Ford, were broadcast on WJR. I remember when Ford celebrated the Golden Lights Jubilee, which commemorated the invention of the electric light. The great inventor, Thomas Edison, attended and was the center of attention.

I was a presenter at the 1939-40 World's Fair in New York City. We had a model of Edison's laboratory. I showed how the phonograph worked. I made recordings. I did this in a rotation during the summer.

Through the Village schools, I worked at the Ford Rouge facility. I worked in Ford's engineering operation.

Through the Village schools I also met Will Rogers.

The second major aspect of my life was my naval career. I enlisted in the U.S. Navy in 1942. I was assigned to the Naval Air Transport Service. While I was not involved in any fighting, my role was important in transporting supplies. In 1944 personnel from American Airlines taught me instrument flying on a DC3. A typical flight would be from Seattle to San Diego or to Fairbanks or Point Barrow, Alaska.

Throughout my career, I was always going to school, building on that fine educational foundation that I got at the Village schools. I studied nuclear energy. I studied chemical warfare.

In 1946 I was involved in Task Force 68. I accompanied the famous Admiral Richard Byrd on his Antarctic Expedition. I was supposed to be the co-pilot on Admiral Byrd's flight, but he chose his favorite pilot instead. We were involved in mineral exploration. We did photo reconnaissance. We tossed out canisters containing American flags and documents over the frozen tundra. In 1947 I sent Easter greetings from Antarctica to Dearborn when the great flood hit and during which Henry Ford died.

In my travels I went to the Will Rogers memorial in Point Barrow, the site at which that great humorist and social commentator's plane crashed.

Beyond that I served in Newfoundland, Iceland, North Africa and the Mediterranean. I was fortunate to be an exchange officer with the British Royal Air Force. I served in that capacity for about 14 months. I trained in Scotland and then was stationed in Northern Ireland.

I served in Guam in an airborne early-warning squad. In the years before the war in Vietnam, I screened for activity in the South China Sea to see which vessels might be near the 7th Fleet. I served in Japan. I served in weather reconnaissance and once flew into the middle of a typhoon.

I only had one major request along the way. I asked to be stationed at a warm-weather base. I got assigned to Jacksonville, Florida, only then to be transferred to Newfoundland and Maine!

I enjoyed every minute of serving in the Navy. I retired in 1964. I worked for Damman Hardware for a couple of years. I then took care of my parents. It was only appropriate that I take care of them after they led me to such wonderful experiences.

When I am gone, I want people to know that I always did what I was told. I learned that in the Navy.

Erwin Spencer passed away on October 4, 2013, at the age of 89.

Santa Survived the Fire — Or Did He?

By Elaine Watson

Standing beside me on our backyard porch, my son Doug, 3, was in tears. "Santa's burning up!" he sobbed.

From the kitchen radio I could hear a reporter from WJR adding details to the news that had brought us running out to the porch on this morning in early November 1962. Now we could hear the wail of fire engines, too. The Rotunda was on fire.

Day after day, Doug's older brother had been telling him about a popular Christmas extravaganza the Ford Motor Company had staged inside its Rotunda during every Christmas season since 1958. The show's reputation had become so widespread that by now it ranked fifth among U.S. tourist attractions.

The architect Albert Kahn had designed the Rotunda as a centerpiece for Ford's exhibit at the Chicago World's Fair, which opened in 1933. After the fair closed, it was taken down and transported to a site not far from Ford's Rouge Plant in Dearborn. There it was reassembled and then erected again.

This time a dome was added to the original structure. It was the first application of a lightly constructed dome, built from a new design by Buckminster Fuller. Residents across the eastern part of the city could admire the dome, rising above the Dearborn skyline.

Inside the Rotunda, every day during the early part

of December, a long line of schoolchildren, of families with preschoolers and of folks from all ages beyond, made their way past dozens of charming holiday displays. Life-size nativity figures gathered around a creche inside a protective grotto. Those waiting in line could enjoy a display, too, of 2,500 costume-clad Goodfellow dolls, a miniature circus, several groups of animated dolls that represented scenes from *Hansel and Gretel* and other children's stories.

A 37-foot, holiday-trimmed tree rose above it all.

Santa sat at the end of the waiting line, there to greet each frightened – or star-struck – or utterly weary child.

We could not see the Rotunda's dome from our porch, but that morning billowing black smoke was drawing folks from all across Dearborn out into yards and streets. The continuing radio report informed us that someone working on the roof had tipped over a burner. The heat then apparently ignited tar on the roof. And the resulting conflagration rapidly became too big to control. The black tar birthed a spectacular sight of billowing, black smoke.

Within an hour, the entire building had been consumed.

Later we learned that many items in the annual Christmas display – the hundreds of dollars, the crèche scene, elegant decorations for the great Christmas tree – were safe, most of them still in storage.

And everyone at the Rotunda had escaped injury, including Santa.

After we went back into the kitchen, I decided it was a good time to have a conversation about Santa with my 3-year-old. About regular, ordinary men who dressed up like Santa to help give little kids some fun during the Christmas season. And that he would probably see more of them. At any rate, after the excitement of the fire at the Rotunda, I certainly did not have to explain anything more that day about who – or if – Santa really was.

This article originally was printed in the Detroit News. Elaine Watson began teaching English and composition at Dearborn High in 1946. She later taught as an adjunct instructor at Henry Ford Community College. Her publications have included novels, short stories, articles and poetry. She writes and guides retirees with their writing. Her latest book is a memoir, CIRCA 1925.

Chapter 15

Experiences

The Long Way Home

By Clarisse Israel Andrus

I have called Dearborn my home for 36 years now and still do. I also call Detroit my hometown, having lived there the first quarter-century of my life. My love of my hometowns comes from a couple of sources – one of them being my dad's lifelong and loving memories of his hometown: Sarud in Heves, Hungary, which he left when he was 12 years old.

My paternal grandfather left Hungary in 1913. My dad was 2 at the time, so his parents decided that his dad would go ahead and bring them over after he got established. World War I intervened, and finally my dad and his mom came to the United States in 1923. My dad loved America but also missed his homeland and his relatives. Over the years as my dad married, had a family and finally retired, he always thought about his hometown of Sarud. He corresponded with relatives and pictures were exchanged, but he never did get back to visit.

In 2008 for my 30th wedding anniversary, my husband asked me where we should vacation. We considered Hawaii, a cruise and Europe. I asked the advice of our daughter, who had been on all three types of vacations, and she said, "Mom, you will love to visit Hungary!" I am not someone who likes things planned out by someone else. So we got our passports, I planned the hotel and airfares about four months in advance and was ready for our trip to Budapest. My plan was to have a nice anniversary dinner on the banks of the Danube, drinking a glass of Egri Bikaver wine.

It was a dream come true to be in Budapest. We saw all the sites and stayed in a hotel on the banks of the Danube. But one thing was missing. I really wanted to visit my dad's hometown. I did some research about his town before we went and found that it is about an hour and half drive from Budapest. We had decided not to rent a car while in Hungary because the public transportation is so good. I didn't think we would be able to take a side trip.

Every day at the hotel I would ask at the desk if anyone knew where Sarud is and is there any train to there, etc. Finally a woman at the desk knew where it was! She said that there is a bus every morning that leaves from the far North side of the city and travels through towns on a six-hour, one-way route to a city called Debrecen. It turns out that Sarud is about the middle point on the route. As a spur-of-the-moment idea, my husband and I decided to take the bus ride the next morning.

We got on the bus around 7 a.m. and arrived in Sarud at 10 a.m. The bus would be back through in six hours, and then it would be a three-hour ride home. We had an address from 20 years before for a family member and tried to find the street. We finally located a map at a little library/museum. I had not thought about this, but, even though most people in Budapest spoke English, no one in Sarud did. I understand limited Hungarian.

One of our stops in town was the city hall because I had found a site online that said there is a book written by a professor from the town that lists all the families from the town for hundreds of years. My attempts to ask for the book in English were not working as I could hear the people in the city hall asking each other in Hungarian, "Does anyone understand English?" Finally I pulled out the paper I had printed and said the name of the author as best

I could and said the word "internet." A light bulb seemed to go off, and the person ran into the other room and came back with the book. I asked, "How much?" and he responded, "Souvenir!" It was exciting to see both my dad's parents' family names in the book being in the town since the 1600s.

Next we looked for the home of my relative. We found the house, but there was a locked gate in front, and no one seemed to be home. We stood in the street for a while, and finally the neighbor across the street came over to help. We struggled talking with her, but I finally showed her a copy of a bunch of pictures of my dad's family that supposedly lived in the house, and she recognized them! I also had made a family tree diagram that showed how I am related. She understood! She explained they were at work but might be home for lunch. She invited us to sit on her porch and drink lemonade while we waited.

Finally about a hour later a car drove up, and a young man about high school age emerged from the house. The neighbor walked over with us and explained to him that we are relatives from America. Thankfully, he spoke some English! Then he and his friend drove us over to his grandmother's house on the other side of the village. His grandmother was my dad's much younger first cousin. We went into her home, and there stood a kindly 80-something lady who welcomed us with open arms.

Her grandson explained who we were, and she was so happy! At that moment I started to have visions of the movie *European Vacation*, in which Chevy Chase and his family think they are visiting his German relatives, but they actually went to the wrong house. My fears were allayed when my dad's cousin Therese went into her bedroom and brought out a picture of my immediate family that my dad had sent her in the 1960s. Seeing that picture of my family, in a relative's home in my dad's little hometown of

Sarud in Hungary, made me realize – I found another hometown, my dad's hometown – where we all came from.

Sometimes people know you better than you know yourself, and before I left for Hungary my older brother had said to me, "If by some chance you get to dad's hometown, bring back some of the soil." I took along a little plastic medicine bottle just in case. And as I boarded the bus for the ride back to Budapest, my husband said, "Don't forget the soil."

When I returned home to Dearborn, I took the little bottle of soil to my dad's gravesite, and as I sprinkled it on his grave, I said, "You are home, Dad."

Clarisse Israel Andrus is a consultant for financial institution retirement plans. She and husband, Bob, have two daughters and have lived in Dearborn since 1978.

His Luckiest Break: 'I Don't Think This Is the Guy'

By Thomas Barszcyowski

Several years ago I was cleaning gutters, and I found out how good Dearborn's paramedics were. I fell from my ladder. After I fell, the paramedics transported me to Oakwood Hospital, where I was treated for a dislocation and a break. The break was the bad part, but the good part is that the doctor who performed the surgery was the orthopedic surgeon for the Detroit Red Wings. I now have two screws in my shoulder and a new respect for ladders. After several months of therapy at the Detroit Medical Center in the community center, I am now somewhat normal. But the real climax to this story comes the day after the fall and the first hospital visit.

I went to Fairlane Sears with my wife. Mind you, my arm was in a sling and my face looked like a bear clawed me, something like Freddy Krueger. On the way down from my fall, I had been attacked by tree branches, which only added to my misery. Next I was approached at Sears by a Dearborn policeman who asked me where I had been (as he was frisking me or patting me down).

My astonishing response was "at home." Now, as my wife approached and the crowd gathered, I asked him why he was doing this. He told me that a man with a sling and wearing a Tiger hat had skipped on his bill at the Big Fish. It was me—NOT. He took my license and wrote my name down and called on his radio and told his partner, "I don't think this is the guy."

My wife, who was now nearby, thought that I knew the officer and he was a friend—NOT. I asked one thing of him before this bizarre thing ended: "Would you tell these people that I didn't do anything wrong?" He did and we parted. But I am not embarrassed or sorry he did this, but happy that we have a police department that does its job. I don't know the officer's name, but thank you, and I am not a criminal!

Thomas Barszcyowski is a retired language arts teacher who has lived in Dearborn for 20 years. He is married to Mary Lou and has two children who attended Divine Child High School.

Forging a Union

By Richard E. "Rick" Danes

In life we have many experiences that upon reflection could be the basis of a good novel or movie.

To set the stage for this true tale, I will go way back–not only in my personal history, but in the history of our country.

To begin with, my wife of 47 years, Irma, was born and mostly raised in the state of Mississippi. Her ancestors were German and English; they were poor but honest dairy farmers, owning and sharecropping in the Mississippi River delta, after migrating down the Ohio and Tennessee rivers from Pennsylvania. Her great-great-grandfather, Abraham Goodnight (from the German Gutnecht), was a private in the Panola County Provincial Cavalry, Confederate States of America during the Civil War, enlisting in 1864 and protecting the area around his home through northern Alabama from a heavy Union presence until he was captured and imprisoned in 1865 at Corinth, Mississippi, until the end of the war.

My ancestors were also German and English and were poor but honest farmers in Ohio and Kentucky after migrating down the Ohio River from Pennsylvania. My great-great-grandfather, James Coleman Franklin, and his brother Reuben went against not only their parents' wishes, but against the orders of their religion to enlist in the Union Army, Reuben in the Missouri Cavalry, James in the 27th Ohio Infantry. For this patriotic act, both were banished both from the church and from the family.

James enlisted in 1861, and his regiment was immediately sent to put down the Confederate uprising in Missouri, but was diverted to Island 10 in the Mississippi River. Keep in mind that in James Garfield's memoir, he noted that when he was in command of the training compound at Camp Chase, Ohio, early in the war, the 27th Ohio arrived to find no barracks or even tents, so they had to build their own – and the regiment was ordered to the field without being outfitted with uniforms, weapons or training–the men would receive them in the field.

Franklin honorably fought with Fuller's Ohio Brigade in Pope's Regiment at Springfield, Missouri, through Tennessee, Mississippi and Alabama, re-enlisting on December 31, 1864. Among his many other trials, he suffered sunstroke while supporting an artillery battery at Farmington, Tennessee, on September 15, 1862. He suffered from the effects of this injury for the rest of his life, as well as from the results of a gunshot wound in the foot at Resaca, Georgia, on May 13, 1864.

Because he could no longer march long distances, James was reassigned to the 1st Battalion of the Invalid Corps (later renamed the Veterans Reserve Corps) at – you guessed it, Corinth, Mississippi!

Although there is no evidence that these two men ever actually met, it is interesting to note that 103 years later, and some 900 miles away from Corinth, the descendents of these two brave men–both Americans–who were both fighting a life-and-death battle for what they thought was right– would meet and would forge a union that could not be accomplished by governments or by armies over 150 years ago.

Richard E. "Rick" Danes is the president of the Museum Guild of Dearborn, commander of the Sons of Union Veterans of the Civil War Camp 427 and immediate past president of the Dearborn Historical Commission. He can often be seen doing volunteer work at the Museum.

Frank Herman, We Forgive You!

By Paul Ganson

My father was a registered professional civil engineer and a project supervisor for the Wayne County Road Commission. He began working for the county in 1920 and retired after a 37-year career – and a debilitating stroke – in 1958. During his active, working years he also built four homes in the area: the first, a two-family home, for his mother and himself on Yinger in Dearborn; the second in Melvindale on Hanna for our family; and a third in Allen Park that was taken, half-finished, by the federal government because it was in the path of the bomber highway being built to enable workers from Detroit to travel as rapidly and conveniently as possible to and from the Willow Run Bomber Plant during World War II. The fourth home owed no small debt to my mother for its creation – and completion. Two or three years following the Second World War, my mother informed my father that she had been paying taxes on a lot on Claremont in Dearborn Hills for 19 years and that she was not going to continue doing so. My father's choice was simple: "Build a house on that lot or sell." My father undertook the more complicated option, which soon became even more complicated than he had imagined.

Having drawn the plans for our new home, my father submitted them to the city of Dearborn for approval. Almost immediately they were rejected, accompanied by a message from the architect for the city of Dearborn: "There shall be no home designed by an engineer built in Dearborn – especially if that home be across the street from the architect for the city of Dearborn!" The architect in question was Mr. Aloys Frank Herman, a designer of some renown; his works included Assumption Grotto on Gratiot near Six Mile Road and many other Roman Catholic houses of worship.

Beyond disgruntled, my father appealed and his plans were approved; however, the brief delay in the construction schedule necessitated by the appeal process meant that we lost the option for natural-gas heating. Every time the oil truck appeared for a delivery (once or twice a year), every time one wiped oil-tainted dust from a marble windowsill, every time the oil-burning furnace clicked on or clicked off, it was as though Frank Herman were grinding the knuckles of his index fingers deeper and deeper into our eye sockets. We never spoke to him, nor in fairness did he to us. My father and I, through no conspiracy but with a refreshing unanimity, avoided any sight or even mention of Frank Herman. We did not cluck our disapproval over anything that might have occurred – or not occurred – around 911 Claremont. Was his house still standing? We could not be summoned as reliable witnesses.

So it remained when we moved from our home in the summer of 1966 – and after my father's subsequent passing in the same year and my mother's sale of the house in 1969. Through all those changes Frank Herman remained as he always had been, no more than a name not to be spoken. Little did I know that through all those years my mother and Frank Herman's wife, Rose, got on famously over bridge tables and at various for-ladies-only events in the neighborhood. If my father knew this – and he probably did – he never confided in me. There remained something, however, that unbeknownst to me would open the silence between Frank Herman and myself.

At 4:05p.m. on Thursday, September 17, 1970, we

musicians, music-lovers, preservationists, historians and architects were foremost among those who were surprised to learn that Orchestra Hall had been sold at noon on that day and was scheduled for demolition in two weeks. At first thought it almost made sense. The boarded-up, cold, dark structure had been stripped and scavenged during the previous 10 years of total abandonment. Before that it had only a decade of occasional, sporadic use as a recording home for the Detroit Symphony Orchestra under Paul Paray – and as the Church of Our Prayer under the Reverend James Lofton. For 10 years before that it had glowed as the Paradise Theatre from the day it reopened in 1941 after the DSO had abandoned the hall in 1939 near the end of the Great Depression. In spite of the miracle of enterprise and engineering that had created Orchestra Hall in only four months and 23 days of 1919 and in spite of the Golden Age of the orchestra under Ossip Gabrilowitsch that followed, the fortunes of the institution seemed to continue inexorably on a downwards path. The end of that path did not seem unpredictable, even though it was unacceptable.

As surprised as I was by the news of Orchestra Hall's imminent demolition, I was shocked when I walked into a meeting of the Detroit Historical Society later that winter to see an elderly gentleman motioning for me to join him. I quickly concluded that he was Frank Herman, not the Prince of Darkness.

He spoke in measured, well-modulated tones. "Hello, Paul. I was hoping to see you. I have been reading about your campaign to Save Orchestra Hall, and I wanted to tell you that I was a boy just out of architecture school in the summer of 1919, and I went to work for the firm of C. Howard Crane. I did all of the exterior drawings for Orchestra Hall." With a quaver in his conservative voice still conveying the stress of those earlier times, he concluded: "That was the fastest project I ever worked on in my entire career.

We just managed to finish the plans the day the building was finished."

During a subsequent interview he confirmed that Orchestra Hall's plans were unique. There were no earlier or alternate sets of plans to copy or to imitate. He recalled that Gabrilowitsch visited a couple of times during that frantic summer and conferred with C. Howard Crane and Rudi Wulf, the actual designer. It was probably as a result of those conferences that William H. Murphy, a major force in the provision of Orchestra Hall, could ascribe a near doubling of the original budget to their midcourse corrections of adding the horseshoe of 26 boxes and extending the balcony all the way to Woodward Avenue. Counterfactual historians might enjoy speculating how those changes affected the acoustics and the overall impact of the final space.

Because these changes were introduced and discussed solely as budget costs, we can only speculate as to the intentions behind them. Perhaps some yet undiscovered memorandum or letter will surprise and inform us as much as Frank Herman's sudden appearance surprised me in the winter of 1970-71 in the basement of the Detroit Historical Museum. Perhaps, too, we shall discover in ourselves the ability to forgive, or at least to understand, those who allowed all those vicissitudes to be heaped upon Orchestra Hall until its demolition seemed a foregone conclusion. After all, if the common consensus had not been "Orchestra Hall is lost," we could not have raised the cry, "Save Orchestra Hall."

A graduate of Dearborn High and the University of Michigan, Paul Ganson retired as principal bassoonist with the Detroit Symphony Orchestra. The campaign he led to save Orchestra Hall was responsible for a listing on the National Register of Historic Places and two decades' worth of renovations. Ganson is researching and writing a history of the DSO.

Last Resort

By Frank "Tom" Jones III

I was out for a midday jog, dressed in my favorite "I Ran Thru Hell" running shirt. I was pounding down the road as I noticed another runner coming toward me on the other side of the street. As the distance between us narrowed, I saw the approaching runner fall – a header, face-down. Curiously continuing forward, I was waiting to see the runner get up and embarrassingly continue down the highway. The runner just lay there. I continued watching, not breaking my pace.

As I drew almost parallel with the fallen runner, it became apparent that I was going to have to interrupt my planned activities and see what I could do. (I want to emphasize that this was not in my character. I am neither a doctor, proficient in first aid, nor a good Samaritan.) In spite of my character, I jogged off to this person's side – if nothing else – to at least extend a hand up. At this time I noticed that the fallen comrade was a female, but in the sweat and dirt a runner is a runner.

Hmmm! Still no movement. "Are you OK?" I asked.

No reply.

The lady wasn't dead. In fact, she was shaking quite violently. Hmmm, the "trap doors" in the back of my mind started giving way. "Boy Scout first-aid data started rolling." Treat and prevent shock ... three blankets under, two on top, elevate feet, encourage the victim ... a lot of words but absolutely no application ... or blankets ... or communication, encouragement (?). The data was pouring out faster than I could sort it. OK, OK, I kneeled down to turn her over by her shoulder. Oh, man, her face was scraped up, not bleeding, filled with dirt and cinders ... and her eyes were rolled back. Tick, tick, tick ... does not compute ... not part of the Boy Scout scenario. Oh, no ... as she rolled over blood started spurting from her forearm. Not oozing– this was a gusher and sprayed out nearly a foot. "Trap door ... send data please!" Tourniquet ... ties ... belts, use a pen or pencil ... tick, tick, tick "Last resort." I definitely remember, "Last resort. Resort of what?"

I took off my shirt and folded it into a band. And wrapped it around her arm. I pressed as hard as I could on the wound and with my other hand pressed at the base of her shoulder. Data, data, ... pressure point, there had to be a pressure point somewhere!

"I called 911," I heard a voice say. Data, data, data, ... blank, blank, blank! I don't remember much more.

"I'll take over," a voice said. A uniform, a belt with scissors, a fire truck! Another voice, "What happened? ... Who is it? ... Where, what, how? ... data, data, data." ... and then the stretcher was going in the truck ... I never heard a siren. People were talking ... murmur, murmur.

What was I doing? Finish the run. Data kept careening out of my mind ... eventually the run was over.

End of the story.

Now, it is a year later ... just another tidbit stored somewhere in the back of my mind somewhere between "tourniquet" and "plans gone awry." The doorbell rings.

"Are you Mr. Jones?"

"Yes."

"Is this yours?" a well-dressed lady I didn't recognize asks as she opens up a T-shirt to reveal the writing: "Run Thru Hell!" Tears were streaming down her face.

"The shirt, yes. What's wrong?"

"I can't believe it," she sobbed. "I have thought about this day for so long ... I am speechless ... You meant so much to me. You saved my life in more ways than one. You were an angel ... and I have never been the same since you brought Jesus into my life."

Duh, ... speechless, speechless.

"When I woke up in the hospital, the past three days were a blur. I remember you, oh, so well, surrounded by a bright light and I remember seeing this T-shirt. And I knew in an instant that my life had been changed."

She unfurled the shirt and there it was ... a picture of the devil himself (pitchfork and all) and the words, "I Ran Thru Hell." ... and on the back of the shirt in small letters "and survived!"

"Mr. Jones, this is the story of my life. I had no meaning or purpose until you brought me the light. I thank Jesus every day for all that you have done."

End of the story again.

You know, I have never talked to that lady again. I think I may have seen her in the distance, but I was never sure.

Never sure of many things.

The "Run Thru Hell" shirt is awarded to participants of a marathon event staged in Hell, Michigan, by the Pinckney Running Club. It is well-known to all Michigan runners.

Frank "Tom" Jones III is a 1965 graduate of Edsel Ford High School. He is retired both from the Ford Motor Company and the United Sates Army as sergeant major (internal/public affairs chief). He splits his residence between Gibraltar, Michigan, and Vero Beach, Florida.

That's Brass

By Loren Moore

The day General Douglas MacArthur came to Dearborn was in 1951. I was in the sixth grade at William Ford School. We got a half a day off. I was with four or five guys from school, and we went to the city hall to see him. It was crowded all the way up the front steps. Being brash kids, we pushed ourselves up to the big block on the left-hand side of the steps. The longer-legged guys climbed up and pulled the rest of us up onto the block. When General MacArthur was speaking at the podium, we were really close.

The next time I would be this close to a general would be in May 1965, when General Harold K. Johnson, chief of staff at the Pentagon, would be giving a farewell to my battalion at Ft. Lewis, Washington, just before we shipped out to Vietnam.

Loren Moore is a retired firefighter. He and his wife, Margaret, have been married for 34 years and are the parents of Laura Lee and Mike and have a grandson, Pauly. He is the secretary of the Early Ford V8 Club of Dearborn.

Going to Prison Saved My Life

By Leno Poli

I began visiting the imprisoned in 1987 at the Federal Correctional Institution at Milan, which has the distinction of having hanged the last man in the federal prison system. I belonged to a Catholic prison ministry group named Cursillo (Spanish for "short course" in Christianity) whose mission was to transform men's lives through a three-day weekend. At the time I had little idea how prison would change my life.

Jesus' words, "I was in prison and you visited me," made him real to me in their faces regardless of what crimes they had committed.

Although a cradle Catholic at age 43 who had a vague, general idea that Jesus had died for my sins on the cross, I came to believe that he had died for me personally and that I owed him my life. He convinced me that I was his brother, in fact, his friend if I would but follow him faithfully. I HAD NEVER FELT SO LOVED. I began to see his likeness in all I met.

Whenever I visited the prison, I would sense his presence in the assembly for he said, "Wherever two or more are gathered in my name, there I am in their midst"; and in the Scripture readings I heard him also; but most importantly his Real Presence in the Eucharist (communion).

I also saw inmates being transformed into his likeness like

the 80-year-old Mafia don, Sammy Rosati; Raphael, a former rebel fighter with Fidel Castro; the drug lords of the Medellin cartel; doctors and airline pilots arrested for drug smuggling and money laundering; former high-ranking government officials from foreign countries and America; and bank robbers and murderers who had made a genuine about-face in life and had decided to dedicate the rest of their lives to serving so noble a lord as Jesus.

Years later I moved to a women's prison and currently serve Michigan's only female prison in Ypsilanti. It is the greatest honor of my life to serve these women as a "cheerleader" for Christ by bringing his name and saving power into their lives so that they might begin new, productive lives and help change the lives of their children and grandchildren for generations to come.

This last year I also began serving as a religious volunteer with two others at the Dickerson County Jail in Hamtramck.

Over the years these men and women have become friends whom I have come to love and who have prayed for and uplifted even my family through crises and medical problems and have made me accountable to live a genuine Christian life myself because "you can't con a con."

The women at the Huron Valley Correctional Facility were especially instrumental in the modern day "miracle" of my wife's receiving a heart transplant three years ago, for which I will be eternally grateful.

My Catholic Christian walk now includes the "tripod" which supports my faith: 1) daily prayer, 2) daily Scripture study and 3) daily action. Daily Mass, reading of the Liturgy of the Hours, Rosary, Chaplet of Divine Mercy and outreach in love, especially to my wife, have become part of my life. They now give me greater joy than I have ever known.

I am striving to be all that Jesus calls me to be and to love God and my fellow man through service so that I might work in partnership with him to change the world. I desire to draw as many as possible into the kingdom that Jesus said, "Man has not seen, nor has ear heard, what God has prepared for those who love him."

My going to prison SAVED MY LIFE.

Leno Poli retired from Ford Motor after 30 years as a tool designer and lives with his wife, Rochelle, in Morley Manor. From their perch high atop the 12th floor they command a "Grand Canyon" view from Southfield to Wyandotte and couldn't enjoy Dearborn more.

You Only Live Twice

By James M. Stanley

When does an adventure begin? You can save a lot of thought and effort by being kidnapped, I suppose, but mostly it's a matter of imagination.

This trip began in the flea market that used to be in front of the Detroit Zoo. I found a stack of National Geographics. Two cover pictures struck me and I bought them: the Grand Canyon and the Pacific Crest Trail. I made it my goal to visit them the coming summer of '75.

I used to hitchhike a lot in those days: exploring the highways and byways of North America, reaching the pure basaltic edge of the continental shelf in Newfoundland, climbing miles-high mountain peaks in Colorado without equipment. When I came back home to tell about it, nobody believed me. They accused me of renting a room above a gas station in Port Huron and making it all up. I wish. The writing would have been better if I had.

This trip began with many minor events. Such as sunburning myself all over on a nude beach in California and attempting to hitch across the desert while fiercely scratching my itchy parts. A troupe of gypsy wanderers eventually picked me up after we met late at the bottom of the Grand Canyon.

I eventually reached the piney scent of the North Rim and gazed over the edge into a different realm. Stories of ghosts, gold, and pink rattlesnakes wafted through my head. I had heard a story of hikers who had died a month before. One stayed stranded on a ledge, and one tried to climb down. No ledges for me, I thought.

Hiking into the canyon was magical. The walls were pure crystal and reflected light differently every time the sun moved. It was a fairyland of scintillating colors.

The trail alongside the stream grew higher and higher – and thinner and thinner. Pretty soon it was just a narrow little ledge one half my boot length.

It was crumbling to pieces behind me as I went. No sweat, I thought. I will just keep on going. No way back is the story of my life.

A couple of time I grabbed onto handholds, and they came apart right in my hand. And so it went.

Finally I came to a spot where the trail stopped. I was stuck on the wall like a fly. There was a handhold and a ledge beyond it. I looked at the handhold. It was in solid rock for many feet. I tested it and it did not crumble. So I put my weight on it to swing over to the second ledge, and the whole big rock, 5 feet by 5 feet, came out of the canyon wall and fell into the stream, far, far, below.

I watched it tumble and turn just like in the movies. I quickly swung back to my little ledge, which promptly began to crumble beneath my feet. Wait a minute!

Perceptions sharpened in a way that happens only in utter emergencies. I spotted a little juniper root dangling down from the edge of the canyon. Junipers are tough. This one was about a quarter-inch thick, just enough to support my weight for a second. And back at school I was a great rope climber.

I scrambled up that juniper root faster than Tarzan. I heaved myself over the edge of the canyon and lay down and just breathed for about five minutes. When I realized what had just happened, I said my first prayer in years:

Thank God. Thank God. Thank God.

Finally, that fall, I reached the Pacific Crest Trail around Mount Rainier. I left the trail (No, no, you might say. Yes, yes, I did) to hike into the valley to be near a glacial runoff stream for my morning ablution. I set up my tent, cooked, night came. Blah, blah, blah.

In the middle of the night I was woken by screaming steam whistles, crashes of locomotives and thundering ground quakes.

Coward that I was, I stayed in the tent crouching and whimpering. Thus I preserved my virtue. It was a herd of rutting bull elk, strutting their stuff.

Next day I awoke to discover hoofprints in the swampy turf over a foot deep.

After hiking out, I got a ride from a couple of college ladies who were thrilled to hear elks bugling in the distance.

"We are so lucky to hear them," one said.

Yeah, lucky.

James M. Stanley is always a student, always a traveler, always an adventurer, always a writer. He retired after teaching both for a Navajo school and for the Detroit Public Schools.

So the FBI Doesn't Know What Bank Robbers Use Nylons For?

By Ron Webb

This event took place on the Friday before Labor Day, 1964. I know that for sure because the next day, the Saturday before Labor Day, 1964, I was getting married. In order to understand the full impact of the events, we have to back up a couple of days to the previous Wednesday.

About a month earlier, my fiancee and I had rented an apartment in east Dearborn. We had spent the intervening time painting it to our preference, making minor repairs, moving in furniture, etc. The last week before the wedding, we were down to moving in books, clothes and other odds and ends.

On that Wednesday, after getting off work, I went over to my fiancee's house to take a bunch of clothes to the apartment. I walked in the back door. Her mother was cooking dinner in the kitchen, and she indicated that my future bride was in the basement. I walked back to her bedroom and hollered down, "Is everything on the bed supposed to go?" She hollered back, "Yes, everything."

In those days, she was a guide at Greenfield Village. They were required to wear a white blouse, black skirt, nylons and black shoes. She had changed clothes after coming home from work and tossed her girdle and nylons (this is the days before panty hose) on the bed next to a laundry basket full of clothes. The reader must also bear in mind that in those days (before Victoria's Secret, etc.) it was considered inappropriate for a young man to be looking at or handling women's underwear. However, since my fiancee and I had a long-standing, very close relationship, I thought it would be

OK to tease her a little. I picked up the girdle and nylons and tossed them on top of the clothes in the basket. I walked out through the kitchen past my future mother-in-law. She immediately saw the girdle and nylons and said, "Oh! You better not let her see that! She'll have a fit!" I replied, "It's three days before the wedding. What she gonna do?"

I walked out and put the basket on the front seat. My fiance came out and got in the car. Of course, the first thing she spotted was the girdle and nylons. "You big dummy!" she said. "What if people saw that? What would they think?" She grabbed the girdle and nylons and stuffed them in the glove compartment. We went on to the apartment, took care of business and returned to her house, forgetting all about the underwear in the glove compartment.

Now, along comes Friday. In those days, I worked as the assistant manager at one of the city's neighborhood pools. Friday was the manager's day off, so I had to wear a white shirt and dark pants to work rather than my usual T-shirt and shorts. It so happened that one of the bathhouse attendants was a girl who lived on the first street to the east of mine. Every day, I would pick her up for work and then drop her off at about 5 p.m. or so before heading home.

Well, late on the Friday afternoon in question, somebody had robbed the Michigan National Bank (now a Bank of America) at the corner of Ford Road and Telegraph. The robber was a young guy, tall, dark hair and eyes, wearing a white shirt and driving an old black car. Well, I was 21, 6 foot, 3 inches, dark brown hair and eyes, wearing a white shirt and driving a black 1954 Ford. I fit the description to a T.

After I dropped off my co-worker, I pulled down the street to the corner, where I had to turn left. As I got to the corner, a newer, very plain sedan was approaching from my right. In it were two men in business suits. I just figured it was two guys heading home from work. To get to my house, I had to turn left, go down to the next cross street and turn left again. My house was the fourth one from the corner. The sedan stopped for the stop sign, and I turned left. As I approached the cross street, where I had to turn left again, the sedan came screaming around to my left at an incredible rate of speed. It swerved in front of me, winding up broadside, blocking my path. Of course, I hit the brakes with everything I had.

I was stunned for a moment or two and then went to reach for the door handle. I was gonna get out and ream that guy a new one. I never got the chance to reach the handle. Of course, this was summer, and I had the window open, As I reached for the handle, I looked up, and there stood one of the guys from the car. He had a little folding card in his hand. He snapped it shut, and right behind the card was the muzzle of a huge handgun.

"FBI!" he shouted at me. "Don't move! Put your hands on the wheel! Eyes straight ahead!"

Of course, I was quaking in my boots. I did exactly as he said.

His partner got in on the passenger side, and the same routine followed: little card snapped shut, followed by "FBI" and the muzzle of another gun. There I sat, with two guns a few inches from each side of my head. I have to say that at that moment, I came as close to soiling myself as I ever have in my entire adult life!

The guy outside started hollering questions at me. "What's your name! Where do you live? What are you doing here? Where have you been all day?" I stammered out answers as best I could. Meanwhile, the guy on the inside of the car grabbed the keys from the ignition, got out and popped open the trunk. Of course, there was nothing in it but a spare tire, a jack and some other odds and ends.

He opened the door and inspected the back-seat area. Then he got back in the front seat. He demanded to see my driver's license, so, very slowly and gingerly, I handed it over.

Of course, by this time, quite a crowd had developed. It was a warm, late summer day, and nobody in that neighborhood had air conditioning. The squealing tires, the blasting horn, the shouts had attracted a lot of attention. Both our cars were ringed by a crowd three or four people deep.

I could hear the murmuring of the people. "Ron Webb. FBI. Bank robbery. Bad kid. Knew it all along."

I looked up the street, and there came my mother, charging along. She was hollering, "What are you doing to my son! Leave my son alone! Don't you know he's getting married tomorrow!!!???"

Just as she approached, the guy in the front seat popped open the glove compartment and, of course, there was the girdle and nylons. I guess by this time, they had figured out that they had the wrong guy.

The guy in the front seat decided he'd have a little fun at my expense. He took the girdle and nylons out of the glove compartment and stepped out of the car.

He held the girdle and nylons up for everyone in the crowd to see and exclaimed, "Hey, it don't matter to us, buddy! Just so long as you didn't take her across a state line!"

The crowd gasped and went silent. Just at that moment, my mother was breaking through the crowd. She took one look at the girdle and nylons, and her jaw dropped practically down to the concrete. She turned around and ran back toward our house.

The guy holding the underwear tossed it back on the front seat, and they both got back in their car. The crowd parted, and they drove off. I turned left and parked in front of my house.

I went in, and my mother was waiting for me in the kitchen. She had her arms crossed across her chest, her right foot was tapping, and she had that look on her face that, from long experience, I knew meant, "Be very careful about what you say next if you want to see another sunrise!!"

"Young man," she said. "Explain to your mother this instant what that girdle and nylons are doing in your car!"

I stammered out the story about the previous Wednesday as best I could. Then my mother said, "Well, I'll just have to ask Lois (my fiancee's mother) about this at the rehearsal tonight!"

My reaction was, "Oh my God, NOOOOOOO! If my fiancee found out that the underwear had appeared, it just might mean cancellation of our wedding plans. In those days, if a young woman wore a white dress to her wedding, it meant she deserved to wear a white dress to her wedding. And my fiancee was going to wear one. Moreover, if my mother brought it up, it would give my future mother-in-law a huge card to play against me in the future, and we weren't even married yet. She had, of course, warned me not to carry out my little prank.

"Mom," I said. Please don't do that! It could be a disaster! Just believe me, OK? I've never lied to you before!" The latter statement was true. I never had lied to her.

"Well, OK!" she said. I'll let it go for now."

I breathed a huge sigh of relief. Thankfully, the wedding went off without a hitch. Finally, several years later, I told my wife what had happened. By that time, we had enjoyed enough marital bliss that we got a good laugh out of it, not only that day, but many times afterward.

Ron Webb is retired from the Dearborn Public Schools, where he was an English teacher for 37 years. He still resides, along with wife, Pam, in west Dearborn about six blocks from where the incident described took place. The fiancée/wife described in this piece is Ron's first wife, who passed away in 1971.

Chapter 16

Life's Journeys

Bookkeeping: All A's; Beating the Hubbards: Incomplete

By Beverly Bazzy

There is some symmetry in life. My condo sits on the site where my deceased husband coached Little League football!

My ethnicity is a bit unusual. I am German, Irish, Jewish and North American Indian. My husband, Allay, was Lebanese, first generation born in the United States. My kids are obviously hybrids.

I moved to Bingham Street from Detroit when I was 7 years old. I attended Lowrey through the ninth grade and then Fordson High School. I got married shortly after my husband was released from serving in the Korean War.

My husband and I lived at 3824 Mayfair for 41 years. When my husband first suggested that we move there, I was hesitant because it was so far in the country. Our home was small, only 800 square feet. Though we had only two bedrooms, we always brought in stray animals and people. We had cots for our strays! The neighborhood kids were always at our house.

Allay worked for 39 years in the city of Dearborn's Water Department. Allay and his co-coaches took a football team that had had no victories in the prior year and turned it into an undefeated, un-scored upon team. They were the Dearborn Thunderbirds, and we were all so proud of those young boys.

We have two sons. Ron is in marketing and finance. David is the president and chief operating officer of Kenwal Corporation. He also serves on the City Council.

I took bookkeeping in high school. I got all A's in those classes. I not only did my homework but my friends' as well. They also got A's. I was hired by the Dearborn Public Schools in 1966. I became the head bookkeeper for the school district's payroll department. I had fun with the knowledge I accumulated along the way.

I worked in various schools along the way. I especially liked working at Edsel Ford. We were like a family there.

In 1970 I decided to run for mayor. Mayor Orville Hubbard asked me, "What makes you think you can beat me?" I told him that he could drop dead and all that I would need is one vote and I would become mayor. "I would hire a bunch of smart people to run the city, just like you did," I told him. Among my concerns was the purchase of the Clearwater, Florida, apartment complex. I find it interesting that the city has finally divested itself of this property.

When I decided to run for office, my dad asked, "Did you lose your brains?" I came in third place, after Hubbard and Doug Thomas. Later I ran for city treasurer against John J. Hubbard. I guess I am a slow learner, running against the Hubbard dynasty.

I'm pretty outspoken. I told my kids that I didn't care what they did for a living, but they should get a college education. I taught them to be sincere, to finish what they start and to be kind to people. I am teaching my grandkids to do the same. I always told my kids, "If you don't like your teacher, too bad. Learn to deal with it with a smile."

I'm proud of David's work on the City Council. He does a great job. When he first told me he was running for office, I told him to make sure and direct the mail to his house. He said, "Mom, I forgot to tell you—you're campaign manager/treasurer."

I like to have fun. I live in this nice condominium. It's funny that I ended up here. Allay came home to Mayfair one day and told me that he put a deposit on a condo in this complex. I told him, "I hope you like it because I'm not moving." He went and got his deposit back. I moved into the complex after he passed away.

Usually everybody gets along in the area. One day, however (while I was the condo president), a neighbor complained that my leaves blew into her yard. I don't know how she knew the leaves were mine, as she had a tree in her yard as well. I told her, "If you show me which leaves are mine, I will rake mine up, but I am not going to rake yours!"

Life has been good to me. I love living in Dearborn. Many of us who have stayed in Dearborn have done so because it is a great place to raise a family, and the city truly cares about its senior citizen residents.

Beverly Bazzy continues to open her home to family and friends. She is the treasurer of the Dearborn Public Schools' 25+ Club.

Mia Famiglia

By Carmen Mattera DeSanto

My family moved from Detroit to Dearborn before I entered elementary school. I attended St. Barbara's and St. Clement's. I discovered that nuns don't like left-handers! I thrived at Fordson. I was on the baseball and track teams. I was in the booster club. However, one memory that jumps out at me was of my initiation into high school. My brother and the brother of my best friend, Beverly Misko, had us clean the steps of Fordson–with a toothbrush! I chuckle when I think of Mr. Bonfiglio's squashing a worm in my hand because I wouldn't touch them.

My mom's name was Louise Mattera, and one day a year – opening day of the baseball season – I assumed her identify to call Fordson and tell the staff that my son (brother) was sick and would not be in school. My now-deceased husband, John DeSanto, followed that tradition and took our kids to the baseball playoffs. One of our kids was fired because of John's pulling him off the job.

I helped my brother, Pete, with his paper route. He figured that I could get more tips than he, so I was to do the collecting. There was only one other girl on the block. There were several boys, so we had lots of fun.

My parents were traditional Italians. The boys could do no wrong. The girls had to be watched! When I went out on dates, my sister had to come along. The tradition that I most remember was having dinner with our extended family on Sundays. My family is Catholic. My cousin, Father Sidera, officiated at the weddings of my two sons and my sister Addy. He baptized all my grandchildren.

My dad came to the United States from Italy when he was 14. He came to Parkersburg, West Virginia, to work in the coal mines. He was buried in the mines three times. After the third time, he came to Detroit to work at "Ford's." He stayed there for more than 40 years. He swore that he would never be buried again. After he died, we placed him in a mausoleum, not a grave. I considered my dad to be my buddy.

My mom was one of eight kids. She was the oldest. She went to school for only three or four years. Then she stayed home to help with the family. As a parent, she was loving but strict.

My first job on graduating from high school was in the payroll department at Montgomery Ward. I worked there for three years. This was my beginning in the service arena.

My husband and I ran the Kenilworth Pub on Ford Road for 28 years. It was a fun bar. We had pig roasts, we took our customers to Camp Dearborn, and we had scavenger hunts. In 1994 we bought the Biergarten from Mickey Misko, whom I considered to be my second father. Coincidentally, my first job was working at Misko's Aviation Bar at the age of 18. In our two bars I met several ball players and hockey players. I met all of the Red Wings. The New York Yankees and the Minnesota Twins were our frequent customers.

At the Biergarten, we had customers bring in their business cards. My daughter-in-law is an artist, and she would copy the business cards on the ceiling. We charged $100 a year for each advertiser. All proceeds went to the Juvenile Diabetes Foundation.

I have three kids. John retired from working on a cruise ship. Dominic is an engineer at NSW, and Carmen is a stay-at-home mom. I have four grandchildren.

One of my fondest memories was of going to Italy. Dominic and his wife paid my way. We visited my father's home, which was on an island not far from the Isle of Capri. Apparently the name Mattera was associated with wealth; everyone thought we were rich. I have had a rich life, though not financially rich. I have been blessed with a wonderful family and good friends.

Carmen Mattera DeSanto lives in west Dearborn, not far from one of her sons and her daughter.

Healing Begins in Here

By Sarah Jane

I am, somehow, a traveler. Born in Grand Rapids, yet keenly sensing that my home is somewhere else, I set out on a journey of both inner and outer space. In July 2013 my path took me to Dearborn. The intent was to help take care of a dear friend's mother, who needed companionship in recuperation from surgery, and to work on my own healing when I could squeeze it in. But then it occurred to me, once I heard myself say it out loud: Why would I give such an important priority the second skimmings of my time and energy? Fate knew better – and forced the issue when I was least expecting it: immediately.

I also consider myself to be a healer. Give me any situation, and I'll give you ways to improve it. Yet the one that always dumbfounded me was the only one I had any real responsibility for: my own. What was going on with that girl in the mirror, and why was I always looking at the reflection, without realizing that what caused the reflection was right in here?

Over and over, the mirror showed to me the same problems, and they seemed to be getting progressively worse, yet I still continued to reach out my hand to the mirror and never to my own being. Until that fateful day, when I finally asked not the mirror, but myself: What is going on with me?

Now that I had the right question and direction, I was

awarded an answer: I had been externalizing everything that was going on within me, and if I really wanted to see a change in the mirror, in the world, I was going to have to start in here. The only one I am able to heal is myself! And the beautiful paradox is, when that happens, when I heal myself, then everyone else will heal too! What I had wanted to find this whole time was so elusive because I was looking in the wrong place. I first had to find it within myself. And now that I am able to find it, see it, accept it, love it, work with it and heal it, I can change my projection, that image I give to the mirror. And that mirror automatically returns a new reflection: the one I had been wanting to see all along.

That's true whether I'm looking at a physical mirror or the mirror of the family, the community and the world and universe at large. It can be tempting to reach out, especially since I hold an inner vision of something so much greater. But it's even more exciting to experience success. As I come to know the truth about myself and see that all of the changes "out there" actually begin in here, I discover more power than I had ever imagined. My power to change myself is my power to change the world. And it began – and begins – with a thought.

I don't know how long I will be in Dearborn; I may be gone before this book is even published. But Dearborn will always be in me, in my heart, because it's the place where this dear was once again born.

Sarah Jane is a creator at heart and loves to experience the beauty of life in the world within and around her.

History 101

By Elvina Korte Taylor

I was born 101 years ago on a farm next door to Henry Ford's farm. My father was in the third grade with Henry Ford.

The first Sacred Heart Church was on Mason between Nona and Park. Back in those days parishioners had to ride a horse and buggy to church on Sundays. If the weather was bad, Mr. Ford would take us in his Model A or Model T. I am not sure which one we rode. He would drive around town and return to pick us up after church services were over and return us to our farm. My brother Eugene took care of Henry's flowers and bushes at his farm next door. I was the youngest of the family of five daughters and two sons. The family sold the farm and moved into a large house on Garrison right behind Kroger on Michigan Avenue. We all graduated from Sacred Heart, except for Elizabeth, who was the oldest but had to quit school to help her mother with the family.

Two of my sisters taught school in Taylor. One of my brothers, John, went to work for Borden's and delivered milk to homes in west Dearborn. My brother Eugene went into the landscape business. Eugene married and bought a farm on Michigan Avenue, west of Wayne Road. Elizabeth married Joseph Penn and lived on Tenny. My brother John married and also lived on Tenny.

I became a nurse and worked at Mt. Carmel Hospital. I married Phil Taylor, and we bought a house on Donaldson between

Elmdale and Monroe. A few years later, with three children, the house became too small so we bought a larger home on Wilson. My husband opened a jewelry store on Warren Avenue. I continued working as a nurse.

After the two girls and son married, Phil and I moved to a home on Lake August in Lake Placid, Florida. After my husband died, I moved into a place on Lake Huntly where my daughter lives. I am very active and like to go visiting and out to eat. I think being a nurse, I had learned to take care of myself.

I sure miss Dearborn, where there was lots to do, and I thought Mayor Hubbard was great. He did a good job taking care of Dearborn and did a good job keeping the town clean and safe to live in. I hope to live a few more years to enjoy all our warm weather here in Florida.

This story was told to James J. Penn.

91 Years
Of Wonderful Memories

By Matt Zipple

I was born in Lansing in 1921. My dad was born in Germany. He ran away from home and became a cabin boy in the merchant marine. He got sick in New York and met a German Jew. My dad asked where he was going. "To Detroit" was the response. My dad decided to go there and ultimately ended up in Lansing.

He became a fire captain and was the first in Lansing to drive a chief's car, an Oldsmobile; before that, the chief rode in horse-drawn conveyances. My mom came from Moravia, which is between Bohemia and Slovakia. She grew up in Elsie, which is north of Lansing, and came there to go to business school. She got a job as a waitress at a restaurant across the street from the fire station. In that my dad worked 24 hours, six days a week, he saw a lot of my mom. The rest is history. They ended up having five children: Karl, Annette, Francis, John and me.

I grew up on the south end of Lansing where weren't many kids. I entertained myself by watching people get off the interurban train coming from Jackson. One of the things that I enjoyed doing was digging holes and covering them with boards or branches so that we could use them as forts.

I was big for my age. At midyear, I went to elementary school earlier than was normal. Two weeks into the first grade, the principal picked five of us and promoted us to the second grade. I started the fifth grade at St. Mary's in Lansing. The school had a calendar that only began in September so I ended up getting bumped up another grade. I graduated from high school at the age of 16.

I entered Michigan State with the idea of studying in the police administration program. The curriculum was changed to five years in length. That didn't appeal to me so I switched to teaching. The University of Michigan was reputed to have a better education program so I transferred there as a junior. I graduated from college when I was 20.

During the summer I worked for Pontiac Motors and for the Yellow Truck and Coach Company. One day I stepped on a spike and it went through my foot. I went to a clinic and was hitchhiking home when a Silvercup bread truck picked me up; the driver asked if I could drive a truck. I could, and so I took that job.

Three days after I turned 21 I was drafted. I was sent to Camp Gruber, Oklahoma. There may be a more God-forsaken place, but if there is, I don't know about it!

I entered the field artillery, and after a week I was offered the job of teaching reading and writing to illiterate soldiers, mainly from Mississippi. I taught them how to write letters home and how to read the bulletin board for their assignments. This kept me off KP (Kitchen Police) duty. After basic training I was sent to OCS (Officer Candidate School) at Fort Sill, Oklahoma, where I became a second lieutenant in field artillery. I was sent to Casablanca and then to Oran in Algeria. One day at the mess hall, somebody said, "Zipple, pass the bread." Somebody else grabbed the bread; it was my brother, who was shipped to Oran from Italy where he had gotten his feet frostbitten!

I went to Italy with the Texas National Guard's 36th Division and landed in southern France. I fought up the Rhone River. I was wounded twice and got a Bronze Star Medal. I finished my tour of duty as part of the occupation army.

I began my master's at U. of M. in education on the GI Bill. When I was not quite finished, the superintendent of schools in Mt. Morris offered me a job. I took the position, but I had to drive a school bus with no extra pay. I complained to the Michigan Education Association, and the superintendent didn't like me after that.

I then got a job in Grand Ledge, some 15 miles west of Lansing. I was able to live at home. I drove a bus there as well. There was a girl, Millie Jones, at the end of the line that I frequently talked to. I saw her as recently as two weeks ago!

I got my certification to teach driver education. I figure that I taught some 4,000 students how to drive. Among the interesting students I taught was a young woman who had no legs. She controlled everything with her hands. Another anecdote: One day my daughter was in Costa Rica visiting a Peace Corps friend. She was introduced to another volunteer. He said, "Does your father teach driver education in Dearborn?" He had been my student!

I began teaching in Dearborn in 1950. In 1953 I got a chance to help plan Edsel Ford. Tony Lawski was in charge of this "Chicago Project." Thirty of us went to Chicago for a semester. We talked to various famous curriculum planners. We traveled around the country looking at model schools. We decided on a unique program. The next year we worked at Greenfield Village teaching our colleagues this new program.

Edsel Ford High School opened in September 1955. We integrated the study of culture into the curriculum. For example, in social studies we studied the culture of the Hopi Indians as well as Ugandans, etc. When I taught sociology, economics and geography, there was an emphasis on the interaction of people. Each teacher served as a guide for a group of students.

The English instructors taught humanities, integrating English, art and music. They really taught students how to write papers. When students graduated, they really appreciated what we did for them.

A government-sponsored program to educate counselors brought me back to Michigan State to study counseling. From there we went to Atlanta University. I took my wife and five kids to attend the school, which turned out to be all black. I was the only white in the institute. We had to have a practicum, but the white schools wouldn't take me because of my attending an all-black college. The black schools wouldn't take me because I was white. I ended up doing my practicum at Morris Brown College. This was the Civil Rights era. I had students asking me what they should do when their parents would not allow them to march in demonstrations. One student said his mom, a school teacher, would be fired if he marched. That was the day of white and black drinking fountains. My kids got as much out of that semester as I did. It was a great learning experience. My wife and I were active in the Catholic Family Movement. We taught Bible school in North Carolina in the summers. That also impacted my kids.

I stayed with Edsel Ford High School until I retired. This was the same year that the ninth-grade students came to the high school building.

My sister went to school at Mount St. Joseph College in

Cincinnati. My brother was in the seminary there, but couldn't come home for Thanksgiving. I decided to take my mom and sister to see my brother. I asked my brother to find us a place to stay. We ended up staying with my sister's friend. Ruth, the friend, was the loveliest thing that I had ever seen. (And I had dated a lot of women.) We spent two days there. I kissed her under the mistletoe. I knew right away I wanted to marry her. I went back at Christmas and proposed.

Ruth and I married on August 20, 1949. We were married for 63 years before she passed away. We had five kids. Mary Therese Lemanek is a retired nurse and social worker, whose main concern these days is caring for her family and conducting church-sponsored programs. Tony is the CEO of a health service in Louisville; he has a doctorate in training the emotionally handicapped. Annette is a pediatrician in Grand Rapids. Katie is a full-time professor of nursing at Wayne State University and is a wound care specialist at Henry Ford Hospital. Daniel (Danny) has a doctorate in economics. He has multiple sclerosis. Danny lives in North Carolina. I have 13 grandkids and two great grandkids.

I hope I taught my kids to help other people. We didn't get here just to make money and get rich. While I never told my kids what to do, I had always hoped that they would be in the service professions. They truly turned out to be quality citizens!

I'm just a 91-year-old retired teacher-counselor who has had a wonderful life and am still blessed with family and memories of a wonderful wife. Few people have been so lucky!

Matt Zipple taught in the Dearborn Public Schools for 36 years and retired in 1986.

(See picture on page 475.)

Chapter 17

Organizations

In Community Service It's a Perennial

By Anina Bachrach
& Patti Mack

The Garden Club of Dearborn played a major role throughout the life of Dearborn. It is the oldest service club in Dearborn. On August 13, 1915, at Mrs. Louis Ives' home, 18 Dearborn women formed the club and named Mrs. Henry Ford (Clara Ford) their first president. She remained for the first five years of the club and an active member for the rest of her life. Their goals were to advance horticulture and gardening and to improve the community. They did this by installing plantings at the schools in the community, securing the first school nurse, supplying milk for lunches and helping to form the first Dearborn Parent-Teacher Association. Their approach was to start a project, demonstrate success and then to persuade the school board or village council to take it over.

An example of this was the development of Dearborn's first public library on Michigan Avenue (originally named the Mason Branch). Through the donation of land in 1923 from Henry and Clara Ford and the hard work of Mrs. Ford's friend Clara Snow and her committee of Garden Club members, the library was established. In 1977 this first library of Dearborn was renamed the Bryant Library in honor of Katherine Bryant (sister-in-law of Clara Ford). Bryant Library served as Dearborn's main library for 45 years. Katherine Bryant was appointed along with Miss Snow to the first library board by the Dearborn Board of Education in July 1920. Both were the representatives for the Garden Club of Dearborn.

The history of the Princeton Branch Library began on November 20, 1958, when ground was broken by Katherine W.

Bryant, using the same spade used exactly 35 years earlier by Mrs. Henry Ford to break ground for the Main Library (now called the Bryant Branch).

A dedication ceremony on July 1, 1962, renamed the library the Clara Snow Branch in honor of Miss Snow, a founder of the Dearborn Public Library system and a charter member of the City Library Commission. Miss Snow had been associated with the public library since 1919, when the Dearborn Garden Club proposed to establish a community library with $200 (equals $2,700 buying power in 2013) of its funds and appointed Miss Snow to make a preparatory study for the project. The Garden Club members were also asked to donate books from their own private libraries to help fill the shelves.

In 1931 the Garden Club of Dearborn was one of 15 clubs to form the Federated Garden Clubs of Michigan. Today this is known as Michigan Garden Clubs, Inc., with nearly 200 clubs and over 7,000 members. In 1932 the Federation became part of the National Council of State Garden Clubs (now known as National Garden Clubs, Inc.), which now has over 276,000 members in 9,300 clubs. There have been 45 presidents of the club with Mrs. Ford being the first. Our oldest member is Nina Kaufman who is 104 years old. She vividly remembers going to Fair Lane for meetings and having tea with Mrs. Ford, with Henry stopping by from time to time.

During World War II the club developed Victory Gardens in Dearborn, giving instruction and help on how to have a successful vegetable garden. The tradition of education and beauty continues today with periodical garden walks staged in members' gardens to help teach the general public about the value and beauty of gardening.

During the 1950s the Garden Club under the leadership of Miss Snow enlisted all the other service groups in Dearborn to get together and help clean up the median on Telegraph from Princeton to Ford Road, after the widening of Telegraph. Monies were raised, and lovely groves of white crab apple trees were planted all along the route. It is amazing these trees have survived and bloom each spring.

Mayors of Dearborn have always turned to the Garden Club for advice and guidance. In 1974 the club was asked to develop ideas for the landscape at Bryant Library to honor the bicentennial year. There is a big tri-color beech, planted in the front yard for that honor, still waving its wonderful leaves. In 1983 we were asked to design the children's garden and planters at the Centennial Library and again in the '90s help with the creating of the Van Mericas Arboretum at the Centennial Library. The club has planted many wonderful specimen trees throughout the city in honor of the club's 50-year members.

Today the Garden Club of Dearborn is a 501(c)3 nonprofit organization that continues to serve the community in many ways such as "garden therapy" with patients at the Oakwood Rehabilitation and Skilled Nursing Center, and installing plantings at the Henry Ford Centennial Library and in downtown west Dearborn. The proceeds from the Garden Club's annual Holly Berry Brunch fund numerous scholarships for University of Michigan-Dearborn and Henry Ford Community College students, internships and garden restoration at the Henry Ford Estate, and landscaping projects at the Ford Community and Performing Arts Center, Environmental Interpretive Center at the University of Michigan-Dearborn and other local schools. The club also provides intra-club scholarships for members attending the Flower Show School, the Gardening Study Courses, Landscape Design and Environment Schools. Members pursuing these studies then bring their knowledge back to the club and community.

Patti Mack is the newly elected president of the Garden Club of Dearborn. Anina Bachrach is an active member who knows the history of this club, takes great pride in the accomplishments of the group and is the number 1 cheerleader for the organization.

Embroiderers Missed Their Morning Fiber

By Patricia Donaldson

The time was January 1974. An enthusiastic group of individuals who loved to do needlework met to form a chapter of the Embroiderers' Guild of America. Officers were elected, by-laws written and application for membership submitted. The Dearborn-Fairlane Chapter officially became affiliated with the national organization on April 22, 1974. After meeting at the Guaranty Federal Savings Bank and the McFadden-Ross House, the chapter found a spacious home at First Presbyterian Church, which accommodated our rapidly growing group. To accommodate our very diverse group of women, two separate meeting groups were set up – one to meet during the day and the other for the working women to meet during the evening.

The chapter continued to grow, offering workshops of many needlework techniques, often taught by some of our own talented members as well as nationally known needlewomen. We became part of the Great Lakes Region, hosted several regional seminars at the Dearborn Inn, as well as the national seminar at the Hyatt Regency in 1981. Over the years, the chapter became one of the largest and most active in the region.

In appreciation of the hospitality extended to us at First Pres, we designed and stitched paraments for the church. We were members of the local arts council, participating at many events, worked with the staff at Meadowbrook Hall to design and stitch luggage rack straps for their guest rooms and donated time and talent to several local charities. Some members assisted the Dearborn Historical Museum in sorting, cleaning, repairing and cataloging needlework items in the collection. One year we made and donated holiday ornaments to the Michigan Women's Historical Center & Hall of Fame – and then drove to Lansing to decorate the tree.

In 2006, after a long run as a very successful chapter, members voted to dissolve due to declining membership and difficulty in electing officers to serve.

However, here's the rest of the story: Many of the members still wished to meet and share their love of the needle arts. So, the Dearborn Fiber Artists was created. We meet monthly at the McFadden-Ross House the mornings of the second Wednesday.

Patricia Donaldson is a long-time resident of Dearborn and charter member of the Dearborn-Fairlane Chapter of the Embroiderers' Guild of America. She is a needlework designer and certified teacher of the American Needlework Guild.

60 Years of Questing

By Virginia Horton

The Questers is a private, nonprofit international organization incorporated in 1944 in Pennsylvania and is presently headquartered in Philadelphia. It was organized by the founder, Mrs. William George Bardens (Bess), as an antique study club and has grown far beyond her initial vision.

The purpose of the Questers is to educate by the research and study of antiques, to donate funds to the preservation and restoration of existing memorials, historical buildings, landmarks and educational purposes.

Cherry Hill Questers #32 was chartered March 25, 1954. The chapter was named for the old local trail called Cherry Hill Road. It ran west from Brady Street to a little settlement between Dearborn and Ann Arbor. The little village was named Cherry Hill because of the great number of wild cherry trees found on a rise of the ground.

Our chapter is celebrating its 60th anniversary March 25, 2014. We have focused most of our fund-raising efforts on the Dearborn Historical Museum. Over the years, we have been able to donate reproduction carpeting, draperies and several china pieces to the Museum for the Commandant's Quarters. A few years ago we were able to sponsor the restoration of a window at the restored Ford Piquette Plant. We continue to meet monthly, often at the

McFadden-Ross House, enjoy programs on a variety of historical subjects and objects and plan field trips to historically significant venues.

We look forward to participating in the International Questers Convention in April 2014. The Michigan State Chapter is hosting this annual meeting in Grand Rapids.

The Quester motto: It's fun to search ... and a joy to find!

In addition to the Cherry Hill Questers, Virginia Horton has actively supported the Dearborn Symphony Orchestra as well as other community organizations.

Compliments of Mayor Michael A. Guido

Books R Us

By Emily Nietering

I have always loved to read. Maybe it has something to do with the fact that both my parents were librarians and met each other at the Detroit Public Library when they both worked there in the early 1950s. For the last 17 years I have kept a journal of all the books I have read, with a short summary of the plot and characters and a recommendation to read or not to read more from the author. As I interacted with my friends and neighbors in Dearborn, I realized many of them were readers too, and the idea of forming a book club began to grow. In fact several neighbors of mine had already been meeting to watch movies together and discuss them and had recently agreed to meet and read and discuss books together. This was in 2001. They invited me to join them, and my first meeting was in June of that year. I distinctly remember our September meeting of 2001. Even though we had read a book in preparation for the meeting, you can imagine what our topic of discussion that day was.

We continued to meet in our small group and read books recommended by each other with a focus on women authors and women's issues. As the months progressed, we each began inviting other friends to join us. Sometime during the next year it was mentioned that the Dearborn Public Library had book kits for groups to check out to read, so we didn't have to buy our own copies. What a concept! To check out book kits you only needed a library card, but your club had to register and needed a name.

We discussed this and became the Second Friday Book Club, since we meet on the second Friday of the month. The book club kits generally have 10 copies of each book, so we have tried to keep our group between 10 and 12 members, so we don't have to share books. The library keeps about 200 kits ready at any time, buying some new titles and retiring some every year, so we haven't run out of choices yet. We expanded our original concept and now read books, both fiction and nonfiction, by all authors and about all topics.

Over the years, members of our book club have come and gone, some moving away or finding a new job that prevented them from attending. We have welcomed new members and relished their perspectives in our discussions. We have different backgrounds, faiths, family and economic situations, and of, course, different tastes in books. That's what makes it fun!

Since we began, we have read 123 books together. Some we liked and some we didn't. In fact the best discussions are often those about a book not liked by everyone. We choose our books from the lists and the summaries of the books found on the book kit tags. Sometimes we have found, to our surprise, that the book didn't really match what we anticipated from the listing. You really can't judge a book by its cover!

Since we have tried to limit our group to what will comfortably fit into a member's Dearborn-sized living room, we have had to turn away some who have asked to join us. We always recommend they start their own book club. Using ours as a model, several other groups have started in Dearborn, meeting on different days at different times. Many groups exist in neighborhoods, at senior living communities, churches, schools and other locations. At one time the Dearborn Public Library had over 50 groups registered to check out book kits. If you like to read, why not start your own book club? Gather a few friends or acquaintances (you'll be friends before long) and choose a time to meet and a book to read. The library book kits come with questions for discussion and often a biography of the author or other material related to the time period or setting of the story. Meeting my friends to discuss our books every month has been a wonderful part of my life in Dearborn. It can be part of yours.

Emily Nietering was born in Detroit and grew up in Elkhart, Indiana. She has lived in Dearborn for 30 years with her husband and three sons. She is an avid reader, gardener and quilter and in her spare time teaches biology at Henry Ford Community College.

The Players Guild in 3 Acts

By Phyllis Tippett

My mother and father joined the Dearborn Players Guild sometime in the 1930s. My father, Bob Shoens, was a ham and found his niche on the stage. My mother, Maida, was happy to work with properties and costumes.

In those days the Players Guild performances were in the Masonic Temple, which is still on the corner of Garrison and Monroe.

I think the auditorium was multi-use, so chairs were placed on the floor for performances. There was a balcony, however, and that was where I spent time watching rehearsals and productions, especially the ones in which my dad had a part.

When he was in a play, I would sit on the edge of the bathtub while he shaved, getting ready for work. We would read through the play. He would say his lines, and I would read those of everyone else in the play. It made me feel important. He was in a play titled *The Male Animal,* later made into a movie starring Henry Fonda.

During World War II the Players Guild moved its rehearsals and productions to an auditorium in Eloise. Sometime later Dr. Arnold, a prominent dentist in Dearborn, spearheaded a drive to raise funds for the guild's own playhouse. Located on Madison in Dearborn, it is going through some renovations.

I don't know what my parents had to do to become members in the 1930s. Much later, however, when I was grown, I decided to join. At that time, maybe the late 1960s or early '70s, I needed a member to sponsor me. My husband, Jim, and I were at a dinner-dance at the Dearborn Country Club, put on by Christ Episcopal Church. There was a lady there of the Snow family who belonged to the church and the Players Guild. I asked her if she would sponsor me and she agreed. I became an active member, but I didn't chase the stage. I was happy to help create stage settings and scenery. Set construction was done onstage, but smaller projects like painting were done in a small room at the back of the building. There were all kinds of tools for those who knew how to use them, and paint and sinks for those of us who didn't.

There are two montages in the club room of the guild today. I have looked at them several times but have never been able to find my father. I have, however, found my high school drama teacher, Miss Churchill.

I buy season tickets now and watch the creative work of others.

Phyllis Tippett has lived in Dearborn for most of her life. She married her husband, Jim, in 1946 while he was in college on the G.I. Bill. She has three children, seven grandchildren and six great grandchildren. She has been taking a creative writing class taught by Anne Gautreau.

Chapter 18

Mother Nature

Just as the Fig Is Bent, The Family Tree's Inclined

By Aurora "Fran" Allen

We were finally on our way. There was no turning back now. My father, mother and I, Aurora, had traveled from our little village of San Pietro in Amantea to Napoli and boarded the ship on that cold January day in 1936.

The fortune teller had told my mother that the first years in America would be like thorns, but later the cycle would change into beautiful roses. The young family was very much encouraged by this prediction.

And yet with all our hopes, there was still a faint twinge of fear. We could feel it deep within our bosoms. We were leaving everybody and everything behind in our pleasant Italia. After all, Papa reasoned, we were not starving like so many of our *paesani*. He was respected in our village as the best carpenter and bricklayer in the entire province. His family owned land and had plenty of denari, and hadn't he gone to school for six Sundays in a row to learn to do accurate mathematical calculations?

Papa had just completed building the largest house on the main street that led to the *spiaggia*. It was our new house, and he hated to leave it. But most of all, he hated to leave his aging parents, who had been so good to us.

Mama's father had lived in America all during her childhood. He would visit his wife and four children occasionally, but the family could always rely on his financial support, which arrived every month faithfully. Now *Nonno* had drawn up immigration papers for the entire *famiglia* in hopes of uniting his kindred together with him under one roof in America. He hadn't counted on the children growing up.

However, since the papers were already drawn up, Mama and Papa decided to leave their beloved *Italia* and come to America with hopes of improving their quality of life.

At the train station in Amantea, Papa's father had handed Papa a small, damp twig wrapped in an old, warn piece of home-made fabric.

"What's this?" asked my father.

"Take it and plant it," replied *Nonno*. "And don't forget us here in *Italia*."

"But what is it?" inquired my father again.

"It's the start of your new fig tree to remind you of your roots. Take good care of it. Nourish it and it will feed you well."

Papa cradled it in his hands and carefully placed the rootling in the trunk full of necessities.

"I won't forget," Papa said as *Nonno* turned his head.

Papa did take good care of that fig rootling. Everywhere the family went he would take special care to tend the fig plant. When he worked in the coal mines of Pennsylvania, where there was always a need for laborers and the pay was good, he would think of *La bella aria aperta* where the fig trees grew in Italy. When he worked in the coke ovens at the Rouge Plant for Ford Motor Company, he would often dream of his family in Italy eating figs plucked fresh from the trees and opened wide to expose the seeds and fleshy sweetness of the fruit. And everywhere Papa and Mama went, the fig tree was part of us all.

Mama did her share too. She cooked and cleaned and she learned to preserve food that she grew in the vegetable garden. She shopped wisely, watching that the merchants were honest and did not cheat her. She had two other children, both born at home, with a home-visiting doctor and plenty of women cousins to help her.

Papa was determined to build a second house—this time in the United States of America. He constructed a solid-cinder-block-and-brick two-story house on Calhoun Street in the east end of Dearborn. It was a peaceful, tree-lined street. And after working many years at Ford Motor Company in the Steel Division, he developed a persistent cough. He was examined by the company doctor who found that Papa's lungs were blackened by the soot and dust of the factory ovens. Papa decided it was time to retire and tend to his fig tree.

Papa decided there is something eternal in an old fig tree. Its limbs so tangled and gnarled, intertwined with its broad canopy of simple, luxuriant leaves. Its branches reaching for Mediterranean sun—hot, fervently converting the sun's energy into succulent fruit. Each rotund purple fruit with its drop of milk harbors a burse of summer sweetness ready to release its goodness in one's mouth. Its roots, well established, strong and growing straight into the rich soil with tender rootlings spread their limbs outward to sustain and protect the plant. Yes, he thought, there is something permanent in an old fig tree.

And yet there is something familial in an old fig tree. He remembered carrying its first few sprigs to America's shores many years ago, carefully protected against the weather in home-spun linens. Its green-stemmed, twisted roots promised new hope in a foreign land where the family could be nourished by its fleshy sweetness. There would be innumerable figs, like children, all healthy, fat, with glowing, blushing faces to be admired by everyone. They would be protected by industrious parents who would feed them a good dose of public education and insist upon excellent achievement along with the watering baptism of the church. They would grow strong and be well established along with the fig tree, prospering year after year with new growth.

And as Papa worked with the family fig, he decided there

is something vulnerable in an old fig tree. It requires warmth, rich loam and watering. And for three summers it needs to unfold itself like a fragile embryo.

The North American winters can ravage the tender shoots and pillage its possibilities. A fig tree needs to be bent over and buried under a blanket of leaves during the winter months. It needs to be sheltered from the cold with an overlay of stacked bales of straw. So too, he thought, the children need nourishment. They need to be cherished and smothered with hugs. They need to be fed plates of pasta thickly covered with home-canned tomato sauce, sprinkled with oregano and garlic and occasionally a small piece of beef or a plump meatball. Add necessary sleep, a good portion of hard work, and a little pleasurable play and the children grow strong and straight. Mama and Papa take a great deal of pleasure in protecting the defenseless weaker members of their family, both children and fig tree. And as we three children grew older and got married and had children and homes of our own, Mama and Papa gave us our own fig tree cuttings.

And in the spring of our togetherness, I asked my husband to plant our fig tree. He protested. Too much work, he said. No room in the garden. No time to take care of it. High maintenance. However, in early May he marched into the yard, dug a deep hole, uncovered the sturdy sprig from the wet newspapers and planted the family fig tree. And in other rooms of that starter home other seeds were planted. The children and the fig germinated, sprouted, put out shoots, developed, flowered and bloomed together. We enjoyed many summer pleasures and abundant harvest from our efforts. And at the winter of our lives, after the divorce, the tree was allowed to die, the roots plucked out by a hired man.

Aurora "Fran" Allen is the mother of 4, the grandmother of 11, and the great-grandmother of one. She retired from the Dearborn Public Schools in 1995 after 30 years of teaching.

Powerless Against Nature

By Jane McCormick

It was described as the worst storm ever in Michigan. Here's how the newspapers reported on it back in July 1980:

"Intense thunderstorms swept across lower Michigan this morning bringing darkness, torrential rains and 75 mile-an-hour winds which blew down power lines and trees and damaged buildings." The Detroit News, Wednesday, July 16.

"The torrential downpour left side streets and viaduct underpasses flooded, while the thrashing winds uprooted approximately 300 trees." Dearborn Press & Guide, Thursday, July 17, 1980.

"...The violent windstorm knocked out electrical power to 300,000 Detroit-area residents last week."

"A Detroit Edison spokesman said yesterday that electrical power for more than 75,000 customers might not be restored until the end of the week." The Detroit News, Monday, July21.

Here's the way it was for me personally:

July 16: I left Dearborn around 8:30 a.m. with Alice Dupler, headed for a day in Owosso with Auntie Nell. We planned to stop along the way and pick peas and perhaps some cherries. As we drove westward along Ford Road through Garden City, the sky began to darken and the clouds got very thick and ominous-looking. Then the sky took on a greenish-yellow cast – a sickening sort of atmosphere. The rain began to fall and the wind picked up as we went along, and I suggested to Alice that maybe we should pull off into a large shopping center parking lot we were passing. But I didn't.

A couple of miles farther on it was raining so hard I knew I had to stop. I just couldn't see the road, and the wind was getting wilder. So I turned into a small side street just one block beyond the main intersection of Newburgh and Ford roads in Westland. It was a residential street, but the houses were not close together. There seemed to be a lot of trees ahead, so I stopped where we didn't appear to be right under any – although I really couldn't see much of anything.

It got very black – lightening flashed continually and the thunder rolled. There were blue flashes in the rear-view mirror now and again – probably on the electrical wire behind us running along the main road.

A large branch fell in front of the house across the street from where we were parked. The wind whipped the trees violently, and I was reminded of scenes from the old Dorothy Lamour/Jon Hall epic *Hurricane*.

Then I became aware of a large tree slowly falling toward us from that same yard. I guess I made no comment – just flattened myself on the seat, while the tree settled down around us, enveloping us actually. There was a thud, a jolt, and then the tinkle of broken glass. Alice said she had no idea the tree was coming at us. She was looking out the other side of the car. The windows were so steamy and the rain so heavy she might not have seen it if she had been looking. I don't recall any particular reaction – unless it was perhaps bewilderment. Certainly not fright – just sort of resignation, I suppose. It must have happened very quickly, although my recollection is of a very slow, graceful drop – nothing violent really. Even the impact was rather gentle and dignified.

Most of the rest of what I recall was Alice trying to keep the rain from pouring into the back seat by moving a glass-filled blanket around – and me telling her not to bother and to be careful not to get cut. There was glass in everything – except the window frame.

The storm stormed on, and we sat and wondered what it was all about, why us and how come we were so fortunate as to be able to sit there and wonder these wonders. Two feet can make all the difference in the world.

We tried opening windows, which provided us with a pleasant, wet-piney-woods smell, but also more moisture than we had need of at that point.

The ferocity of the storm eased off somewhat, and there was a smell of gas, which made me uneasy. So we decided to attempt an escape from our woodsy prison. My door wouldn't open, but Alice's did – about a foot. We twisted and turned and wiggled and waggled our way out. We climbed through the grasping branches and slogged our way to the front porch of a house on our side of the street. Looking back, nothing could be seen of the car. Uneasy thoughts crept into my head. Supposing we'd been hurt. No one would have known we were there – for hours perhaps.

Alice's knock on the door was answered by a tousle-headed young man – barely awake. His brother was still asleep on the couch in the front room. They had no phone but donated a sturdy black umbrella so we could go in further search of some line of communication. For some reason I kept hoping we could find someone with a CB who could get help for us. At that point we had no concept of how widespread the storm was or how extensive the damage, and we imagined ourselves to be the most urgent emergency.

I've no idea how long all this took, only that everywhere we went (even back home in Dearborn) all the clocks had stopped at 9 a.m.

We started back toward Newburgh Road, looking for a phone and soon realized that no one had any power. There were no traffic lights at the corner, and all places of business were dark.

When a young man in a pick–up said the place he worked – a couple of blocks back – had one phone line that was working, he took us there.

Alice tried to call her husband, Jerry, but couldn't find him. I called my husband, Alan. He told me that Mrs. Boor's house had been damaged, the garage next door totaled, wires were down all over, and he couldn't get his truck out of the driveway.

Alice caught up with Jerry, and he said he'd be out with a saw as soon as he could.

I went over to see if D. & L. Towing would tow my car across the street (it was almost directly opposite) when the tree was removed, so it would be protected from vandalism, and I wouldn't have to spend the next six to eight hours sitting around there waiting for something to happen. They decided they could, so I called AAA again to see if it was OK to handle things this way. I got a claim number, but the girl kept insisting that if the car was drivable, they would not pay any towing charges. The guys at D. & L. were sure it was not drivable, but the girl (bless her) was very insistent that I realize I would be liable for the charges if it was.

Meantime Jerry arrived, and when I got back to the car, he was sawing away for all he was worth on a large limb that seemed to be what was really holding my little green Hornet captive. Lots of small boys and large men joined in – taking turns with the saw (though Jerry did most of it) – moving branches as they were freed.

The woman who lives in the house belonging to the tree was watching the proceedings. She said she'd seen the triple-trunk terror twisting and turning in the wind from her upstairs window. She grabbed the baby and rushed to the basement so didn't see it fall. It must have twisted one turn too many as it came right up by the roots. Besides this leviathan of the woods, we discovered we had a large piece of a pine tree on us as well.

There were several people with cameras taking pictures. I do wish someone had offered to send me a copy.

My friendly neighborhood tree-removal crew finally decided that if the car was indeed drivable, it could be driven out from under rather than trying to remove the tree from the car. So Jerry got in and – it started! A 300-pound man and his 200 pound buddy clambered around on the hood pulling off branches and worked the car free enough so Jerry could drive it right out. Unbelievable!

The whole thing was unbelievable from start to finish. Fortunately it was not a finish for the car. We drove home with the wind whistling through the rear and the muffler doing less and less muffling as we went along. At the time I assumed the impact of the tree had knocked the muffler loose, but in retrospect, I wonder if the overweight good Samaritans might have been the cause.

Before leaving the area, we went back to the D. & L. boys to say we were out of the woods and cancel my request for a tow. While we were there, a city truck arrived and began cutting up the tree. I hated to tell Jerry.

When I got home, I found Kathy hard at work mopping up the side porch, which was very wet and very muddy, and the chairs had puddles of water on them. The yard was blanketed with branches and leaves, and a few large limbs had fallen on the fence by the driveway, breaking one rail, but not really doing much other damage. The biggest end was in the center of one of the evergreens, but none of it was broken, and everything sprang back into place when I finally was able to haul the limb out the following day.

We were lucky – really lucky. No damage to house or garage, and we had a phone and hot water, although no electrical power. Some houses had trees embedded in them (Margery Mielke McLeod's for one) – or corners knocked off their roofs (Mrs. Boor) – or trees uprooted (Mrs. Boor again). Chunks of sidewalk and/ or driveway were upended in some places – torn out by the force of the tree roots as they came up. Many of the cross streets between Cherry Hill and Rockford were blocked with several trees across them.

I took my car to the AAA Claim Center at Inkster and Schoolcraft, traveling out Inkster Road. At one intersection there would be a policeman directing traffic – at the next four-way stop signs had been posted – at another a "civilian official" in a brilliant orange vest was wildly orchestrating the traffic (and doing a fine job, too) – and every now and then the traffic lights would be operating normally.

After an hour's wait, a girl looked at my car, wrote up the apparent damage and told me where to take it for an estimate and further AAA check. We compared notes on damage at home. Seems like everybody, everywhere got it.

Actually this was not so. There were sections of the Detroit area that had no concept of what the rest of us had gone through, and even parts of Dearborn, not far from here, never lost any power.

I got home around 4:00, I guess, and began to do what I could about cleaning up the yard – hauling the big stuff out to the street. Alan had done some in the morning.

Alice, Jerry and I went out to dinner – the only part of the day that went according to our original plan.

We made the papers that day:

"WESTLAND: Power lost in a quarter of the homes in the southwest part of the city, which has 90,000 residents. All traffic lights also were out. In addition, falling trees damaged two homes and five cars. Numerous wires, trees and branches also were down." The Detroit News, Wednesday July 16.

Thursday, July 17

I took my car to Dearborn Collision on Ford Road and walked home through the devastation to the north of us. The rest of the day was spent carrying huge branches to the street and sawing up what I could of the ones that had fallen on the fence. I did a dumb, stupid, careless thing, and for the second day in a row had the feeling that someone was looking after me, keeping me from serious injury. When I found the saw too slow to suit me, I got out an ax and finished two or three branches that way. Then I thought if a little bit was good, why wouldn't a lot be better, and went at a branch without sawing it first. I was leaning over, quite close to my "opponent," and as I gave a good healthy chop, a small chip flew up and struck me in the eye. It frightened me more really than the previous day's events, I think. A look in the mirror showed nothing but small, broken blood vessel. I breathed a sigh of relief, put the ax back in the shed and returned to my sawing.

As I trudged from yard to street, practically hidden under the branches I was carrying, I felt like something out of *Macbeth*, Act V.

Another night of going to bed by candlelight.

Friday, July 18

I finished what sawing I could do in the morning, and Larry McNab (Winters' house) came over with a power saw to finish it up for me. The day was spent raking up most of the yard, loaning the phone to assorted neighbors who were without, begging ice water from Barb Hoatlin across the street and generally chatting with everyone who went past. I've never seen such a parade of people walking around – people I'd never seen, for the most part. Reminded me of the way folks used to roam the neighborhood looking at Christmas decorations.

Good news from AAA – finally. They will cover the damage on my car except my muffler.

In the evening Helen Ransom called offering a bag of ice cubes and space in her freezer for anything I had still frozen. Louise had arrived unexpectedly in the afternoon so she, Kathy and I loaded all we could into my cooler and one borrowed from the Duplers, and we headed for Livonia to Helen's. Most of the meat seemed OK – only one package was soft, and we gave that to Helen's dog.

Saturday, July 19

I finished the raking, and, all things considered, we looked pretty neat. Food was getting pretty scarce by this time. We were reduced to hard-boiled eggs and cheese and fruit and bread for the most part.

Sunday, July 20

I spent the whole day cleaning the refrigerator – throwing out food—mopping the porch, which was very muddy – and mopping the kitchen floor because the refrigerator had leaked yucky-looking stuff all over.

Peg VanHaaren, who lives in Redford, brought me a five-pound block of ice and two bags of cubes, so I transformed the top of the fridge into an old-fashioned ice box, and it proved to be quite successful. I didn't expect the ice to last more than a day, but by supplementing it with plastic jugs of ice, there was still a piece of the block left four days later.

Toc Dunlap was roaming the neighborhood taking movies and stopped by for a visit. She's had power since yesterday. I also learned later than Mrs. Geiger has hers on, but not the Hoatlins next door to her.

After dark that evening, sitting on the back porch, I could see no lights anywhere except what I decided must be candlelight at the Turpins' on the corner of Denwood and Rockford. But no, I was mistaken. The street light was on at that corner, so probably the Turpins had power, too.

Monday, July 21

Still no power here. Alice called to say theirs came on early in the afternoon. About 3 p.m. we were hit by an absolute deluge (rain, not power). There was some thunder and lightning but mostly in the distance. No wind–just a lot of water. Of course it leaked in the bay at the end of the living room – but not in the basement for once. Fortunately I had gone to the bank and grocery (by bike) a couple of hours earlier.

The city picked up the garbage – our regular day – fortunately. Ours, as that of most everyone else, I expect, was full of decaying oddities from a hibernating freezer. The disposal didn't work, of course, so there was no other way to dispose of even our normal, everyday garbage. It was getting rather fragrant sitting out in the heat of the day, and I noted a similar aroma all along the street as I rode home from shopping. I don't remember ever experiencing that before around here. The collective food loss must have been monumental. We were lucky, I'm sure, to have ours under $50.

I took four half-gallon plastic jugs to the Kennedys to freeze today. The block of ice was still doing well. I heard a cheery report on the radio that some folks might be without power into the next weekend.

About 9 p.m. those who had power around us lost it, and then all of a sudden, three-quarters of an hour later, a few lights flickered on here and there. Our basement light went on and seemed extremely bright. I thought perhaps it was because we'd been without for so long, but I guess we were getting too much power. Only a very few of the lights in the house seemed to work, and those that did didn't seem to be related. Some rooms had an overhead light, but the floor lamps didn't work. My bedroom had everything. Kathy's next door and the bathroom had nothing. The back hall light worked; the front hall light did not.

Indicative of something perhaps – there were fireflies all around that night. It was the proper weather for them, I'm sure, but it almost seemed Mother Nature was trying to make up for her unpleasantness of last Wednesday and all the resulting problems by trying to give us a little light at least.

Tuesday, July 22

We still had only partial power – for example, the stove. The clock was running, but the lights didn't come on. The burners gave forth some heat on high only, and the oven worked, but with noticeable lack of enthusiasm and really only warmed things slightly.

I took two gallon jugs to the Dunlaps' freezer and brought back half a dozen frozen "freezer packs."

I made an early morning call to Detroit Edison and was

told not to use any appliances as there is danger of burning them out. I couldn't figure if this applied to lights as well, so didn't turn any on.

On my third call to Edison, later in the day, I learned that I could turn on anything. If it worked, OK – if not, I should turn it off, especially appliances.

The TV did not work. My clock radio ran, but the electric clock in the master bedroom did not. I didn't try the refrigerator or deep freeze. I planned to clean the latter the next day and then see what happened after that.

So we were on the road to recovery, but there was still a block of homes across the street with zilch.

Wednesday, July 23

We were indeed a strange mixture of two worlds on Wednesday. I would turn on the electric light in the basement so I could see to light the gas stove because the electric stove in the kitchen wouldn't boil water. No more candles necessary down there anyway.

The refrigerator was still a primitive ice box, but I was able to freeze large jugs of ice in the deep freeze in the basement to keep the ice box going. No more running to the Kennedys and Dunlaps and Gumps or calling Peg for help to replenish my supply.

I did three loads of laundry successfully – including two lots of things from the car. Hopefully I got all the glass bits out.

Thursday, July 24

A rather uneventful day for the most part. I made my daily pilgrimage to the grocery store on my bike, did a couple more loads of laundry and spent the afternoon figuring out how to get dinner to come out, even using the gas burners for some things and the oven in the kitchen for the rest.

6:30 p.m. – the witching hour, or perhaps better, the de-witching hour. Anyhow, the oven light began to give off a dim, eerie light, blinked a few times and then shown forth in all its glory. Hoorah! Back to the 20th century.

That night I went to sleep with my friendly neighborhood streetlight shining in the window for the first time in eight days – a sure sign all was right with our little world again.

P.S. Got my car back on Friday.

Jane McCormick retired from Visitor Services at The Henry Ford. She then worked as a volunteer there and is now a volunteer at the Dearborn Historical Museum.

Going Green

By Maureen McIlrath

I moved to Dearborn over 20 years ago when I was pregnant with my first child, Berlyn Quinn Noland, who is now a graduate of Edsel Ford High school. My second child is Ian McIlrath Pitoniak, and he is 8 and attends Long Elementary School.

A few years ago when the mortgage crisis hit, I like many others had a mortgage that was flipped. I had a choice to let go of my home of almost 20 years or fight to stay in a community that had helped me as a single parent through so much. Not only did I fight, but I also saw an opportunity to bring the community together by starting a community garden through the city's adopt-a-lot program. The city could not find a lot, but offered me 2.5 acres behind Long School to develop. I thought this would be a great way for me to help my community by starting an organic sustainable farm; it would give me the ability to help bring the cost of organic foods down so that everyone had the opportunity to eat healthier. The farm is now in the city's master plan and is registered as a farm through the USDA.

I then started a nonprofit called the Going Green Foundation to help raise funds. I also took a grant class and hired my teacher to help write federal grants for the farm. The farm is now in its fourth year, and we have donated over 2,000 pounds of food to our local food banks and are offering our produce at the Dearborn Farmers Market. The foundation is also working with Henry Ford Community College and its Culinary Arts Department to bring locally grown produce into the school, restaurant and training programs. We have also implemented the Chefs Move to Schools Program at Long School, along with a recycling and composting program.

We offer children's gardening and community garden spots for people interested in gardening but don't have the room. This offers the community a way of coming together and helping others in need.

Since starting this project, I have become more involved in the community. I sit on the City Beautiful Commission, Telecommunications Commission, Environmental Commission, the Dearborn Federation of Neighborhood Associations as vice president, and Long School's PTA as president. I recently ran for a seat on Dearborn City Council and continue to look at ways we as a city can be more sustainable.

I believe that one person can make a difference; I believe that we are all stewards of the environment, and more than that I believe we all have the ability to do more to help our city be the best it can possibly be.

We have plans on building a container house as well as pushing the city to do more solar and wind. I have made sustainability a priority in my life, and I hope I can convince the citizens of Dearborn to do the same.

The foundation has been present at the Dearborn Homecoming for the last three years, and we have taken on the role of organizers for the Green Alternative Expo that is now a part of the Homecoming.

We would like to finish developing the farm. We still have two acres to go and are always looking for volunteer help, donations and grants.

Maureen McIlrath is following in the footsteps of one of Dearborn's most respected residents, Henry Ford, with her take on a sustainable Dearborn beginning with her first project a sustainable organic farm in Crowley Park.

Victory Plots

By Isamay E. Osborne

During the early to mid-1940s, citizens were encouraged to plant gardens for victory. The concept was not a new one. History tells us that hundreds of years before, England encouraged its citizens to plant gardens in times of war.

As students at the Greenfield Village Schools, we, too, participated in this activity and planted Victory Gardens. I remember that a large tract of land on Village Road (near Southfield Road) was prepared for us. Students were assigned a plot to garden. With the help of family members, we planted an assortment of vegetables in our designated area—tomatoes, lettuce, carrots, beans, onions. Now any garden requires quite a bit of attention in order for it to be productive – hoeing and weeding – on a regular basis. So I remember making several trips to the garden each week to work.

The gardens were regularly inspected by "student generals," and flags were staked at each plot indicating the condition of the garden. Blue: great! White: needs work! Red: not good! Everyone hoped to see a blue flag by his or her garden.

At the end of the season, just before school began again, a family picnic was held on the lawn of the Secretary House (now referred to as the Giddings Family Home), where the student generals awarded blue flags to each child who had kept his/her garden clean all summer. The flag was printed in gold and read:

The Edison Institute
Greenfield Village
Victory Gardens
1944

I happily received a blue flag in 1943 and 1944, due to my family's helpful participation with the weeding. A great memory – and the veggies were good too. I still have those two blue flags and recently found a group picture of the flag recipients at the picnic in August, 1944.

Isamay E.Osborne is a lifelong resident of Dearborn, director and past president of the Museum Guild of Dearborn and a former member of the Dearborn Historical Commission.

Tending the Compost, Coping With Life

By Margaret Wilkie

We always had a compost pile. In the '50s there was considerable opinion against such quaint notions. I conjecture, sometimes, about why. There was talk among the adults about rats and vermin. These people had been through a war and lost friends and endured. Here was their little Shangri-La, their castles, complete with a view. They wanted to put the bad behind them and live a perfect life. Everything was trucked in and found at Foodfair. Dirt, the decomposing side of things, chaos, had no place in the life they were planning, and they worked hard to keep it that way. No one was allowed on the grass; we had to play in the street.

Automobile paint became an obsession. Many men spent their Saturdays off from the automobile plants in careful, meditative cleaning and touching up of the family car. My young self recalls these men to be very surly, caring only for their cars and lawns. Seems like the women took care of any messes, and they did so promptly. We used to joke that Mrs. L. next door would wear out her carpet vacuuming it, she spent so much time at it.

There was emotion underneath. People were working very hard not to acknowledge it, lest the world fall apart, and more explosions and dead buddies and shattered lives emerge. People coped by putting the horror of the war away, not allowing the hardships inside. Things were different now. We had won, and as victors, only good could come to us by every law of life. Also, science was bringing us penicillin, the UAW had brought white people a car in every garage, utopia was in reach for suburban America. If only the malcontents, communists and do-gooders didn't ruin it by bringing in stray concepts like sustainability and race and finite resources (read oil) that didn't seem to have anything to do with the ideal life. I recall an uncle saying at a family gathering, "We gotta have more oil, that's all there is to it. We gotta have more oil."

There were a few diehard gardeners like Mother, like Mr. Rodriguez. The Rodriguez family lived behind us. I realize now they are Mexican—suspect in our waspish enclave, but tolerated. They lived by Dartmouth at the very edge of the suburb, grew many tree fruits. There was a man over across Dartmouth, in the "township," who had a pond and raised goldfish.

The township had many open spaces. My sister used to catch butterflies for her collection in a field that is now St. Sebastian Church. She had a net. After she caught the "specimen," she'd bring it home and put it in a bottle with ether to kill it "humanely." Then she would stick a pin through it and mount it with the others. I am amazed at the species diversity in our meadow. It was probably a farm before the postwar housing boom turned it into a suburb. Most of the area was farms. Before the farms, it was beech-maple forest.

There was not a lot of thought given to diversity of butterfly species in the '50s and '60s. Rachel Carson's *Silent Spring* was new and controversial. Most adults were busy trying to raise their children. In my block, there were three families that had seven children. We counted: There were 42 children on our block. That made for a lot of playmates for us. My friend Janet and I set up child-sitting services.

Mother made the compost piles discreet so Mrs. G. wouldn't complain. When she cleared out an area, masses of green swelled the pile. If it was warm, the little hill of damp green would quickly reduce in volume and turn into rich brown dirt. She would toss the dirt here or there and use it in the hole if she were transplanting.

I liked to be around when she was transplanting. The soil in her garden was dark and rich, even when it was dry. Years of adding compost made our heavy clay friable. Mother became all business, but she'd let me help. There was plenty of stuff to tote around. Compost to bring to the site. Water was set out for and hour or so before the planting to "take the chill off so as not to shock the roots." If the plant was large, the hole was filled with compost, then dirt, then water, then the plant, dirt and compost again. Then she would step all around the area to tamp it all down and then set the hose on a trickle for the afternoon. If the plant was small, every hole was filled in with compost, the old soil on top. I think plants responded to the healing thoughts she surrounded them with. They would certainly grow for her.

Mother had gardening clothes. Old pants and a shirt. She wore a straw hat and gloves and would change into this outfit before going out to garden. It is true, she would pull out a weed or two if she were in the vicinity even if she wasn't in uniform. The magic, communing with the garden, happened when everything was prepared and thought-out and planned. Once out in the garden, she could putter for hours, as there was always this and that to do in a garden, if there was time. If not, she'd often say, "It'll keep."

Chapter 19

Literature

Good Morning to You, Too

By Nabeel Abraham

In life we don't always get what we want. When we do, we expect to be content. But are we?

This is the story of Musa Kurd, a young Arab American who had just bought a corner house on Theisen and Morross in Dearborn's east end. It was the mid-'80s and Musa was an aspiring artist who by day worked as a social worker.

This was Musa's first house and his first time in Dearborn. He was familiar with the old Southend Arab neighborhood. He was now in his mid-30s, and Musa's meanderings had taken him to capitals in Europe and the Middle East. He was determined to make the best of his move to Dearborn because he needed the steady income of his day job.

Although he was proud of his Arab heritage, Musa valued his personal freedom, especially his privacy. He thought he could protect his privacy from what he assumed would be the prying eyes of neighbors, especially Arab families, and thereby preserve his freedom to date, drink and dance with whomever he wished. To that end, Musa resolved from Day One to keep a distance from his neighbors. He hoped to re-create the anonymity of Big City life in small-town Dearborn.

When Musa, with the help of a motley crew of friends, moved into the new house, it was already late autumn, and the neighbors had rolled back into the warmth of their houses along with the lawn furniture. As a result, Musa saw very little of his neighbors that winter, and this pleased him.

As spring opened her arms, Musa started to notice his neighbors more and more. He especially noticed the couple who lived in the corner duplex across Morross, the side street. His kitchen window opened directly to their house. So exposed was the house that Musa was able to see people entering through the front door as well as what was happening in the back yard. Even though it was the house farthest from his own, it was a regular fixture in Musa's field of vision.

As the days of spring grew longer, Musa detected a pattern in the behavior of the neighboring couple. Every time he stepped outside, they invariably avoided making eye contact with him, especially the old man. At first Musa chalked this up to coincidence. As the weeks passed, however, the pattern was so consistent that Musa began to rule out coincidence. He knew this because his daily path to his garage forced him to directly face the neighbor's house and back yard. In other words, the L-shaped configuration of the walk to his garage forced him to make eye contact with the house across the street during the short part of the L, and then walk along the sidewalk to the garage on the long part of the L. Yet, it never failed that when his portly neighbor was tending to his garden, he was careful to never look up when Musa made his morning trip to the garage.

Now, this state of affairs began to wear on Musa. True, he had wanted to keep his distance from his new neighbors, but the studied avoidance of his neighbors was more than he had bargained for. Keeping one's distance was one thing, but a deliberate snub was another thing entirely. Musa's personal dignity and self-esteem were on the line. What had he done to be ignored? Or, could all this still be a matter of coincidence?

Musa decided to test his neighbor. One morning as Musa was making his way to the garage, he spied the old man working in his yard. His heart quickened as he made the turn toward the garage. Out of the blue, Musa turned his head in the direction of the old man bent over in his garden and burst out, "Good morning!" in Arabic.

Seconds ticked ... No response ... Musa turned his head and walked on. Then, out of nowhere came "Sabah al-Ful." Excited,

Musa looked over his shoulder, hoping to greet his neighbor's smiling visage but only found him still bent over in his garden.

Musa was flabbergasted. He pulled his car out of the garage and drove past the old man, feigning indifference. On the inside, however, Musa's self-esteem was melting in a pool of humiliation. Musa couldn't help wondering why the neighbor hadn't met him halfway. What had Musa done to deserve this?

To be fair, the neighbor had met Musa halfway – technically at least. Hadn't he met Musa's greeting with a perfunctory retort? True, but human interaction even among strangers is more than merely perfunctory. The vibes have to be right. Even a passing greeting requires some eye contact, a smile, wave, something beyond a simple grunt. When so little is known about a stranger, trivial details acquire an exaggerated sense of importance.

Most troubling, what would Musa do the next time he and the old man were within sight of one another? He resolved to ignore his unfriendly neighbor and pretend the previous day's awkward exchange had never happened. "When all else fails, play dumb," someone once advised.

The next morning, Musa looked out the kitchen window, hoping not to find the old man in his garden. "Rats!" he exclaimed. "He's out there." Musa waited as long as he could for him to return indoors, but the need to get to work on time forced his hand.

Musa took a deep breath, pressed the garage door opener and headed out the back door. He quietly closed the door, so as not to alert the old man of his leaving. Stopping at the gate, he lifted the latch slowly to avoid a clang of metal. He gently pushed the gate open just far enough to get through. It gave off a soft moan from an unoiled hinge. Musa felt the dryness of his mouth. His carotid artery throbbed. He thought about the absurdity of leaving his own house in a stealthily manner.

He kept his gaze downward as he negotiated the 90-degree

turn left along Morross Street to the garage. He, nevertheless, caught sight of the neighbor working in his back yard. Musa stuck to his silence. The old man remained silent, too.

"If I can pull this off another two or three times," Musa thought, "I will have gotten the toothpaste back in the tube." He pulled out of the garage and went down Morross, careful to keep his eyes fixed on the road ahead.

The next day Musa awoke to rain. Normally the sight of precipitation would be occasion for gloom to set in, but not this particular morning. An open umbrella would provide a perfect shield for his walk to the garage. Musa desperately wanted to return to the safety and anonymity of his pre-contact life.

On the fourth day following the opening to his neighbor, Musa lifted the shades in his bedroom to find a glorious spring morning. The rain clouds of the previous day had blown over. Soon dejection set in as Musa wondered whether his neighbor would be outside.

As he shaved, Musa berated himself. "Come on, what am I afraid of?" he asked himself. "I don't owe him anything." Musa had conveniently forgotten that it was his own discomfiture at being ignored that had precipitated his current dilemma.

Just the same, he consoled himself with the thought that enough time had elapsed since the fateful encounter for the genie of contact to have been put back into the bottle. Musa would pretend that nothing ever happened.

True to form, the old man was working in his garden. Musa proceeded as he had done previously. He would exit as quietly as possible and move with deliberate speed to the garage without making eye contact with the old man. "After all, the old man himself doesn't want any interaction, so, there is nothing wrong with ignoring him despite my original opening to him," Musa reasoned.

Oddly, Musa was more nervous than ever. He closed the back

door with a loud thud. The gate squealed as never before. Musa's heart pounded so hard he was sure the old man could hear it 40 feet away. Musa was falling apart at the sight of his neighbor. The absurdity of what he was doing did not escape him and probably contributed to his self-conscious clumsiness.

He was only a few short steps shy of the garage when the unexpected sounds landed on his ears . . ."Sabah al-Khair!"

Stunned, Musa paused for a moment. And then reflexively responded, "Good morning," in Arabic.

By the time Musa laid eyes on the old man, all he saw was his neighbor bent over working nonchalantly in his garden.

Musa had been ambushed! The genie had let himself out of the bottle. The old man had bested him. As Musa drove past him, a smile came over his face as he nodded in the direction of the old man, affirming his neighbor's triumph. The old man never looked up.

Postscript:

Musa and his neighbor eventually become friends. All the things Musa had feared – loss of privacy, intrusiveness into his private life, endless conversations, and reciprocity over food and drink – came to pass.

After several years Musa married and moved away. The passage of many years saw a wistful Musa on a return visit to the old neighborhood. He was saddened to see a vacant lot where once stood the old man's house. What happened to the duplex and its former occupants is unknown. Musa also quickly saw that anyone occupying his former house would be assured of a good deal of privacy as a result.

Nabeel Abraham recently retired from Henry Ford Community College, where he taught anthropology and also directed the Honors Program for 28 years. Some of his short stories are published in Dinarzad's Children: An Anthology of Arab American Fiction. *Abraham is co-editor of several works, including* Arab Detroit 9/11 *and* Arab Detroit: From Margin to Mainstream.

Sky Afire

By Frank M. DeBoever

The sky's afire
A backdrop of resplendence
In the shadow of Ford World Headquarters
I drive on thinking many things in this rare juxtaposition
Rare for me...
My thoughts turn to death on this fiery morn
But not in a way that makes me sad
I am emptied
Death to my hauntings
And imagining heaven
If there be such a place
A brilliant nothingness that stirs my desires
Color abounds in an unimaginable rainbow
Yet I see it so clearly
Morning and death seem like queer company
But I praise its marriage
Oh how I sing its marriage...
Two tickets to Paradise is a pale soundtrack
Sorry Eddie
You will grace me once again when the sky is not afire.

Frank M. DeBoever is a "late in life returning student" who fell in love with poetry after taking a class in poetry at Henry Ford Community College. He now works for Howe-Peterson Funeral Home after spending many years in the automotive paint business. He and his wife, Nancy, are empty nesters, and he has more time to reminisce about days gone by and loving Dearborn.

Eggs

By Anne Gautreau

Each spring my father motored north to check mills and miles.
At a farm in West Branch he'd buy morning
eggs and cackle with the proprietor who reminded
him of his feisty-French-Canadian mother.

Driving south for hours through Michigan
snows and muds and rains he'd haul
news, business papers, crafts and half-a-dozen
cartons of farm-fresh eggs for family and friends.

Once home he'd set egg containers on smooth-white
Formica just left of the refrigerator.
Then he'd crack lids, inspect shells, grin and
take silent satisfaction in shock absorbers.

With weekly ritual he'd lift one egg,
cup it in palm, hold it like a host and
exclaim, "Just look at the size!"
Family members would cluck and lower their eyes.

One Saturday at the Eastern Market in Detroit
turkey eggs gobbled up my attention.
I bought one, brought it home, and
hid it in one of Father's famous-egg cartons.

When he discovered it after Sunday mass,
he could not bear to crack his
prized-astounding-suspended-gelatinous mass.
into the anonymous oblivion of scrambled eggs,

For a week he showed every single person
who entered the house that "Can-you-believe-it-egg?"
Exclamations and hyperbolic jokes filled the air,
delight was wondrous and nature truly rare.

I never should have told.

Father's face froze momentarily then cracked chagrin.
To the boy inside taunts echoed and egged him on.
If only I had tripped and smashed shell before that good
lie died to be reborn into such an ordinary world.

Storm: July 23, 1998

the day after
that perfect-horizontal storm
when profound clouds
whipped together theatrical
pratfalls and hurled everything
stage left to stage right
from one-neighbor-to-the-next
(as if the shrew herself were being tamed)
one-ferocious lover flung
object-after-object at the other
in one-frenzied through-line of
envy, rage and jealousy

reality bounced
outdoor plastics–
chairstablesbinsbarrels
outdoor woods–
a timber tirade of decks and
branches outdoor greens–
plantingpotsstrippedlimblessbushes
outdoor plumbing–

full-spigoted drips-dropping desperate drizzles
gushed
drained
finally spent

then neighbors crept forth from
homes banged-bumped battered and bashed
whispered, giggled together in
clan gatherings
awed titillated survivors
torn from TV to tumultuous
reality

the next day
at dawn
crowded urban campers awoke
to a fresh storm of contumacious
helicopters, TV news crews and
the sobs of buzz saws

trees
had risen like beaten
egg whites and left
stiff-pale peaks of compound fractures
bloodless bones exposed
roots risen from graves
tree giants sprawled
framed by perfect rectangles of now-
vertical lawns
gamed by nature into
crazy-perpendicular greens dented with
hyperbolic divots of perverse delight

The Autumn That Followed The Dreadful Drought

The magnolias bloomed that fall,
the autumn that followed the dreadful drought,
when compassionates assuaged the thirst of critters;
and crabapples carpeted newly loomed lawns.

The sweet-fruit-stench stuffed nostrils; and
Old-Man Tippett claimed that the trees, knowing
beneath bark they had to trick death,
gave all to their seed. And the flies harvested
great storm of life on the fruit. At the golden
hour aerial ballets stirred dusty light.

Most of all I remember magnolia blossoms,
luscious as fruit, turning trees into singular-gigantic
blooms so fabulous that people stopped
rushing and gazed at them, ending wondrous
reveries with shakes of heads and sighs.
Glimpses of such off-season beauty
birthed infinities of bittersweet memories.

Premature frost unsettled that fall,
the autumn that followed the dreadful drought,
and foreshadowed blustery snow.
Dearborn awoke in a carved ivory world.
Cracked-satin petals pillowed the ground.
The spell had been snapped.

Leaf litter came later, that autumn
that followed the dreadful drought;
And beneath bark, fecundity flourished.
And Old-Man Tippett nodded as he plucked
bright-orange pods of tangling bittersweet.

The EFHS Bird-Court Caper

A golden pheasant skipped school to grace gray-suburban snow
like a commemorative medallion on Woodside Drive. (Was he
simply in search of Snow Avenue?)

Under clipped-crisp evergreens he glimmered against dross
darkening day like a
sun-pierced storm cloud.

Then two classy keepers came with net and glove and cage, tricks
and stealth to
reclaim freedom.

One mesmerized the metallic bird
as the other slid slowly and silently
then slipped
    his
      net
        over
blossoming wings and neck. A marigold of feathers!
Hokusai himself could not have carved a better woodblock.

*Anne Gautreau was raised in and resides in Dearborn. She holds
degrees from Western Michigan University and the University of
Michigan. She has presented at conferences for the National Council
of Teachers of English and participated in numerous panels and
symposia on the brain, learning and writing.*

Schaefer Ave. '66

By Christopher Martin Jones

Mother and I would go up Schaefer

back when the world was bluish black and white.

There were two Kresge's

stacked nearly atop one another

and Monkeys swung kitty-corner

from Cunningham Drugs

where the soda fountain

filled me with malts and hope,

while the juke box

filled me with visions

of Nancy's walking boots

and Petula's downtown.

I dreamt of growing taller

with no concern of growing older

as I watched the parade of grown-ups

through the misty windows

all marching to get nowhere fast.

The ladies wore scarves

and the gentlemen wore hats

and the bad news of the day never sat beside a small boy.

After a stop for a few bits and bobs at Frank's,

Ziggy the Polish butcher

would impress me with his blood-soaked apron

before we moved on to visit Julius and Bernard Pesick

who had bees dancing atop the pyramid of melons.

Packers had a big barrel of pickles to pick from

and just up the street the Buster Brown store

had top-secret, decoder-rings, never mind the shoes.

United Shirt confused me by selling pants

and Maryann's was torture for a small, impatient boy

shopping with his overly patient mother

so I would escape the monster of boredom

finding refuge inside of the folding mirrors,

surrounding myself with an army of me's

each appearing to get a bit smaller

than the one in front of him

as I grew a bit taller than the day behind me

but as far as growing older and tomorrows,

they were nowhere to be found for a small boy

on Schaefer Avenue in 1966.

(copyright 2013 Christopher Martin Jones)

Christopher Martin Jones, a Fordson graduate, was born and raised in east Dearborn. He currently resides in west Dearborn with his wife, Michele. His love of poetry was passed on to him by his father, Renwick, who was also a poet.

The Rock

By Diane Kaye

When I was a child to the park we'd go,
Just me and my Grandma, hand in hand.
We'd walk down the block and around the corner
Then straight to the "promised land."

Just before we came to the swings and the slides,
Sitting all alone in the field of green
Was a great big stone gleaming in the sun.
The biggest rock I'd ever seen!

I always tried to climb on it,
Kept searching for a way.
It was so high that I was sure
If I climbed up on top, I'd have to stay.

We walked to the swings. Grandma pushed me for a while,
Then several times down the slide I went.
We did some turns on the merry-go-round,
And then our time was spent.

Hand in hand, we passed the rock once again.
What was always puzzling to me
Was how in the world, in this flat field of green,
This giant rock came to be.

Well, the years went by and I grew up.
    My dear sweet grandma passed away.
        I brought my own two little girls
            to the big rock to see what they'd say.

We drove down the street, 'round the corner, and then
    There was the rock in the field of green!
        "It must have shrunk," I said in disbelief.
            "Or the weather wore it down,
                know what I mean?"

We got out of the car to see for ourselves
    Just what happened to the humongous stone
        still sitting on the edge of the field of green.
        Just sitting there all alone.

We started to laugh as we reached the rock.
    We laughed and laughed 'til we cried.
        The rock that I thought was gigantic back then
        Was really just barely waist high!

Diane Kaye is a retired teacher who enjoys writing poetry and stories for children. She describes the background of this poem as follows:

"Upon their arrival from Germany in 1914, my grandparents built a house for their brood of seven in the Michigan Avenue/Wyoming area. In the 1950s, my grandmother and I often walked to Kielb Park, named for a heroic soldier of World War II whose family lived on Porath Street. There was a large stone in the park, on which was mounted a plaque giving the details of Walter Kielb's heroism. The park was located between Porath and I-94, where the 'infamous rock' stood until the late '90s when the park was closed."

The Tickle Bear Family

By Irving Orne

Once upon a time in the deep forest lived the Tickle bear family: Papa bear, Tickle-He, Mama bear, Tickle-She, and baby bear, Tickle-It, and their Uncle Tickle-Who and Aunt Tickle-What.

The Tickle bears loved to eat honey. One summer morning, they gathered near a field of beehives. The bees were busy, buzzing around the hives while other bees gathered nectar from the flowers in the meadows.

Tickle-He, Tickle-She, Tickle-It, Uncle Tickle-Who and Aunt Tickle-What could smell the sweet scent of honey. They could see it dribbling from the beehives. They surrounded the hives.

Each bear began to shove and push each other away from the hives. They clawed their way through the hives, and the sweet honey began to pour out and coat their paws. The bears began to lick the honey.

The bees were very angry. They began to attack the bears. They buzzed around their eyes. They buzzed around their noses. They began to sting Tickle-He, Tickle-She, Tickle-It, Uncle Tickle-Who and Aunt Tickle-What.

They tried to cover their noses from the bees' attack. They began to howl. They began to shriek in pain. The bees stung their noses. The bees stung their paws. The bees stung their ears. All the bears scattered.

Some headed deep into the forest. Some headed for the lake and dove in head first.

Uncle Tickle-Who and Aunt Tickle-What felt the cold lake water soothe their painful noses and paws and toes while Tickle-He, Tickle-She and Tickle-It headed for a cool, dark cave deep within the forest to lick their wounds. Their eyes and noses were swollen from the bee stings.

But, my little boys and girls, as I am sure you know, bears never learn.

After their bee stings healed, the bear family once again gathered around new beehives and broke into them for the sweet taste of honey. Bears love the sweet taste of honey so much that they are willing to be stung by the bees.

Remember, boys and girls, you can never change the nature of bears or the nature of bees. Bears must have their honey, and bees must sting.

Irving Orne would rather be an artist than a poet, but his hobby is writing.

Ford Field Memories

By Charles J. Sharney

"Do you want to go to 'old' Dearborn?" My mom would say.

"We'll go to Sanders for ice cream and Ford Field to play."

...And play we did and I would stand and look from the bridge.

Did you know in 1898 the bridge was a giant tree trunk that fell across the river?

And the kids would walk across without a quiver.

In 1900, planks were nailed two feet wide with a wooden rail.

Children would build and navigate homemade boats with sail.

More planks were added just in time.

Yelled boys with a football they were tossin'.

And soon came children pulling a wagon

Tied on the back tin cans a 'draggin'.

In 1929, Dearborn High played football and baseball by the hill.

"Casey" up to bat...what a thrill!

In 1940, thousands would frolic on "Dearborn Day."

In 1976, "Homecoming" came to stay.

...I still look back in time to dream and reminisce

As I lean on the rail to enjoy the view,

I recall my children and grandkids, too.

We went on picnics and jamborees.

Smelled the flowers that made us sneeze.

Then we would sing a jingle that goes like this,

"We always say gesundheit when someone goes, 'Achoo.'

We always say gesundheit and sometimes God Bless You!"

And we would laugh and go along

And listen as the wind made the weeping willow branches sway in song.

The weeping willows bloom first in spring and go last in fall.

Green then golden and oh so tall.

In winter the kids would slide down the hill when it snowed.

We stoked the fire till it glowed.

We'd walk the trail along the river bank.

Happy and contented with God to thank.

Spotted deer and beaver and raccoon, too,

And visited with Indians at Rendezvous.

Pretended and played with arrows and bows.

Rolled down the hill and dirtied our clothes.

...Now I am in the twilight of my life...

Ford Field has helped to make life sublime

Can't wait till the morrow to go back in time.

Charles J. Sharney was named after Dr. Charles Castrop, who brought so many children into the world at the old Dearborn Medical Center. He was a teacher and principal in the Romulus School District. He has four daughters teaching in four different school districts. His son is preparing for a dental career. His wife and he reside in Dearborn Heights but his spirit is forever Dearborn!

Henry Would Be Proud

By Ellen Weston

Henry Ford Village - the perfect way
To bring Henry Ford's birthplace into today...

We think he'd be proud of the park on his land;
In fact he might even be lending a hand --

With the beautiful grooming,
The fine loving care
Of the flowers and trees -
The gazebo - so rare!

And the good senior living -
what joy and good cheer!
In fact, he might even be
living Here!

Ellen Weston has been married to Raymond Weston for 42 joyful years. They have three daughters: Sally, Heidi and Pamela. They have three grandchildren: Marika, Hannah and Ben and a step-granddaughter, Maggie. She used to be an Arthur Murray dance instructor. She does ballroom dancing one night a week. She had been a secretary for 10 years at Ford Motor Company.

Henry Ford and his dog.

Joseph and Barbara Reckinger (1893). Reckinger Road was named after them.

Dort School serving primarily German families (1903).

Interurban Transit (c. 1900).

Dearborn police with tommy guns (1928).

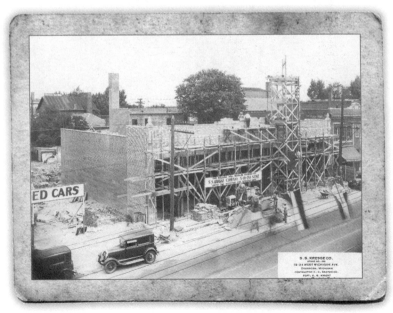

Kresge Building on Michigan Avenue (1928).

First Communion: Fr. Arthur Reckinger, Sacred Heart School's first ordained graduate; from left - Don Junoles, Lavern Reckinger, Anna Marie Forner.

Flag-raising ceremony at Oxford School (1975).

Marguerite Assenmacher Baumgardner & Magdalene Assenmacher (1946).

Wagner Hotel, Michigan Avenue (early 1900s).

Iris Becker (c.1955.)

Marathon runner in front of Palms Café (1929).

Matt Zipple & fellow educators at Atlanta University.